OU-YANG HSIU

OU-YANG HSIU

(Courtesy of the Gest Oriental Library, Princeton University)

OU-YANG HSIU

An Eleventh-Century Neo-Confucianist

JAMES T. C. LIU

STANFORD UNIVERSITY PRESS
STANFORD, CALIFORNIA
1967

This work was originally published in 1963, in Hong Kong, under the title *Ou-yang Hsiu ti chih-hsüeh yü ts'ung-cheng*. In preparing this translation, the author has made extensive revisions for the benefit of Western readers.

The author acknowledges his debt to the following for allowing him to quote from the works named, to which they hold the rights: to New Directions Publishing Corporation and Kenneth Rexroth for Mr. Rexroth's translations of "In the Evening I Walk by the River," "Fisherman," "The Spring Walk to the Pavilion of Good Crops and Peace," "Green Jade Plum Trees in Spring," and "East Wind," from *One Hundred Poems from the Chinese*; to Columbia University Press and Theodore de Bary for selections from *Sources of the Chinese Tradition*; to Grove Press and Cyril Birch for selections from *An Anthology of Chinese Literature from Early Times to the Fourteenth Century*; and to George Allen and Unwin, Ltd., for Arthur Waley's translation of "The Cicada," from *The Temple, and Other Poems*.

TO HUI-CHEN WANG LIU

PREFACE

THE SUNG PERIOD is interesting in terms of both Chinese history and comparative historical studies. It was during the Sung that the ancient Confucian heritage evolved into the new pattern that was to permeate Chinese society for the next thousand years. To modern man, who lives amid bureaucratic tensions, the Sung is especially significant, for it was the earliest centralized empire in history to be managed by non-aristocratic civil servants. What is presented here is the intellectual and political life of an outstanding scholar-official of that period.

This volume is not, strictly speaking, a new book. Rather, it may be described as a compact version in English, with some minor revisions and hopefully some slight improvements, of my book *Ou-yang Hsiu ti chih-hsüeh yü ts'ung-cheng,* originally published in Hong Kong in 1963. It was my humble hope, in originally writing the book, that I might make a small contribution to scholars in my fatherland who might happen to be interested in the Sung, in neo-Confucianism, and in Ou-yang Hsiu; and it is now my hope that this English version will serve the same purpose in the West.

I am grateful to the Bollingen Foundation for an initial grant awarded me when I was at the University of Pittsburgh, and to the East Asian Studies Committee of Stanford University for its summer grants, which made my research possible. I am also indebted to the Committee on Chinese Thought of the Association for Asian Studies for the intellectual stimulation I received at three conferences held under its auspices between 1954 and 1959. My many helpful friends and colleagues will perhaps pardon me for not mentioning them individually here; in other ways, they know already how much I appreciate their kind assistance. Let me name but one colleague, the most helpful of all: my long-suffering and forgiving wife, Dr. Hui-chen Wang Liu, to whom this volume is dedicated.

James Tzu-chien Liu

Princeton University

CONTENTS

CONTENTS

OU-YANG HSIU

CHAPTER ONE

PROLOGUE

ONE HAS THE URGE to climb a mountain, as the saying goes, simply because it is there. The desire to study a great man is similar: he cannot be ignored. And as climbing a mountain gives a grander view of the country surrounding it, so studying a key historical figure gives us a finer perspective of his whole era. These are our interests in Ou-yang Hsiu (courtesy name Yung-shu) who lived from A.D. 1007 to 1072, in Sung China. Talented, energetic, and versatile, he is known to this day as a classicist, a historian, an archaeologist, a statesman, a political theorist, and above all an essayist and a poet. In these capacities he played a pioneering and sometimes pivotal role in the early political and intellectual development of neo-Confucianism, a system of thought and a way of life that was to dominate China for nearly a thousand years. As a man he was remarkable, and as a historical figure he merits close attention.

Previous appraisals of Ou-yang fall into three categories: the traditional evaluation, that of Western scholars, and that of the scholars and educators in contemporary China. On the traditional scale, he ranks among the greatest men Confucian China ever produced, to judge from his persistent appearance among the historical exemplars invoked by Confucian scholar-officials in later centuries, the epitomized images with which they identified themselves and molded subsequent generations in the hope of inspiring renewed dedication to reinforce the Confucian tradition. An adequate discussion of these images obviously lies beyond the scope of this work. Let it suffice to attempt some brief profiles, at the risk of oversimplification.

For a Confucianist to be regarded as outstanding among his contemporaries, he would have had to be not only gifted but upright, not only worthy but influential. Even in his childhood, he would be noted for remarkable conduct. In his youth he would achieve literary fame at least in prose, if not also in poetry. As time went on he would win further respect for his scholarship in the classics and their philosophical principles, in historical studies, and often in the theory of statecraft as well. He would achieve prominence in government service, where he would demonstrate his moral leadership and wise statesmanship. This would be enough to make him outstanding in his own time. But to be more than this—to be one of the great Confucianists of all times—he would have to pass another test, that of "historical competition." He would have to attain the same heights as the great masters of the past, to make his influence felt in later centuries. In short, the image of an outstanding scholar-official was that of a "universal man" of lasting stature, personifying the tradition and adding something significant to it.[1] In the long history of China only a few hundred men were ever so honored in the Confucian Hall. Ou-yang Hsiu was one of them.

Ou-yang is more interesting than others in this exalted category, for his true worth was repeatedly disputed. One complaint raised during his life was that his private morals left something to be desired. This issue was raised again a century later by the great Chu Hsi (1130–1200), sometimes referred to as the Thomas Aquinas of neo-Confucianism. According to Chu, despite Ou-yang's impressive contributions in many areas he had not fathomed Confucian philosophical principles deeply enough to qualify as a great master.[2] Another condemnation was political. Ou-yang once wrote a famous letter to his friend Fan Chung-yen, a reform leader, in which he upheld the principle that the emperor should delegate power to his ministers, and should respect their opinions even when he disagreed with them. Particularly renowned was a memorial in which Ou-yang asserted that superior men may form a political faction, so long as it is based on moral and ideological principles. These views were denounced in the eighteenth century by Emperor Yung-cheng as deviations incompatible with the loyalty all officials must maintain toward their sovereign. So infuriated was this energetic absolutist that he wanted to box Ou-yang's ears.[3] However, none of these criticisms succeeded in altering the majority opinion, which through the centuries has held Ou-yang in great respect.

Ou-yang's stature is recognized outside China too. He is among the few Confucianists who have become known in the West. Western scholars, though not culturally bound to the Chinese heritage, have nonetheless found the traditional evaluation essentially correct. However, from their modern, cosmopolitan viewpoint they have emphasized its various aspects differently. They have been more interested in Ou-yang's historiography and archaeology than in his interpretations of the classics, more interested in his contributions to neo-Confucianism and his political thought than in his career. What impresses them most of all is his literary work, which even in translation has a universal appeal.[4]

This view is largely shared in China today. Revolutionary China holds Ou-yang in high regard not as a great Confucianist—a dubious honor at best these days—but chiefly as a paragon of classical literature. Recently compiled anthologies invariably include selections from his works. Teachers in modern schools, like tutors in the old days, would hardly neglect to remind their students that Ou-yang was one of the eight great prose masters produced by the T'ang and Sung periods, masters whose model compositions have been recited through the ages. But since classical prose now holds little appeal, current admiration has shifted to Ou-yang's poetry. Only a few years ago a selection of his poems appeared with a translation into vernacular Chinese for reading by those not sufficiently versed in classical literature to read the originals.[5]

Strange as it may seem, few works give us an integrated view of Ou-yang: accounts of his manifold accomplishments are scattered among numerous books in various specialized fields. The traditional accounts of his life are unsatisfactory, as is perhaps inevitable given the circumstances and assumptions under which practically all Chinese biographies were written in bygone centuries.[6] An eminent person in Confucian China was honored after death by a series of commemorative and didactic accounts of his life. These were begun at the family level, usually by someone of prestige either close to the family or working with background information it furnished. Such accounts usually included the compositions made soon after the subject's death—a brief obituary, a lengthy "account of conduct" (submitted to the authorities as a reference for an eventual official biography), numerous odes delivered at the funeral and on subsequent memorial occasions, an inscription buried with the coffin, and the epitaph or epitaphs cut on the tombstone. Many of these documents were then incorporated, occasionally in abridged versions, into the family genealogy. The major shortcoming of these accounts, understandably enough, is their eulogistic nature. They are not otherwise unreliable, however, for traditional practice granted no license to go beyond artful exaggeration of a man's merits and discreet understatement or silence about his faults.

Above the family level, the standards of precise historiography were applied with increasing rigor. The tone of flattery definitely diminished, and concern with the subject's social and political worth became more pronounced. This outlook became evident to some degree at the regional level—in the biographical sections of local gazetteers, for example—and more apparent in the standard histories compiled by official commissions. At this government level other complications set in, such as prejudice, nepotistic pressures, political considerations, and conventional biases about what constituted historical success or failure. Finally came works by private scholars, who usually attempted to improve or otherwise supplement the standard compilations. In both the private works and the official histories the basic objective was didactic: to determine the essential character of the subject, to compose his biography as an illustration of that character, and to assign him to a category of comparable persons. In short, these biographies (which appear in groups according to didactic classifications) may be regarded as assessments in the Confucian value-scheme. Strictly speaking, none of the accounts at any of the levels so far discussed satisfy the standards of biography in the modern or Western sense of a work investigating a man's character and particularities for their intrinsic interest, or for the light they shed on the man's times.

One type of traditional account, however, must be excepted from these general observations. This is the annalistic or chronological biography compiled long after a man's death by a private scholar, out of his own interest and curiosity. Such a biography often involved considerable research. Its compiler's emphasis was more on ascertaining the facts than on interpreting them. Presenting a man's activities chronologically, item after item, helped reduce the didactic overtone. Admittedly, the biases of the author's time and of his own scholastic outlook are still there, as is the author's admiration for his subject. Yet these factors tend to interfere with objectivity less in this genre than in the others. When available, annalistic biographies are the most helpful to present-day historical research.[7]

Beyond the traditional biographical accounts, the modern researcher has no choice but to read as widely and as cautiously as he can in other useful sources: elsewhere in the standard and privately compiled histories, in the chronicles, in collections of government documents, in encyclopedias, in local gazetteers, in the works of the subject himself and those of his contemporaries, in the informal writings of the period (ranging from serious essays to anecdotes and gossip), and in the commentaries written by scholars of later times. Fortunately, in the case of Ou-yang there is a fair amount of information available in these sources.[8]

Chinese historical sources, biographical and otherwise, have yet

5

another common deficiency: they generally neglect the historical setting. This deficiency stems only partly from the writers' persistent emphasis on the didactic value of history, an emphasis that leaves relatively little room for concern with time and change. It is due mainly to the assumption in Confucian China that the few interested readers, highly educated as they were, would be either well acquainted with the historical events or quite capable of easily becoming so. Yet even if this questionable assumption is granted as being valid to a point, a knowledge of historical events does not necessarily entail understanding of the framework in which they took place. In our modern thinking, a man reacts to his time: the two are inseparable. To study Ou-yang, we must first look at the period in which he lived.

CHAPTER TWO

THE HISTORICAL SETTING

A GREAT DIVIDE in Chinese history occurred around the eighth century, in the middle of the T'ang period (618–907). Between the eighth century and the founding of the Sung dynasty (960–1279), a China run by aristocrats slowly evolved into a China run by bureaucrats. Aristocratic families generally ceased to exist. Nor did the military exercise regional control. The government, effectively centralized from the capital down to each walled city, was staffed by professional bureaucrats, most of whom had risen by their own merits through the competitive examination system and years of service. Most bureaucrats were still landed gentry, but it was essentially their earned status as administrators, not their inherited status as landowners, that made them members of the ruling class. Many other factors contributed to the transformation from aristocracy to bureaucracy: the development of commerce and of a money economy; increasing urbanization; the spread of movable-type printing, and thus of education; and the opportunity for some commoners to rise through the civil-service examinations to the ranks of the elite. This set of conditions remained largely characteristic of China from the early Sung to the early twentieth century.[1]

What is the chief significance of the Sung period in Chinese history as a whole? Scholars generally agree that it was the formative period of a new social and cultural pattern. Some historians have described the new growth as a kind of "renaissance," in a

7

rather special sense of this overused term. Others have gone further, contending that the Sung was the beginning of an "early modern" period. These characterizations share a basic fault: they attempt to fit Chinese history into a European frame of reference. At best, they are more analogous than explanatory; they do not help to explain why after the "renaissance" China did not continue going forward, why no "late modern" period ever ensued, or why and how the new pattern became the established order and lasted so long.

To achieve a balanced view of the Sung one must neither overestimate the momentum of these changes nor underestimate the inertia of historical continuity. After all, continuity and the forces of change are by no means mutually exclusive: they interact with one another. While the forces of change modify continuity, continuity determines the kind of change that can take place. Given a high degree of Chinese cultural continuity since antiquity, sustained up to the T'ang by a firmly rooted and actively functioning heritage, the changes that occurred from then until the Sung could not help but be slow rather than sudden, and partial rather than total. They created a new pattern that took the place of the earlier one rather than encouraging further change. This is why I have suggested elsewhere the concept of a "neo-traditional" stage of development, beginning in the late T'ang, taking definite shape in the early Sung, and continuing for nearly a millennium.[2] By neo-traditional is meant in essence an integration of selected elements of the ancient heritage with selected elements of change to form the ingredients of a new tradition. In permeating the whole society, reaching a vast number of commoners instead of confining itself mainly to the elite, the new tradition was even more tenacious than the earlier one. Because it came into being through a gentle interweaving of old and new, it was always opposed to sudden and sweeping changes, let alone those that appeared revolutionary. Ultimately, its basically conservative orientation led to stagnation.

The early Sung was of course far from stagnant: the new tradi-

8

tion was then young and robust. Many forward-looking spirits appeared, Ou-yang Hsiu among them. They drew on the old heritage to define new issues, advance new ideas, and attempt both new solutions to old problems and solutions in response to the new and challenging problems of their time.

The Sung period had its share of serious problems.[3] Militarily, the agricultural empire was not exactly weak, but it could hardly match the power of its northern neighbors. The reunification it carried out was triumphant everywhere in China except the north. A strategic portion of North China immediately below the Great Wall remained firmly in the hands of the Liao empire, whose Khitan rulers were experienced in controlling these farming areas along with their own pastoral domain farther north. The inability of the Sung rulers to recapture what historically had been an integral part of China caused national humiliation and resentment. Worse was the fact that in choosing peace the Sung agreed in 1004 to make an annual appeasement payment. As time went on, the formula of defeatist diplomacy persisted. With successive crises the terms became increasingly unfavorable to the Sung.

During the eleventh century tension mounted. From the northwest, below the desert of Inner Mongolia, the new state of Hsi Hsia organized by the Tangut tribes started an invasion in 1038. Taking advantage of the situation, the Liao made threatening demands. At the same time, scattered uprisings occurred within the Sung empire itself. The compounded crises produced the minor reform of 1043–44. However, international and domestic order was restored soon afterward, and the reform was discontinued. Subsequently the major reform of 1069–85 undertook, among other grand measures, to build up the empire's military power. Victories were gained toward Annam in the south, and also in the northwest. Yet half a century later disaster struck. A new power, the Jürched (or Jürchen) people, from the part of Manchuria just northeast of the Great Wall, destroyed the Liao and established their own Chin empire. In a few years they moved down into the Yellow River valley and conquered the Northern Sung, which had been their nominal ally for a brief time. The surviving part of the empire, known as the Southern Sung (1127–1279), maintained itself below the Huai River valley in what is roughly Central and South China. In the end the Mongols came and conquered both the Chin and the Southern Sung.

Despite repeated setbacks and humiliations, the Southern Sung survived the attacks of the Mongols for about half a century, much longer than the Chin lasted. This record is attributable mostly to its internal solidarity. The Sung government had learned an important lesson from the military and regional usurpations that had destroyed the previous T'ang empire and the short-lived Five Dynasties (907–960). It guarded its military power jealously, concentrating a large part of its best troops around the capital and deliberately keeping its territorial forces so impotent that sometimes they could not even cope with local disturbances. No military command was ever given more than limited authority, which was always subject to restraint. Whatever this policy's faults, it well served the ends of internal security. Regional separatism never had a chance to emerge, and no would-be usurpers threatened the throne. The two puppet rulers temporarily installed by the Chin invaders are hardly exceptions; their inability to stand on their own is additional evidence of the solid support the Sung enjoyed. Two other factors making for solidarity were the largely unswerving loyalty of the scholar-officials and the widespread aversion to the alien invaders. Perhaps because of this aversion, there were remarkably few large-scale peasant uprisings in this period, compared with other periods in Chinese history.[4] The peasants were occasionally helped by tax remissions and exemptions, emergency food distributions, and efforts to reduce corruption and abuses of landlordism. Most important of all, the general prosperity of an expanding economy kept the dissatisfaction of most poor peasants below the flash point.

Financially, the Sung started off in a healthy condition: centralized control secured adequate regional revenues to meet the government's needs; income rose with the general economic growth; and government spending was watched with care to ensure a surplus. So the annual payments to the Liao and the Hsi Hsia presented no serious difficulty. The total cost of appeasement in the eleventh century has been estimated to be probably under 2 per cent of the state budget, if we exclude the heavy cost of military preparedness. Even more costly, ironically, was the maintenance of the civilian government. It was the cardinal policy of the Sung dynasty to treat its bureaucrats well. Eventually, the effects of something like Parkinson's law began to be felt. And prosperity was not free from undesirable side effects. The bureaucrats' standard of living moved upward, stimulated by the luxurious style of city life. Expanded demand led to rising prices, and to a higher cost of living.

By the middle of the eleventh century, the fiscal picture looked cloudy. Not only did expenditures exceed revenue; revenue fell short of expectations. Although the deficit was made up in part by increased income from urban areas, a serious problem lay in the decline of rural collections, probably resulting from a combination of maladministration, tax evasion, and a shift of the burden onto the helpless poor peasants, who could hardly meet the increased quota. Repeated efforts were then made to economize on government expenditures. When such retrenching measures brought little improvement, the pendulum swung to the alternative of assertive government roles, especially in trade and finance. The New Laws that came with the major reform of 1069–85 instituted a series of unprecedentedly vigorous measures, such as a reorganization of the budget, a more equitable land tax based on revised assessments, a new scheme for collecting and transporting tribute revenues, direct state participation in commerce, the issuance of interest-bearing state loans to farmers, and conversion of the corvée from labor to cash payment. These efforts did achieve a great increase in revenue. Unfortunately, the resulting surplus was soon dissipated, and although the major reform wiped out some class inequities, much to the displeasure of the elite, the common people's tax burden became heavier than before. It would not have been so crushing had the reform measures been administered as efficiently as intended. But the government's new economic activity created many more opportunities, especially in local government, for abuse and corruption, to the advantage of the officials, the clerks, and the merchants who connived with them. Moreover, false complacency about the reform program's temporary success gave rise to shameless extravagance on the part of the imperial house and to ill-advised military ventures, both of which contributed directly to the fall of the Northern Sung. The Southern Sung was never fiscally healthy. Its heavy taxation, snowballing irregularities in tax-collecting procedures, widespread corruption, and inflationary issuance of paper currency are well known.

What saved the Sung economy from collapse was its basic strength, both in agriculture and in the extractive industries. The Sung empire was beyond doubt the richest in the world in its time. Agriculture flourished. Along the southern and southwestern frontiers new lands were brought under cultivation as the difficulties of mountainous terrain and inferior soil were overcome. Old lands were reclaimed in densely populated areas, and marginal lands were also utilized. Better seed was introduced, a strain of early-ripening rice in particular; irrigation and many other improved techniques of intensive farming gradually spread from the prosperous regions to the backward parts of the country.[5] Production of food, silk, tea, and cotton increased greatly. The volume and quality of the products of the extractive industries (salt, copper, gold, silver, lead, tin, alum, and others) increased as well, adding to the wealth of the nation. Technological advancements in the coal and iron industries were particularly noteworthy. Despite the stunting effect of tax impositions and certain state monopolies, the economy continued to grow, apparently indefatigably. The processing and manufacturing trades throve, turning out textiles, metalware, paper, printing, painted merchandise, lacquers, and much else. The art objects of the Sung, especially porcelains, are famous. Regional specialization developed, and in time there grew up an increasing international demand for products of Chinese manufacture. Commerce expanded by leaps and bounds in local fairs, district markets, and regional and long-distance trade. Goods moved along the major waterways, along the coast, and overseas. Improved transportation made commerce easier; so did the increasing availability of credit and banking facilities. Of particular significance was the wide use of paper money.[6] For an agricultural society the extent of economic diversification and the expanding use of money are remarkable. Both were unprecedented in Chinese history.

In this affluent society (affluent by pre-modern standards) the cities grew in splendor.[7] The total population of the Northern Sung was probably not much more than sixty million people. The capital, Kaifeng, and a few other cities each claimed a million inhabitants or more. A score of lesser cities had populations over 100,000. A beautiful contemporary scroll, extant today principally in the form of copies made in subsequent centuries, reveals a vivid picture of Kaifeng, starting with a busy river scene, then moving over the rainbow bridge to crowded streets lined with the stores of many trades, where performers entertain crowds of adults and children with a variety of tricks, and peddlers sell sundry goods. The exquisite mansions of the elite stand nearby; in the background are the secluded palace grounds in all their grandeur. Records of the time contain minute details of the manifold activity of the capital. Later on Lin-an (now known as Hangchow), the capital of the Southern Sung, became an even more dazzling metropolis. Not much hurt by the coming of the Mongols, it made an indelible impression on Marco Polo, and, through his accounts, on the world.

Urbanization had social as well as economic effects. Among

other things, it brought the elite and the common people closer together, enriching the lives of both. The elite prided themselves on diverse refinements, among them classical literature, other sophisticated literary forms that absorbed not a few popular ingredients, critical scholarship, creative philosophy, painting and other fine arts, and the appreciation of sophisticated comforts and delicacies.

These refinements had considerable appeal to those of the lower classes who were exposed to them, and many proved apt emulators of the elite's tastes; while the upper class, for its part, found amusement in the popular entertainments of the city, notably dramatic performances and storytelling. Gradually, the old class barriers wore away. The ruling elite of scholar-officials was reasonably open to men of common birth who could pass the civil-service examinations. The merchants grew in numbers and importance, and other urban groups acquired a measure of prosperity. The urban way of life spread from the metropolitan centers to the lesser cities, carried by officials transferred to new posts; by printed books available to the distant corners of the empire; by the web of trade, of fairs and markets, of restaurants, wineshops, and teashops, even in remote small towns; by traveling performers of all kinds. In short, urbanization helped the diffusion of culture throughout society.

At the apex of Sung society stood the scholar-officials. Politically, they were the men in charge. Socially, they were the elite beyond challenge. Culturally, they were also leaders: steeped in their culture, proud of it, active in refining it. Economically, most were from landed families, though many rose from relatively modest backgrounds. Once in government service, they received excellent pay in both cash and goods, official gifts and rewards on special state occasions, various favors and perquisites for themselves, and additional favors for members of their families, not to mention honorary titles and pensions for retirement. They invested their surplus income in land, and land owned by officials was tax-exempt, within certain limits. A few of them had interests in businesses run by relatives or friends. Some merchants, though comparatively few, were as rich as the richest scholar-officials, but commerce had little prestige. Status came principally from office, only secondarily from wealth. The only way for a wealthy merchant to increase his prestige was by gaining the friendship of scholar-officials, or, better yet, by having a son join their ranks.[8]

The ascendancy of the scholar-officials was due to the Sung emperors' distrust of the military and of aristocrats with hereditary regional influence. Rather than rely on these traditionally ambitious and potentially subversive elements, the Sung preferred to recruit a class of professional civil servants. So the gates of the examination hall were opened to all qualified candidates, including those of plebeian origin, and the successful were rewarded with honor, glory, and a secure and well-paid position.[9] Descendants of formerly illustrious families had little choice but to live with the new system of equal opportunity, and those who rose by it from humble backgrounds were particularly grateful and loyal to it.

All the power a bureaucrat had he owed to his appointment, which was subject to change according to the rules and regulations of the civil service and ultimately dependent on the emperor's will. He was the emperor's creature, without any power base of his own. This derivative nature of the bureaucrat's power was the best guarantee of his loyalty, a loyalty reinforced by Confucian precepts.

The Sung government was a machine owned and directed by the absolutist emperor, but operated by the scholar-officials. Promotions were generally made in accordance with merit, seniority, recommendations, and special sponsoring; nepotism and favoritism were as a rule kept at a minimum, except under degenerate administrations. Demotions resulted from unfavorable reports, obvious faults, charges made by the censors, and sometimes political backstabbing. The standard of performance was fair enough, especially early in the Sung. This standard was also reinforced by Confucian moral precepts, which revived and achieved new strength in the Sung. They were built into the improved social conventions that were evolving at the time, and assiduously practiced by the better scholar-officials.

From the first, the Sung emperors ruled by determining policy themselves, with the advice of their leading councillors, then delegating to these councillors the major responsibilities of implementation. By the middle of the eleventh century, however, some idealistic scholar-officials were boldly demanding a greater share of power. Their demands were based on the Confucian principle that assigned the emperor's moral guardianship to their care. They were his tutors, both before and after he ascended the throne. They had the privilege, and theoretically the moral responsibility, of remonstrating with him when he failed to act properly. In fact, those who were appointed to be policy critic-advisers had the specific duty of pointing out his mistakes. It followed, from the idealistic point of view, that the scholar-officials knew best how to manage the state. The emperor, then, should confine himself to choosing the best available scholar-officials as his councillors and advisers and should grant them sufficient power to govern in his behalf.

Inherent in the Confucian state was a basic antagonism between Confucianism as ideological authority and the state as power structure.[10] To respect the scholar-officials for their ideological authority while carefully limiting their power was an ambivalent attitude. Had many scholar-officials ever acted in unison they might have attained a far greater measure of both authority and power. After all, withdrawal of their collective support would have meant grave danger for the empire. However, their divisive political nature precluded any such possibility. Individual ambition, conflicts of personal interests, and honest differences of opinion all played a part. Whenever a leading official became more influential than usual, others would insinuate that he was verging on usurpation of power, if not exactly disloyalty. Whenever a group of officials remained in power for a considerable length of time, those out of power would begin to accuse them of forming a faction, monopolizing access to the emperor, misleading him and preventing better advice from reaching his ears. In factional disputes, both sides tried to invoke the emperor's support, which contributed to a further rise of his absolute power, an eventual decline of their delegated power, and even a weakening of their ideological authority. United, the scholar-officials might stand; but they never were. Divided they could only fall, and they inevitably did. The eleventh century seemed like a golden opportunity for them to rise to greater political heights than ever before. Paradoxically, they ruined their own chances.

In the non-bureaucratic reaches of ideology, the Sung scholar-officials had a more lasting effect. They not only revived Confucianism, but enriched it with new content. For nearly a millennium before the Sung, Confucianism had been losing ground to neo-Taoism and especially to Buddhism, which gained tremendous popularity among the common people and an important following among the educated. During the T'ang dynasty, for example, many literati studied at Buddhist temples, then the leading centers of learning. But under the Sung, Confucian learning soon came to the fore again, thanks in great part to the state examinations. Confucian schools expanded rapidly. Wealthy citizens endowed private academies with buildings and income-producing lands; local officials set up some schools at government expense and solicited individual gifts for others. By the middle of the eleventh century, it was the declared policy of the state to establish government schools eventually in all prefectures and important subprefectures. As printing progressed and the use of movable type developed, books became much cheaper, and thus much more accessible to those of modest means. An increasing quantity and variety were produced by the imperial educational offices, local governments in prosperous regions, interested scholar-officials, the schools themselves, and book merchants in many cities. Serious works, belles lettres, classics, and new works all circulated more widely. Reference books especially useful at the state examinations came out in pocket form. The educated grew rapidly in number, and the keen competition among them stimulated an advance in Confucian scholarship much beyond the achievements of the past. This upsurge was the beginning of neo-Confucianism.

European sinologists since the Jesuits have long used the term neo-Confucianism in a narrow sense, to refer mainly to the Confucian orthodox philosophy established in the twelfth century by Chu Hsi—the school of thought known to the Chinese as the *Tao-hsüeh chia,* the School of the True Way. In accordance with the practice of other scholars in recent years, I shall use the term more broadly here, to designate an extensive, pervasive intellectual system and way of life, a system based on key Confucian precepts that was developed beginning in the eleventh century to meet the changing needs of a more complex society. In short, neo-Confucianism, in this sense of the term, is the intellectual and ethical fabric of neo-traditional society.[11] It was an extension of classical Confucianism, and never assumed a separate or independent identity: together with classical Confucianism, it formed China's new orthodoxy. Nonetheless, one may discern important distinctions between the two philosophies.

Neo-Confucianism had four main characteristics: ethical fundamentalism, restorationism, historical-mindedness, and humanism. Ethical fundamentalism—a belief in the fundamental importance of ethics, and in the need to obey the moral instructions of the ancient texts literally—was central to all forms of Confucianism, but neo-Confucianism was the most elaborate in systematically exploring the metaphysical underpinnings of ethics, and in developing vast and detailed codes of conduct. Restorationism was the belief that great efforts should be made toward the restoration of the Golden Age, an ancient utopia reconstructed by the neo-Confucianists from the ideal principles they believed to be embodied in the classics. Historical-mindedness helped balance this belief in the superiority of antiquity by cultivating a more realistic awareness than earlier Confucianists had had of the actual changes that had taken place since antiquity. History was studied to see how and why society degenerated, so that degeneration might be prevented and ways by which society could change for the better might be found. Humanism, as we shall use the term, refers to an emphasis on men, on self-cultivation, on human possibilities and human limits. Unlike classical Confucianism, which concentrated on indoctrinating the aristocratic elements, assuming that the rest of society would come under their moral influence, neo-Confucian humanism extended to elite and commoners alike, as befitted a society in which elite status was conferred by competitive examination. Neo-Confucianism was in no sense egalitarian; like classical Confucianism, it saw proper hierarchical relationships as fundamental. It implemented Confucian precepts by designing various codes of conduct, according to each man's station.

Neo-Confucianism had a few forerunners in the middle and late T'ang, but its main development took place during the Sung. Its proponents in the early Sung possessed a zeal that overflowed the bounds of their official careers. They took up Confucian learning for its own sake, confident that their scholarship surpassed that of earlier times and linked them directly with the ancient masters. They believed that they were recapturing the original vision of Confucius himself. They were activists, both by conviction and by temperament. Their supreme ideal was to apply the Confucian vision, characteristically with some modifications of their own, to the improvement of society. This reforming spirit, particularly common among the eleventh-century neo-Confucian leaders, might even be described as a sense of Confucianizing mission.[12]

The scholarship of these pioneering neo-Confucianists covered a wide range. They were innovators in metaphysics, and in ethics they reached greater psychological depths than any of their predecessors. Cosmology aroused much interest, but practical issues remained at the center of attention. The ancient classics were subjected to textual criticism, and also given pragmatic interpretations in the light of existing circumstances. The drive to improve society led to varying philosophical emphases: most scholars stressed individual morality through self-cultivation; a significant minority advocated reforms of governmental institutions and policies; still others promoted social reconstruction at the family, clan, and community levels. Seeking lessons from the past, they wrote histories of all sorts—dynastic, annalistic, institutional, local, topical, and encyclopedic—and made important advances in the related disciplines of archaeology, historiography, and bibliography.[13] This new growth in scholarship was also reflected in literature: a new style of prose was developed. It belies its name, the "ancient style," for though it followed old models in spirit it was nonetheless a major innovation. In poetry the Sung masters not only rivaled their T'ang predecessors, but developed a new song-form, the *tz'u*, or lyric meters, into the prize achievement of the Sung.[14]

Neo-Confucianism had a characteristic way of enriching itself. Onto the Confucian tree it grafted new branches, which bore new fruit. It recaptured what was thought to be the vision of Confucius and attempted to use it to reform contemporary life. It invoked the authority of antiquity, not really to turn back to the past, but to sanction a mixture between the selected heritage and the innovations of the present. Ou-yang Hsiu, as we shall see, exemplifies this balance of Confucian ideals and contemporary concerns. Another outstanding example was Wang An-shih, the leader of the major reform. He placed tremendous faith in the classics, particularly the *Rituals of Chou,* but only in accordance with his own interpretations and mainly to justify his New Laws, many of which were without precedent. The same was true of the five founders of neo-Confucian metaphysics. They were honored in later centuries for having re-established philosophical orthodoxy, which had not existed since the time of Confucius and Mencius. The neo-Confucians' main contribution, however, was in metaphysics, a field about which neither Confucius nor Mencius had much to say.

Neo-Confucianism developed in the face of considerable opposition. Although most people accepted the convention of honoring the past, few were willing to let its lessons interfere with their own interests in the present. Every proposed change, be it restoration or innovation, had its opponents. It was argued that what had long been dead could hardly be revived for use in a different age, or it was argued that lack of precedent made new departures unjustifiable. Another difficulty was internal. The leading neo-Confucian scholars disagreed among themselves a great deal: on the proper interpretation of the classics, on what direction political and social development should take, and frequently on both.

Quarrels over political thought were particularly intense. At the beginning of the Sung, most scholar-officials had a conventional outlook and took little interest in political theories.[15] But less than a century later the situation had changed altogether. Dissatisfied with the state of the world and impelled by idealistic beliefs, a number of leading scholar-officials made increasingly strong criticisms and advocated various reforms, sometimes at the cost of their careers. There is a resemblance, in a way, between the diversity of eleventh-century political thought and the diversity of the thought of the Hundred Schools period, the most creative period in ancient Chinese philosophy. Sung thought, being all under the umbrella of neo-Confucianism, was of course far less diverse. Still, the Sung was the liveliest age for political thought since remote antiquity.[16]

The central problem of the political storms and theoretical disputes was that of orthodoxy. Some pioneers were so charged with zeal that they often replaced earlier Confucian interpretations with their own, insisting that only theirs were right. Such claims to orthodoxy aroused much antagonism, particularly among neo-Confucianists with different ideas.[17] The Correct School of the Ch'ing-li reign (1041–48), which gave an ideological underpinning to the minor reform in 1043–44, claimed orthodoxy in this way. The factionalism provoked by this school (and by the reform it supported) went on for a long time, poisoning both the political and the academic atmosphere. A similar sequence of events, on a much larger scale, took place after 1069, when the major reform swept across the land. Several claims to orthodoxy were made, although generally the scholar-officials split into two clear-cut camps: for and against the reform. The dispute went on for decades, with political control switching back and forth and neither side hesitating to use official pressure to establish its version as the truth. Gone was the fairly free spirit that had nurtured the growth of varying opinions.

Political thought was less dynamic in the Southern Sung; the times were stiff with convention, and criticism of the established order was regarded with suspicion. Early in the dynasty, Chu Hsi and his followers made their claim to be the School of the True Way. Their opponents had them officially denounced as the "False School" and dismissed from active government service. Nevertheless, their superior scholarship, high standard of conduct, and voluminous writings eventually won great respect for their teachings in academic circles. Much of what they had advocated in social improvement and self-cultivation came to be widely accepted. The state, though powerful, did not go so far as to deny their claim to intellectual and social leadership. At the end of the thirteenth century—under the Mongols, ironically—their school finally won official recognition as the orthodox Confucianism. The elaborate system of neo-Confucian philosophy this school created was without question of lasting importance. However, the long struggle for ideological supremacy had sapped the school of any political vigor it might once have had. Its political outlook had become tame, narrow, and conservative.[18] The great paradox of neo-Confucianism is that having been a vigorous ideological guardian of state affairs during the Northern Sung, often in conflict with the emperors and the less ideologically oriented scholar-officials, it ended as a state-sponsored system of thought that stifled questioning and criticism.

The Sung was a period of splendid attainment that established the neo-traditional pattern for later centuries. Despite frequent disagreements among many neo-Confucianists, it largely succeeded in combining old and new into a dynamic, effective tradition. Thus it seemed to the scholar-officials of later eras a near-fulfillment of their common ideals. True, their admiration for the Sung made them overlook its cultural retrogressions—the decline of the martial spirit and of the status of women, the deterioration of Buddhism, and the tendency toward cultural ethnocentrism, to name a few—and made them excuse such faults as absolutism, bureaucratic abuses, and the general poverty of the peasants as well. However, the elite were not alone in their affection for this remarkable age. As can be heard in the oral tradition kept alive in popular plays and vernacular literature, the common people of later centuries shared a generally favorable impression of it. To this day, the Sung stands high in the minds of many Chinese.

CHAPTER THREE

EARLY CAREER

IN THE LATE T'ANG the best-developed region in China, both culturally and economically, was the lower Yangtze valley, particularly the Yangtze delta from Nanking eastward. During the military chaos and political instability of the Five Dynasties period, many low-ranking scholar-officials assigned to posts inland and upriver, in what is now Kiangsi, chose to settle there permanently. The region was quite mountainous and not very fertile, but it was relatively secure from disturbances. There the seeds of the traditional culture borne by the immigrants from the lowlands blossomed anew. In the middle of the eleventh century, a new crop of bright, energetic, and forward-looking scholars emerged from Kiangsi and broke the monopoly on high court positions that the northerners from the Yellow River valley, the birthplace of the Sung, had held ever since the founding of the dynasty a hundred years earlier. Among the best-known of these southern scholars, in addition to Ou-yang Hsiu and the famous reformer Wang An-shih, were Wang Ch'in-jo, the first southerner to attain the high rank of state councillor; Yen Shu, the second; Wang An-kuo, Wang An-shih's younger brother; and Tseng Kung, Ou-yang's leading disciple.[1] The family histories of all these men show successive rises, in a few generations, from relatively obscure literati backgrounds to the top of the political and social ladder.

The genealogy Ou-yang compiled for his own family traced its origins to some illustrious names of the T'ang period. This claim is at best dubious: there were several obvious gaps in the lineage of which nothing was known or said.[2] Actually, the family remained obscure until the generation before Ou-yang himself. All three of his uncles attained court rank in the early Sung, the first men in the family to do so.[3] His father also had a promising start, earning the degree of doctor of letters in 1000, but he died in 1010 after serving at minor posts up and down the Yangtze valley.[4] Ou-yang's mother's family was said to be "a clan of note in the lower river valley," but since the clan was not identified, its eminence is presumably exaggerated.[5]

Ou-yang, though counted by custom and law as being from Kiangsi because of his paternal lineage, was not a true native of that region. He was born in 1007 in Mienchow, in what is now Szechwan, where his father was an official. He was brought up in Suichow, in what is now Hupeh, at the post of his uncle Hua, where his mother took him after the death of his father.[6] Only once—for the burial of his parents—did he make an important visit to the ancestral home in Luling. Although on this occasion he composed a moving burial ode expressing the deepest feelings of filial piety, he never returned to the ancestral graves as a pious son should, but left them to the care of some Taoist priests. He was more attracted by the beautiful lake scenery in Yingchow (modern Fu-yang in Anhwei), where he bought some land and eventually retired.[7] His seemingly un-Confucian conduct toward his ancestors earned him rather sharp criticism in later centuries. However, his critics failed to take changing historical circumstances into account. In the early Sung, there was considerable upward social mobility and accompanying family migration, much more so than later on. Many officials from relatively modest backgrounds, after years of service in different parts of the country, chose to settle down in a place they themselves liked rather than to return to the home of their clan. Like Ou-yang, his uncles and their families never returned to Luling.[8]

There is a story about Ou-yang's childhood, based on a statement in the *Sung Standard History*, that appears even today in Chinese children's books. According to this story, Ou-yang's family was so poor that he learned to write by using a reed-stock to draw on the ground.[9] This is not literally true; Ou-yang's uncle Hua, under whose protection he spent his childhood, was a doctor of letters and a government official—hardly a poor man. But the story is symbolically true, and was so intended by the compilers of the official history, to reinforce the implication that Ou-yang was essentially a self-educated man. He never attended a formal school, and as he himself testified, there were no notable scholars teaching in the rather backward region of Suichow. But Ou-yang was a brilliant, eager child, and he studied hard. According to Su Ch'e he read rapidly, about five lines at a glance, even though he was nearsighted.[10] In his youth, as he said himself, he had few books, but he had a wealthy friend named Li whose family owned many volumes. During a visit to Li's home Ou-yang discovered in a broken storage basket an incomplete set of the works of Han Yü, a great author of the T'ang period and a forerunner of neo-Confucianism. Ou-yang was taken by the ancient-style prose of Han Yü, and developed an ambition to master it himself. This early exposure had important consequences in the future, but for the time being he had to forgo his wish. The ancient style was not well known or respected at all: it was the current style that counted at the examinations.

In 1023, when Ou-yang was sixteen, he took the examinations for the first time and failed on the technicality of a wrong rhyme. He tried again in 1027 but had no better luck. By an old custom of the T'ang period that was still followed to some extent during the Sung, young candidates might seek recognition by presenting their compositions to high officials who were authorities on literature; and in 1028 Ou-yang took some of his work to Hsü Yen, a court academician, who was then at nearby Hanyang. Hsü liked ancient-style prose; he had already befriended a handful of authors, such as Liu K'ai, who deplored the current style. Hsü found Ou-

26

yang promising and asked him to stay on. The next year he took Ou-yang with him to Kaifeng, where he introduced him to other high officials with literary inclinations. Ou-yang learned a great deal at the capital, and attracted further attention. He passed the first examination in 1029, and in 1030 earned the degree of doctor of letters.[11]

It was customary at the time for a promising degree-holder of modest origin to be taken as a son-in-law by an eminent official. Ou-yang, in accordance with the custom, married Hsü's daughter.[12] She died three years later, having borne him no children. In 1037, Ou-yang married the daughter of another high official, Hsüeh K'uei. Relationship by marriage usually but not necessarily strengthened personal bonds in politics; in Ou-yang's case it did not. In 1036, when the reformer Fan Chung-yen attacked Lü I-chien, the chief councillor, Hsü Yen supported his friend Lü, but Ou-yang, Hsü's protégé, sided with Fan. To Ou-yang, political principles came before personal relations; but Hsü never forgave him. The death of Hsü saddened Ou-yang deeply, for his wish to repay his benefactor could never be fulfilled.[13] By his second marriage, Ou-yang became related to Wang Kung-ch'en, who had also earned his doctorate in 1030 and married one of Hsüeh K'uei's daughters. But Wang remained an arch-opponent of all reformers throughout his career.[14]

After Ou-yang received his degree, he was appointed to serve at Loyang, which for centuries had been the leading cultural metropolis of northern China. His duties as a junior staff member were light, and he had plenty of time for writing and social activities.[15] Several colleagues of established literary fame were of great help to him. From Yin Shu, a leading writer and historian, Ou-yang learned to write excellent prose in the ancient style, following Han Yü and other early masters in spirit but developing techniques of his own. Stimulated by Mei Yao-ch'en, perhaps the best poet of the time, he perfected his ability to work not only in the traditional poetic forms, but in the increasingly popular *tz'u* as well. So rapid was his progress in both prose and poetry that his literary fame soon matched that of his friends.

Ou-yang and his friends studied and discussed a broad range of subjects besides literature: interpretations of the classics, philosophy (which they occasionally discussed with some learned Buddhist monks), and practical matters, notably military affairs.[16] The Sung empire had never been strong along its northern frontiers, and under the appeasement policy, as Ou-yang and his friends perceived, it was getting weaker.[17] Ou-yang harbored youthful dreams of someday playing a military role,[18] and was eager to make friends with anyone knowledgeable about military problems. The man who impressed him most as a potential military leader was Shih Yen-nieh (better known by his courtesy name, Shih Man-ch'ing). Shih was learned but virile, unbridled and exhilarating, a drinker of heroic capacity. He was too unconventional to please most people, and died in the prime of life without ever being given a chance to distinguish himself.[19] In the preface to a collection of poems by a Buddhist monk who was one of Shih's best friends, Ou-yang lamented how lack of attention had kept Shih's talents buried:

> For forty years past, the state had held all within the four seas in unity, a stop had been put to armed strife and the world had been nourished and fostered in freedom from troubles of any kind; therefore it must often befall that men of worth, skilled in stratagem, bold and of high purpose, men far removed from the common run, would find no scope for their abilities but prefer concealment to emergence on the public scene. Among the wooded hills they might live as butchers or pedlars, grow old and die without ever becoming known to the world; nor was it possible to seek out such men or draw them forth.
>
> Then, later, I found my friend, now dead, Shih Man-ch'ing. Man-ch'ing was a man of broad vision and high mind. If those in power could find no use for such material, neither could Man-ch'ing stoop to seek any compromise. Lacking an outlet for his

ambitions, time and again he would carouse with commoners and yokels, never to grow weary though soused and staggering drunk.[20]

Ou-yang was never able to realize his youthful military aspirations. But his interest in making friends and discovering talented newcomers never left him. It remained a habit with him to carry a dozen or so blank cards for social calls. Whenever he heard an unfamiliar name praised highly, he would ask for the man's address, have a card filled out, and proceed to call on him.[21] When he ascertained that someone was promising, even at second hand from friends whose judgment he trusted, he would recommend the newcomer to someone who could help him. In this manner he helped a whole generation of young talents. His interest in giving aid to the deserving was fully in accord with the Confucian tenet that the good man is the basic asset of state and society; it may also have derived in part, psychologically, from the struggles of his lonely youth. In any event, Ou-yang seems to have been extroverted and energetic, fond of lively conversation and serious discussion alike.

The years at Loyang turned out to be the most enjoyable of his life. Study and writing seemed to blend well for him with women, wine, and song.[22] However, it is said that his intimacy with a courtesan went so far as to interfere with the discharge of his official responsibilities. His superiors, one after another, advised him to drop the affair to avoid a scandal, but Ou-yang persisted.[23] At the time, Ou-yang's indulgence brought no serious consequences, but years later it was used against him by his political opponents.

Ou-yang's high aspirations and dynamic personality soon involved him in a political controversy, the clash between Fan Chung-yen and Lü I-chien that preceded the minor reform. Essentially, this was the first clash between neo-Confucianism, which was then growing in zeal and strength, and the established order of the Sung, which had never before been challenged. Fan had

risen by his own efforts from an even lower background than Ou-
yang. His famous maxim—that a scholar should be "first in worry-
ing about the world's troubles and last in enjoying its pleasures"—
characterizes his crusading spirit.[24] Repeatedly and fearlessly, he
overstepped the conventional limitations that generally prevented
the lower-ranking scholar-officials from speaking out, beyond their
official concerns, on the shortcomings of the state, and criticized
the court for what he as an intellectual considered to be deviations
from Confucian teaching. In 1029, early in his career, he antago-
nized the reigning empress dowager and her leading councillors
by maintaining that the young Emperor Jen-tsung should not
kneel before the empress dowager on her birthday, as the officials
did.[25] This bold protest attracted much attention, and Fan was
dismissed from the court, but those who admired his courage in
defending the emperor's dignity regarded his dismissal as a "glorious demotion." In 1033 Jen-tsung, by then reigning himself,
brought Fan back as a policy critic-adviser. However, Fan's grate-
fulness did not silence him—he soon criticized the emperor himself for unjustifiably divorcing the empress, and Lü I-chien by implication for abetting the divorce.[26] The immediate result was a
second glorious demotion.

Fan's protests foreshadowed other, similar controversies. On the
surface these were part of a power struggle: Fan and other ideologically oriented scholar-officials against the emperor and his
leading ministers. In the background were class and regional antagonisms. Most ministers were highborn northerners, whereas
many of the outspoken scholar-officials were southerners of modest
origin. But the fundamental cause of these controversies was the
conflict inherent in the Confucian state between ideology and the
power structure. What the idealists wanted was an official say in
policy making. What the state wanted was able and loyal administrators to implement its fixed policies.

Fan was sent to Soochow, where he proved a most successful administrator, especially in irrigation development. In 1035, he was

brought back to the capital city as its acting metropolitan prefect—not exactly a court position, but one with easy access to the court.[27] The next year, Fan presented the emperor with four famous essays on the need to appreciate the value of virtuous officials; to select learned and capable scholars for court positions; to accept the ideological authority of their advice; and to delegate power to them according to their responsibilities, without concentrating power in his own hands or in those of his chief councillor. Fan also presented the emperor with a chart showing how Lü I-chien had played favorites in appointing various officials. Jen-tsung took the essays and the chart as implying that he and his chief councillor had been managing state affairs improperly, and demoted Fan for a third time.[28] By doing so he created an opposition faction within the bureaucracy, for the scholar-officials who sympathized with Fan now rallied to the cause of maintaining their ideological autonomy and encouraged one another to continue criticizing the policies followed by the administration of Lü I-chien.

Lü was in many ways an exemplary civil servant. Familiar with government intricacies by virtue of family background and long experience, he won much respect as a meticulous administrator and astute politician.[29] One of his major administrative achievements was the compilation of a handbook summarizing all bureaucratic regulations and precedents, in order to prevent the common device of using the latter to circumvent the former. He was especially adept in dealing with delicate matters at court. It was he who quietly cautioned the empress dowager to be kind toward Jen-tsung, her adopted heir, lest her family suffer from retaliations after her death.[30] Later on, when Jen-tsung ascended the throne, his consort advised him that Lü had been too close to the old lady and should not be trusted. Jen-tsung removed Lü from court for a short while, but soon realized that Lü, with his long experience at court, was probably the best possible choice for chief councillor. Restored to power, Lü supported Jen-tsung in divorcing the empress, in part to please him and in part for revenge. Lü was much criticized for his part in this affair, but not all his actions were known at the time. After the divorce, he discreetly persuaded the emperor to take another consort without delay, for Lü saw clearly that otherwise Jen-tsung's amorous involvements with numerous ladies-in-waiting would soon bring even greater dissension and intrigue than normal to the court. Lü was perhaps overly involved in court life; he could claim little credit in matters of policy, with which Fan and the other idealistic neo-Confucianists were most concerned.[31]

By 1036, Lü was firmly entrenched as the recognized leader of the conservative northern bureaucrats. Lü saw the new breed of aspiring southern scholar-officials as a threat to the status quo, which he was determined to preserve. The northerners' control of the administrative organs of the state was strong enough to prevent Fan and his friends from gaining much power in the executive branch; their only means of expanding their influence was by demonstrating their superior scholarship, which meant presenting challenging new interpretations of Confucian theories, or adroit use of the critical power that scholar-officials were privileged to exercise in opposing the administration. Criticism bred attempts to silence the critics; the two groups crystallized into full-fledged factions; and the conflict between them became bitter strife.[32]

The storm soon swept Ou-yang into it. On Fan's second demotion, Ou-yang wrote him from Loyang, enjoining him not to become discouraged.[33] After Ou-yang's term at Loyang, he was appointed to the Imperial Academy. At that time Fan was again serving at the capital, and a close friendship developed between them. They agreed that to be effective, or at least to provoke attention, Fan must break out of conventional bureaucratic channels with his criticism.[34] This was precisely what he did in 1036. As administrator of Kaifeng, Fan had no call to criticize the way the emperor and his councillor conducted affairs of state. In doing so, he flouted the rules of proper procedure. Lü realized that Fan's act must not be allowed to set a precedent. Not only was Fan demoted; a special injunction was proclaimed, forbidding all officials to speak on matters outside their jurisdiction. This step raised the issue of the privilege of criticism. On the one hand, the injunction had its justification in the traditional Confucian value of submission to the hierarchical order. On the other hand, it conflicted with an equally important and characteristically neo-Confucian belief: that loyalty required the scholar-officials to contribute their honest opinions to the best of their ability. In Ou-yang's eyes, the injunction was a measure meant to suppress the worthy scholar-officials. He was particularly angered by the slavish silence and pathetic lack of response among most of his colleagues.[35] But how could he take action? The issue of the injunction was far outside the jurisdiction of his minor position; to speak up on it would be to disobey the injunction himself. Consequently, he attacked one of Lü's key supporters, Kao Jo-no, a northerner whose position as a policy critic-adviser would enable him to speak out on the injunction, for not opposing it![36] Ou-yang wrote to Kao in the most insulting terms:

After the demotion of Fan, I saw you at the home of Chang Fang-p'ing and heard your disparaging remarks about Fan.... Fan has always been an upright official, just as he is a learned scholar of the classics. His service at the court has adhered strictly to high principles, as the whole world knows.... Yet you denounce him after his downfall and consider it well-deserved.... This means that you care so much about your post ... that you dare not, even once, oppose the chief councillor.... Why, if Fan were really not virtuous ... did you not so inform the emperor previously, when Fan was promoted to a high position? Instead, you did not murmur a single word. Why have you waited till his downfall to add your abuses? ... The day before yesterday, the Censorate posted the injunction forbidding all officials to speak on matters outside the scope of their duties. This means that the only persons who still have a voice are the policy critic-advisers. If you do not speak up, no one else in the world can.

You alone are in an official position to speak, yet you do not; then you ought to resign! ... But still you make your appearance among the scholar-officials in and out of the court, and still you call yourself a policy critic-adviser. This means you no longer have the sense of shame of any decent human being! ... I wish you would forthwith bring this letter of mine to the court so that my offense may be duly penalized by capital punishment![37]

This letter sent Kao off to the court in tears, complaining of the deliberate humiliation he had suffered. Lü was forced to take some action, for his own authority was being indirectly challenged, but he realized that a brilliant young man like Ou-yang was bound to rise high someday, and therefore did not wish to appear any harsher than necessary. So he merely demoted Ou-yang to the subprefecture of I-ling, below the Yangtze gorges, not far from Suichow, where he had been raised.

The setback was not without some blessings. To begin with, Ou-yang's reputation was greatly enhanced among the southern faction. A widely circulated poem by Ts'ai Hsiang, a well-known scholar-official, praised the independent stand of Fan, Ou-yang and his old friend Yin Shu, and Yü Ching, who were all demoted at about the same time.[38] It also depicted Kao Jo-no as a dishonorable person with no sense of shame. Ou-yang reacted to the demotion without self-pity or resentment, and devoted his years at I-ling to study and reflection. He dissipated less, and started to write a new history of the Five Dynasties, since many scholars had been dissatisfied with the old official history. This work eventually established him as a leading historian, for it was officially adopted as a standard history—a unique honor for a private work.[39] Ou-yang also gave much thought to the problems of administration, and soon came to the conclusion that excellence as an administrator depended to a great degree on substantive knowledge of practice, of the various ways and means by which policy might be implemented. Confucian theories and lofty ideals alone would hardly help. This conclusion led him to formulate a new set of administrative principles, as will be discussed in a later chapter. It also changed his political outlook. In retrospect, he realized that he had been hotheaded in attacking his adversaries, and that he should have been more constructive in criticizing their policies.[40] In the future he would temper his idealism with realism, giving due consideration to contrary views, allowing for practical difficulties, and settling for modest reforms rather than making grandiloquent but ineffective gestures.

In 1040 the vassal kingdom of Hsi Hsia declared itself independent of the Sung empire and began to invade the Sung's northwestern border areas. By that time the antagonisms roused in 1036 had lost much of their heat, and the emergence of an external military threat made it desirable to compose internal political differences. The man most instrumental in reconciling the two factions was Han Ch'i, a high-born northerner who had spent considerable time in the south, and who had a distinguished record both as an administrator and as a policy critic-adviser. Sharing the background of the men in power and the ideals of the opposition, he commanded the respect of all. When the Hsi Hsia invasion began, he recommended entrusting Fan Chung-yen, as a man of proven courage and ability, with the defense of the northwestern frontier, pledging that he would be willing to be penalized himself if Fan should turn out to be a poor choice.[41] Lü I-chien responded with characteristic smoothness. He knew that Fan and his friends, who had gained in prestige in the years since their defeat, could not be kept down forever. Besides, they were highly capable officials whose services would be valuable in the crisis then mounting. Lü might also have been thinking of protecting the future careers of his sons, who were in the same age group as many of his political adversaries.[42] In any event, he not only supported Han's recommendation, but suggested that Fan be given a higher rank than Han had proposed. It was then Fan's turn to be conciliatory; on taking up his new duties, he could hardly give his enemies a chance to attack him at court while he was far away and unable to defend himself. In a formal letter to Lü offering an apology for their previous clash, he complimented Lü for having been so broadminded as to forgive him. He expressed his wishes for cooperation between them in the future, citing a historical precedent in the T'ang period in which two feuding officials had reconciled their differences in the interest of the state.⁴³

Several of Fan's friends were also given new duties, and they too made conciliatory gestures to Lü. Ou-yang hoped to gain a military post, but was disappointed. Fan recommended him for the position of staff secretary, but Ou-yang declined it, saying in a letter to Fan:

> The responsibility of considering and discussing strategies, of anticipating the enemy and making sure of victories, rests with the military staff. The preparation of reports, memorials, and other correspondence is a minor matter, easily taken care of so long as there is no shortage of officials.... Besides, secretarial work involves the use of parallel-style prose, which I do not like. While preparing for the doctorate in letters, I could not help writing it, but since then I have given it up. At the time of my secretarial position in Loyang, though duty called for such prose, I declined to write it.⁴⁴

Ou-yang's refusal brought him high praise from many people, who interpreted it as showing willingness to suffer demotion with Fan but unwillingness to rise again through his influence—both as a matter of principle. Actually, as he wrote his friend Mei Yao-ch'en, Ou-yang would not have minded working for Fan, nor have been bothered by the false allegation that their working together constituted factionalism. But he would not serve as a mere secretary, for he considered the offer of this position to be an implied underestimate of his capabilities. Anyhow, Ou-yang stood to gain by the changed political atmosphere. Ostensibly in recognition of his progress in scholarship, he was soon assigned to catalogue the imperial library. Upon the completion of this task he was promoted again.[45]

In concluding this chapter, an incident that took place years later should be mentioned. After the death of Fan Chung-yen, Ou-yang was asked by Fan's family to compose a tomb inscription. To do it took two years, many drafts, and much consultation with Fan's friends, particularly Han Ch'i. The main difficulty was how to describe the reconciliation between Fan and Lü I-chien. By that time, Fan was looked on as seemingly faultless and morally a "superior man" (*chün-tzu*). His admirers looked down on Lü as an "inferior person" (*hsiao-jen*), in accordance with the Confucian dichotomy of good men and bad. They therefore assumed that Fan had never made any conciliatory gestures toward Lü; to have done so would have been a compromise of Fan's unimpeachable moral integrity. Ou-yang refused to go along. In retrospect, he did not regard Lü as a villain; and he was not about to conceal an important historical fact. Moreover, he had heard Fan himself say late in life that he harbored no lasting grudge against anyone. This, to Ou-yang, showed a truly great spirit.[46] Hence the pertinent passage in his manuscript for the inscription reads: "Thereupon, the two gentlemen gladly promised each other to exert themselves to their utmost, in order to defeat the rebels. For this they were admired by all the scholars in the country. Nevertheless, the allegation of factionalism, having been raised, could not be stopped."[47]

Fan's sons had this passage deleted from the tomb inscription and their father's conciliatory letter to Lü expunged from his collected works. Fu Pi, an old friend of Fan, wrote a separate epitaph implying that Ou-yang, out of political considerations, had failed to use "crystal-clear words" to make "the distinction between right and wrong." Ou-yang defended himself vigorously: "In my manuscript ... Fan's virtue of forgiveness is shown to be as expansive as the cosmos. Loyal and righteous, he placed the interest of the state above all. On Lü, my manuscript also notes the facts."[48]

Fan's stature was even greater in the eyes of many scholars of succeeding generations, who found Ou-yang's account so upsetting that they often questioned its accuracy. Only a few scholar-officials were keen enough to appreciate it. For example, Su Hsün, the father of Su Tung-p'o, commented that Ou-yang deserved much respect for being profoundly considerate.[49] Yeh Meng-te, at the end of the Northern Sung, wrote that "Ou-yang's version tells of what Fan hoped would occur; the version his sons insisted on was the negative result [of Fan's hopes]."[50] Indeed, no real cooperation ensued from Fan's conciliatory gesture. He continued to watch his steps carefully, while Lü set other officials to finding fault with him.[51]

Chu Hsi, though often critical of Ou-yang, praised this account of his for being based upon "broad principles," and rejected the speculation that Ou-yang refrained from criticizing Lü because of his friendship with Lü's sons.

> Ou-yang touches on the effort toward reconciliation, for he knows that Fan wanted a reconciliation. Lü was at fault when he at first caused Fan to be demoted, but his being helpful in bringing Fan back to prominence deserves fair evaluation. Neither his fault, nor his merit, factually described, should obscure the other.... Besides, Ou-yang mentions Lü only in this connection; he does not have any other favorable comment elsewhere. This implies that Lü should be blamed for the previous dismissals of worthy officials. To say nothing more about Lü's fault might seem to be an attempt to conceal it. Actually, Ou-yang's version has the effect of making Lü's character all the more apparent.[52]

Ou-yang did not imply that a reconciliation was actually reached; after all, the reference to the promise of cooperation in his manuscript was immediately followed by the statement that factional conflicts persisted nonetheless. Ou-yang was not giving Lü undue credit, as many neo-Confucianists with narrow doctrinaire mentalities mistakenly believed in later generations. Political adversary though Lü was, Ou-yang simply described him with the broadminded fairness and compassionate understanding that he brought to all things.

CHAPTER FOUR

THE MINOR REFORM

REFORMS SELDOM HAPPENED in Chinese history unless there were compelling reasons and unusual circumstances. The traditional accounts of the minor reform—the first reform of the Sung period —tend to give the impression that Han Ch'i and Fan Chung-yen, having demonstrated their capability by organizing an effective defense against the Hsi Hsia invasion, were summoned to the court and given a free hand to improve on general administration.[1] Actually, the reform resulted from an unprecedented set of crises.

The Hsi Hsia invasion in the northwest created an ominous situation, for the Liao empire in the north, taking advantage of the invasion, also threatened to make war on the Sung.[2] Internal security was in danger too: bandits became rampant, some in areas near the capital. An uprising led by Wang Lun assumed the proportions of a rebellion, the first in the history of the Sung.[3] In many places, bold bandits and rebels, in small groups or large, encountered little effective local resistance. They easily "stormed into the cities in broad daylight, waving their flags and beating their drums."[4] The policy of concentrating the best troops in only a few strategic points was costing dearly.[5] Many local government officials, instead of mounting what defense they could, tried shamelessly to buy off the attackers to save their own skins. "Some officials requisitioned supplies from the population and delivered these to the bandits; others surrendered, turning over arms and armor; yet others tried to appease them with elaborate banquets."[6]

In the best chronological history of the Sung, the Wang Lun uprising is followed immediately by the appointment of Han and Fan to court.[7] The sequence is deliberate, implying a causal relationship. The draft biography of Ou-yang in the Veritable Record compiled shortly after his death makes the connection explicitly clear. "While the war on the northwestern border was going on, many groups of bandits rose in the areas to the east and west of the capital. Both externally and internally, the empire felt disturbed. Emperor Jen-tsung, in replacing his leading councillors, wished to see due changes made to cope with various matters."[8] It was only natural to summon those who had successfully defended the border to return and guard the court.

Even so, it took many sharp criticisms and repeated recommendations before the emperor acted. The ban of 1036 forbidding officials to speak on matters outside their jurisdiction was rescinded in 1040, and only then did some officials begin to express in their memorials dissatisfaction with those in power. Some private citizens also submitted petitions that were critical of the administration.[9] Lü I-chien suffered a stroke and finally resigned in the spring of 1043. However, because of the confidence the emperor had long had in him, he was given in semi-retirement the unusual privilege of "consultation on important state and military affairs"—a privilege to which his critics, Ts'ai Hsiang in particular, objected.[10] Ou-yang was made a policy critic-adviser shortly after Lü's resignation, and one of his first official statements was that Lü had reaped all the glories of a high official but had left the emperor with all the worries. In his opinion, Lü should not have been given the privilege of submitting confidential memorials, and thus the opportunity to continue his manipulations. This criticism persuaded Jen-tsung to rescind the privilege.[11]

With Lü completely removed, power at court was shared for a time by several high officials, none of whom was eager to introduce changes. One of them, Yen Shu, had originally been a patron of Fan, but now felt that Fan was too outspoken and eager for fame. He thought Ou-yang was also making too many comments on various matters.[12] Another, Chang Te-hsiang, pretended not to hear suggestions for making improvements. He told his friends that people who tried to stir things up were like unruly children who could not be stopped from jumping up and down but would quiet down when they ran head-on into a stone wall. He did not oppose them openly, but tried to undermine them behind the scene, to make sure that his own political fortune would outlast theirs.[13] Chia Ch'ang-ch'ao, another powerful councillor, was a northern conservative close to palace circles and friendly with some of the eunuchs. He was not at all sympathetic to the officials who demanded reform.[14]

At first, Han and Fan were both appointed assistant military commissioners. They repeatedly declined these appointments, for they were reluctant to serve under the men then in power, but in the end they had to obey orders.[15] While they were en route to the capital, a court intrigue developed. Hsia Sung, the military commissioner, had often in the past disagreed with Han and Fan. Lü's retirement gave him some hope of becoming chief councillor, but he had opponents working against him on both sides of the political fence. Wang Kung-ch'en, who was generally favorable to the retired Lu, attacked Hsia in as many as eighteen memorials. A leading scholar named Shih Chieh admired both Han and Fan. Highly opinionated and temperamental, he campaigned against Hsia day and night among the censors and policy critic-advisers, and succeeded in persuading several of them to speak out against him.[16] Hsia vigorously denied his alleged faults, but to no avail— he was transferred to a regional post. Tu Yen, who succeeded him as the military commissioner, was sympathetic to Han and Fan. Shih, much elated, composed and circulated a poem celebrating "the advance of the worthy officials," meaning Han and Fan, and "the removal of the scoundrel." Hsia had a copy of Shih's poem delivered to Han and Fan on their arrival at the capital, accompanied by an oral message half protesting the insult and half warning them that a supporter as reckless as Shih would not, in Hsia's opinion, prove a source of comfort. As will be seen, Hsia later made his warning good.[17]

Meanwhile the supporters of Han and Fan, flushed with victory, pressed their advantage as much as they could. Han and Fan had been at their new posts only a few months when Ts'ai Hsiang and Ou-yang recommended that they should be promoted again, to the position of councillors. At the time Jen-tsung put a high value on outspoken advice, and in the summer of 1043 he gave the policy critic-advisers, including Ou-yang, more power than ever before, by having them come to the court daily to take part in policy deliberations. Simultaneously he made Fan the assistant councillor, and from then on he treated Fan as if he were the leading minister. The post of chief councillor thus became in effect little more than a titular honor.[18] Ou-yang soon made another suggestion—that the emperor should order Fan and Han to submit their policy goals in full. Again, Jen-tsung approved. Fan and Han were summoned to the sanctuary of an imperial library and told to set down in writing what they thought should be done. The result was their famous Ten-Point Memorial, which included some ideas that Ou-yang himself espoused.[19]

The ten points that the memorial proposed were as follows:

(1) strictness in evaluating the bureaucrats' performance, for the specific purpose of eliminating entrenched incompetents;

(2) vigilance against favoritism, to begin with a reduction of the number of privileged appointments a high-ranking official was allowed to request for his sons and relatives;

(3) a reform of the examination standards, de-emphasizing poetry and poetic prose and stressing essays and discussions of statecraft problems;

(4) careful choice of regional officials, who would be charged with the responsibility for recommending and sponsoring their subordinates;

(5) an increase in the land attached to local posts, to ensure a

sufficient income for the officeholders and to minimize the temptations of bribery and squeeze;

(6) promotion of land reclamation and dike repairs beneficial to agricultural productivity, and implementation of measures to make the grain transport system more efficient;

(7) creation of local militias among the peasants, to strengthen internal order and external defense;

(8) the taking of steps to ensure that orders for amnesty and reduction of criminal sentences would be fully implemented, and that the people so pardoned would feel grateful to the government;

(9) elimination of contradictions, loopholes, and inequities in the codes and government regulations, and insistence thereafter on strict law enforcement;

(10) reduction of the corvée, including a measure to reduce the need for it by consolidating several prefectures or subprefectures into one.[20]

The Ten-Point Memorial inaugurated the minor reform. In comparison with the major reform a quarter of a century later, the minor reform was a modest administrative program, seeking improvements within the existing framework and not advocating any radical changes in either law or policy. Its objectives were more effective control over the bureaucracy, and better-qualified bureaucrats, who would receive larger incomes in exchange for more satisfactory performance. But this reform was significant as the first attempt to improve on a system that had been largely unchanged and uncriticized since the beginning of the Sung. Its inauguration was the first open admission that the system had degenerated deplorably and the bureaucrats had become entrenched and lax, with their minds closed to all but their own interests.

Ou-yang, a key figure of the reform, forewarned the emperor that many bureaucrats would be against it.[21] The proposal that generated the most opposition, of course, was the reduction of appointments by official patronage. Each year nearly a thousand young men entered the civil service not through the examination system but through the back door whereby officials above certain ranks were allowed to request appointments for their sons (even when the sons were mere boys) as well as for their relatives, their dependents, or the retainers of their families. Under Fan this privilege was limited to only one son, and only on the occasion of an imperial celebration, for administrative posts. Other relatives would be given mere titles, without office. Furthermore, those who received administrative appointments through this variety of patronage would be permanently disqualified for such high positions as censor or academician.[22]

Another measure that disturbed the entrenched bureaucrats was the change in examination standards, which Ou-yang had much to do with. The change was an effort on the part of the reformers to encourage refreshing interpretations of the classics, application of Confucian ideology to practical matters, and lively discussions in ancient-style prose. However, it was viewed by many of the reformers' opponents as implying that they were unqualified for their posts. It also dimmed the prospects of their sons and followers, whose education had dealt little with essays and statecraft. Moreover, according to the opposition, the new standards inadvertently produced irresponsible criticism, denunciation, and sarcasm on the part of many candidates who knew little about government affairs.[23]

Yet another issue was promotions and demotions. The opponents of reform charged that in promoting men of like mind the reformers were guilty of the favoritism they were pretending to do away with. It was unreasonable, these opponents said, for policy critic-advisers such as Ou-yang to recommend that men who made heated and exaggerated attacks on others be promoted on the dubious grounds that the attacks showed their straightforwardness and daring. Above all, it was argued, reliance on sponsorship had a demoralizing effect. Opportunistic officials would lose all dignity and integrity in rushing to ingratiate themselves with those in power.[24]

Ou-yang was especially concerned with the large number of unsatisfactory local officials. Even before the reform, at his first appearance at court as a policy critic-adviser, he brought up the need to appoint special intendant-inspectors in every region to check the performance of the local officials and demote those who were corrupt, incompetent, or too old or sick to be effective.[25] However, it was not until the reform that Ou-yang's recommendation was put into effect, and then it did not last long. Covert opposition managed to hinder its implementation. The validity of the unfavorable evaluations that these newly appointed intendant-inspectors made was seriously questioned. Ou-yang responded that such questioning was itself suspicious. It took considerable courage, he said, to make an unfavorable evaluation of someone who might well turn out to be the friend of a minister or the son of a high official, or to have other influential backers. Another criticism was that this new system encouraged toadying. This criticism, Ou-yang replied, was not valid; it could be made of any system that dealt with promotions and demotions.[26] By the time these objections came up, the reformers had lost power. Ou-yang's counter-arguments were pigeonholed, and the court issued an order that the inspection of local officials should be neither harsh nor deliberately faultfinding, so as not to contravene, in characteristically bureaucratic words, "the emperor's august wish to treat his officials well."[27] The principal satisfaction Ou-yang gained from the adoption of his proposal came from the inspection he himself made of the area of Ho-tung, to the east of the Yellow River, where he rectified many administrative defects and demoted many incompetent officials.[28] He commented that "if the government were to choose officials who could do their duties properly, and to eliminate those unfit for office, along with the waste they cause," it would make other reforming measures far less necessary.[29]

By the winter of 1043, some improvements were already apparent, although the reform program had barely gotten under way. The fiscal picture began to brighten and the tribute transport system to look better.[30] But as Ou-yang had forewarned, complaints and criticisms about the program soon began to weigh on Jen-tsung's mind, and by summer 1044 there were signs that he was having second thoughts.[31] What tipped the balance against the reform was Jen-tsung's decision to negotiate for peace with the Hsi Hsia. Most officials were in favor of the decision, and the objections of several reformers failed to take hold. A series of subtle shuffles soon followed. Fan was sent to pacify and consolidate the area near the Hsi Hsia border. Fu Pi, another reformer, was dispatched on an important mission to avert the threat of a Liao invasion, and Ou-yang himself went to Ho-tung. With the national security no longer in jeopardy either externally or internally, the emperor seemed to lose interest in supporting the reform. In the winter of 1044 allegations of factionalism were raised against the reformers, and Fan, Han Ch'i, Fu, and several others were one after another dismissed from their key positions. In the spring of 1045, the reform measures, with few exceptions, were rescinded.[32] But the issue of factionalism remained alive.

To a significant extent, the reformers themselves were to blame for their downfall. Most of them probably did not anticipate that a theoretically desirable principle might be difficult to implement, and that its implementation might have rather mixed results. Moreover, they tended to be self-righteous, and to ignore their partial failures. Their overconfidence generated overeagerness, and they tried to introduce too many changes too fast. Their self-righteousness also manifested itself in careless intolerance of other views—a handicap in politics, especially for a minority group. Fan Chung-yen, for example, had such strong likes and dislikes that he would not easily compromise even on details; sometimes a slight disagreement would enrage him. Ou-yang Hsiu, Fu Pi, and Yin Shu always made a sharp distinction between the officials they considered worthy and those they considered unworthy. Naturally they ran into animosity and malevolence.[33] Han Ch'i was the only

47

exception: he never lost his temper and never allowed discussions of issues to involve personalities. Nor did he put on airs of virtue, as many reform leaders did, at least in the eyes of their enemies. These traits, coupled with his personal integrity and illustrious northern background, eventually enabled him to rise to power again, and to carry some of the reformers with him.[34] Many followers of the reform shared its leaders' faults, exercising little restraint in criticizing others and thus creating unnecessary trouble.[35] Shih Chieh was the worst. Even his friend Ou-yang found him too arrogant and critical, too ready to assert egotistically his own superiority, whatever the cost. Self-righteousness and intolerance bred favoritism. The prefect T'eng Tsung-liang, for example, greatly overspent his office's appropriation, and when inquiries began to be made he had the insolence to burn the pertinent records. Ou-yang originally maintained that T'eng should be impeached, but Fan used all his influence to ask for leniency and persuade Ou-yang to reverse himself, as a result of which T'eng was merely demoted and transferred.[36]

These actions and attitudes of the reformers furnished good grounds for their opponents to complain of their factionalism. Their more bitter enemies accused them of being disrespectful, or even disloyal, to the emperor. Jen-tsung originally had considerable respect for and confidence in the reformers. Even in the summer of 1044, when he began having second thoughts, he still trusted Fan enough to ask him point-blank whether or not he and his friends were, as alleged, a faction. Fan's response was straightforward, perhaps tactlessly so. He said that since ancient times superior men (*chün-tzu*) and inferior persons (*hsiao-jen*) could never help being divided into opposing factions, and that it was up to the emperor to tell which faction was which.[37] This response apparently did not satisfy Jen-tsung. Ou-yang, realizing the seriousness of the situation, promptly submitted his famous memorial "On Factions." Since Fan had not denied that the reformers were a faction, Ou-yang could hardly do so. Instead, he argued that factionalism based on honest principles and true friendship was no crime. Since the issue of factionalism will be taken up in the next chapter, let it suffice here to say that the emperor was not satisfied with Ou-yang's argument either, impressive though it was.[38]

While Jen-tsung was still pondering it, a palace eunuch reminded him of the poem that Ts'ai Hsiang had written in 1036, praising the officials who had opposed Fan's third demotion, and claimed that the poem was documentary proof the reform faction had existed for nearly ten years. The eunuch warned that the faction now surrounded the throne and controlled much of the administrative machinery; that in another few years its followers would occupy all key positions, there would be no one to oppose it, and not even the emperor would be able to break its grip on the state.[39] The accusation of conspiracy was clearly a smear, but it made Jen-tsung uneasy. The more he inquired about the reformers' loyalty the more allegations he heard against them, and the more suspicious he became. It was at this point that Ou-yang was sent to Ho-tung, and another enemy struck a blow. Hsia Sung, who had been demoted to make way for the rise of the reformers, had long planned revenge. For over a year he had kept a maid practicing the calligraphic style of Shih Chieh, which was as markedly unconventional as Shih himself. Now Hsia had a letter forged, purportedly from Shih Chieh to Fu Pi, suggesting a conspiracy to overthrow the emperor. Jen-tsung did not believe the letter to be genuine, but a vague rumor that Fan had such sinister intentions had circulated in 1036, as Hsia well knew.[40] Taken together, the letter and the memory of the old rumor shook Jen-tsung's trust in the reformers. It was further undermined when a few more eunuchs, displeased by Fu's strictness with their promotions, continued to insinuate that Fan and Fu were disloyal. As a result, Jen-tsung sent the two away on temporary missions.[41]

While several reform leaders were gone from the capital by the end of 1043, their followers were still influential.[42] But in the winter of 1044, Su Shun-ch'in, Wang I-jou, and several other young supporters of the reform held a banquet at which, after much toasting, they sang poetic songs in which a few careless lines seemed disrespectful to the emperor. Li Ting, a social climber who was not invited to the banquet, heard of the songs and spread the story in revenge. It soon reached the ears of Wang Kung-ch'en, the censor who had married the sister of Ou-yang's second wife, but who opposed both Hsia Sung and the reformers. Under Wang's expert guidance, his subordinate censors built a case of *lèse majesté*. The incriminated supporters of the reform were promptly arrested.[43] Chia Ch'ang-ch'ao (the titular chief councillor) and several other high ministers advocated a criminal investigation of the affair, which was prevented only when Han Ch'i reminded them that the folly of drunken young men was hardly a serious crime. As a result, these young men were merely demoted, and not given legal punishment. But neither Han nor anyone else could soothe the resentment the emperor now felt against the entire reform faction. An edict of admonition was issued, declaring that the case should be a lesson to all those who formed factions, promoted their own fame, conducted themselves in an unconventional manner, held strange opinions, and behaved disrespectfully toward the emperor. Wang Kung-ch'en boastfully exclaimed: "I caught all of them in a net."[44]

The handwriting on the wall was clear. Fan, far away in the northwest, realized that he was indirectly under attack, and felt that he should submit his resignation as a councillor.[45] Chang Te-hsiang, a quiet enemy of the reform, suggested that given the high esteem Fan enjoyed throughout the country an eager acceptance of his resignation would create a bad impression. Besides, an initial rejection of it would serve to test his sincerity. If, after the rejection, Fan should thank the emperor for not allowing him to resign, it would prove beyond doubt that he had merely been making a gesture. In that case, Fan would deserve an outright dismissal. The trap was set, and Fan fell right into it. Jen-tsung, convinced that Fan should never be trusted again, forthwith demoted him to a mere prefect.[46]

Fan's demotion signaled the defeat of the reform and the discrediting of the reformers. The councillors whom the emperor chose to succeed them were conservatives who had no particular desire to distinguish themselves in policy matters. They merely undertook routine administration in the conventional ways.[47] However, no real stability was achieved. The bureaucracy relapsed into stagnation, but the issue of factionalism remained unsettled.

CHAPTER FIVE

FACTIONALISM AND
CRITICAL POWER

THE IDEOLOGICALLY ORIENTED neo-Confucianists, like most men, preferred the company of men of like mind. The frustrations and attacks they suffered in common drove them together even more. But they grouped together more socially than politically. It was in the context of social relations that they discussed desirable policies, the best ways to implement them, and, unavoidably, the best kind of officials to do so. The group's leaders owed their position, as a rule, to their followers' recognition of their superior qualities —recognition the leaders won in social situations. When the group took political action, it was as a loose conglomeration of friendly colleagues. They would have been far more effective had they been able to organize themselves into a political body, but the state absolutely forbade it. Confucius himself had said that "a *chün-tzu* while sociable is not factious," or connected with a faction. Hence, the reformers were something between a group of friends and a loose political association—they were unified in opinion, but incapable of concerted action. They were, however, quite vulnerable to attack as a faction, a label that traditionally had connotations of conspiracy and selfishness. The absolutist emperors were always suspicious of any group that might bring pressure on the throne or threaten its security, so such a group could always be denounced as a faction working for its own interests rather than for the good of the state.[1]

How should the ideologically oriented elements face this diffi-culty? Should they deny their common bond, and abandon the kind of *esprit de corps* it gave them? If they did not, how could they avoid being labeled a faction? Fan Chung-yen was the first to take up the challenge, by accepting the label. As early as 1029, at the time of his first demotion, he argued that the straight and the crooked always belong to two opposing factions.[2] In the confron-tation of 1036, Lü I-chien made factionalism a formal charge against Fan and his supporters, escalating what had up to then been regarded as a personal fault into a public offense. Incidentally, Lü used the same charge in 1041 against an entirely different group of political opponents.[3]

What Lü did not foresee was that the label of faction would become a symbol of prestige. Some aspiring and reckless scholar-officials took pride in identifying themselves as "members of [Fan's] faction."[4] Their actions greatly strengthened Fan's self-confidence. Thus when Jen-tsung put him on the spot about his alleged factionalism in 1044, he boldly reiterated his long-held be-lief. "If through friendship men should work together for the good of the state," he asked, "what is the harm?"[5] Nor was Fan alone—Fu Pi and Yin Shu made the same point on other occa-sions.[6]

The memorial "On Factions" that Ou-yang submitted soon after Fan's bold response to the emperor was considered a brilliant, original contribution to Confucian thought. A standard transla-tion of it, titled "On Party," reads in part as follows:

Your servant is aware that from ancient times there have been discussions on the worth of parties. It is only to be hoped that a ruler will distinguish between those of gentlemen [*chün-tzu*] and those of inferior men [*hsiao-jen*]. In general, gentlemen join with other gentlemen in parties because of common principles, while inferior men join with other inferior men for reason of common profit. This is quite natural. But your servant would contend that in fact inferior men have no parties, and that it is only gentlemen who are capable of forming them. Why is this? Inferior men love profit and covet material wealth. When the time seems to offer mutual advantages, they will temporarily band together to form a party, which is, however, essentially false. But when they reach the stage where they are actually competing among themselves for advantage, or when the advantages they have sought fail to materialize and they drift apart, then they turn about and begin to attack each other, and even the fact that a man is a brother or a relative does not spare him. Therefore, your servant maintains that such men have no real parties.... But this is not true of gentlemen, who abide by the Way and righteousness, who practice loyalty and good faith and care for honor and integrity.... When they employ these qualities in their personal conduct they share a common principle ... unite in common ideals and mutual assistance, and from beginning to end act as one. These are the parties of gentlemen.[7]

Actually, the idea that good people have factions originated not with Ou-yang, but with Fan. What Ou-yang added was the rather startling point that bad people are not even good enough to stay together as a faction.

Through the centuries, neither the admirers nor the critics of Ou-yang paid enough attention to the fact that he himself actually did not believe in this argument. In spring 1045, when the reform leaders were being dismissed from court and Ou-yang was still in Ho-tung, he presented another memorial in which he completely denied that the reformers were ever a faction. Since this second memorial was historically overshadowed by the first one, it deserves to be quoted at length:

From ancient times ... when inferior persons wanted to endanger superior men on a wide scale, they would merely point them out as a faction. Why is this? If they remove one good man, other good men will still remain.... The only way to get rid of them all ... is to point an accusing finger at them, alleging them to be a faction.... These four men [Tu Yen, Fan Chung-yen, Han Ch'i, and Fu Pi] have quite different temperaments, but they all put loyalty to the emperor first. Yet among themselves they hold quite different opinions. In deliberation, they frequently refuse to yield to one another.... When at their leisure, in private, they praise each other's fine qualities as friends. But when they discuss state affairs at court, they argue openly, in the public interest, uninfluenced by private considerations.... They differ honestly, as a matter of principle, and thus truly achieve what the history of the Han period has described as the virtue of loyal ministers. Yet inferior persons insinuate that they are a faction. Oh, what a false accusation it is![8]

In Ou-yang's *New History of the Five Dynasties* he pointed out that the term "faction" could easily be stretched to cover any social group—he mentioned clansmen, relatives, old acquaintances, close friends, schoolmates, and colleagues, among others—and that historically the charge of factionalism had often been trumped up against the innocent by the *hsiao-jen*.[9] In other words, factionalism did not in fact exist in most cases.

In retrospect, Ou-yang realized that the supporters of the reform had brought the label of faction down on themselves. In a memorial written in 1056 discussing the problems of government schools, he made an important admission:

The custom at the time of the Eastern Han made the *chün-tzu* take so much pride in their reputation and moral integrity that they were eventually charged with being a faction, which brought many disasters all over the country. The trouble really began with the private scholars, who in voicing their opinion denounced others without restraint.... They also conducted themselves in peculiar or strange ways, seeking lofty reputations for rare virtues. They haughtily discussed their high ideals and abstract theories in order to win acclaim as talented and knowledgeable people. Recently, the scholars in the Ch'ing-li [reform] era had precisely the same kind of faults.[10]

Long afterward, Chu Hsi commented that the leaders of the reform had provoked their opponents sorely, citing the poems by Ts'ai Hsiang and Shih Chieh, and Ou-yang's memorial "On Factions," as examples. In Chu's opinion, the reformers' arrogant classifying of themselves as good and their opponents as bad led surely to disaster.[11] Incidentally, Chu and his followers were not cautious enough in observing this criticism themselves: their strong sense of self-righteousness made them subject to allegations of factionalism too.

If Ou-yang honestly did not believe that there was a reform faction, why then did he argue as he did in his famous memorial, in contravention of what Confucius himself had said? Yeh Shih, a leading authority on statecraft in the Southern Sung, had the best answer. He correctly surmised that Ou-yang had advanced this brilliant thesis only "in desperation." Since Fan had already admitted to the emperor that the reformers were a faction, Ou-yang could hardly deny it at the time, no matter what his personal opinion might be. In the hope of saving Fan and the reform, he had to argue like a lawyer, turning the admission of his client into an impressive defense.[12]

Ou-yang's defense of factions inspired the next generation, throughout Wang An-shih's reform, the subsequent anti-reform, and the post-reform period.[13] Many leading scholar-officials wrestled with the hard fact that on the one hand, the old Confucian ideal of good people's not having a faction did not seem attainable; and that on the other, contrary to Ou-yang's analysis, bad people apparently formed factions too. A brief survey of the solutions to this difficult problem that were attempted during the next generation is pertinent at this point both to assess Ou-yang's influence and to show that the problem of factionalism remained unsolvable in Confucian theory.

Generally speaking, the next generation came up with four hypotheses. The first, following Fan and Ou-yang, stressed the unavoidable conflict between good and bad factions and therefore maintained that it was urgent for the emperor to tell them apart from the very beginning. For example, Ssu-ma Kuang, the great historian and leading conservative, lamented that the emperor had failed to realize that Wang An-shih and his fellow reformers were a bad faction.[14] The second hypothesis was pessimistic, predicting the inevitable defeat of the good factions because their high principles left them relatively defenseless against the political trickery of their opponents. According to Ch'in Kuan, the defeat of the minor reform itself, along with many other historical instances, proved this hypothesis.[15] The third was an admixture of Taoist and Legalist sophistication, and was conditionally optimistic. Agreeing with Ou-yang that no genuine solidarity held bad factions together, Su Shih (Su Tung-p'o) suggested that good officials should assume a Taoist appearance in order to avoid premature confrontation with their opponents, and should wait, as Legalist strategists would, to strike the opponents down when they were divided.[16] The fourth hypothesis recognized that a simple dichotomy between good and bad factions was unrealistic: opposing sides would each have some good members and some bad ones, and in a clash neither side would be faultless. The only hope for the preservation of the good members of both factions would be mediation and conciliation.[17] For example, Fan Ch'un-jen, the eldest son of Fan Chung-yen, opposed Wang An-shih but criticized many of his fellow conservatives for their vindictiveness. Tseng Pu was an example from the opposite side: having become disillusioned with his fellow reformers, he attempted when he returned to power in his old age to mediate between the reformers and the conservatives, though without success.[18]

The first hypothesis left all action up to the emperor, giving no assurance that his action would be wise. The second was defeatist, simply giving up hope. The maneuvers of the third required such cleverness that probably only a few people were ever capable of them. And the fourth, when followed, proved unsuccessful. In short, no feasible means of preventing factionalism, or even of coping with it, was ever found by the Sung Confucians. Their failure would seem to be attributable to three reasons. First, Confucian theoretical discussions tended to take established institutions as given conditions, neither conceiving that the roots of the problem might be in some of the institutions themselves, nor proposing new institutions as solutions. Second, the absolutist emperor always regarded a recognizable group of scholar-officials as a potential threat to his power: to him, any assertion by the scholar-officials that they possessed ideas superior to his own implied a denial of his legitimacy. Third, the state structure, to function well, required a consensus among the bureaucrats; but it lacked the flexibility to provide a forum where divergent views could be aired and honest differences composed.

The last point must be qualified. A large bureaucracy usually contains some mechanism for internal control that provides a limited channel for the expression of critical opinion. In the Chinese empire, a fixed number of officials were appointed as policy critic-advisers and censors to act as a check on the executive branch of the government. Occasionally, some academicians performed the same function; their high prestige and direct access to the emperor enabled them to do so. For the sake of convenience, the term "critical power" will be used here to refer to the weight of critical opinion that these separate categories of officials could collectively bring to bear.

In the early Sung, these critics had little power. The first two emperors worked energetically as chief executives, supervising their councillors much as a general would his staff. Criticism was not encouraged; it was not felt to be necessary. The jurisdiction of the censors was confined to minor malpractices that violated laws, and that of the policy critic-advisers to helping the emperor improve his personal attitude and conduct.[19] Under the third emperor, Chen-tsung, critical power began to grow, as more learned scholars came up through the examination system. At first, a few censors were appointed to look into general administrative matters. Then, the privilege of expressing an opinion on general administration, and of backing it up in court, was extended to every censor.[20] More important, the jurisdiction of the policy critic-advisers was expanded. They were permitted "to express opinions on and to rectify the deficiencies and mistakes of the policies of the court, the incompetencies of all officials from the councillors downward, and the actions of various departments and bureaus."[21] While nothing important lay outside their jurisdiction, in practice they almost always refrained from either exercising their power to its fullest extent or making sharp criticisms.

The decisive enlargement of critical power came with the minor reform. Lü I-chien's attempt in 1036 to block officials from raising issues unrelated to their duties did not stem the tide for long. When Lü's injunction was rescinded on the eve of the reform, all court-rank officials were officially called on to submit their frank opinions. At that time, Jen-tsung believed that affairs of state should be thoroughly discussed in court with the policy critic-advisers present, and that then either the best opinion would prevail or a consensus would emerge. This procedure put the executive branch on the defensive before the critics. The loudest voice of all happened to be Ou-yang's. It was his attack that cut Lü I-chien's last strand of influence, and his recommendations that set the reform program in motion. Critical power was carrying unprecedented weight. It continued to do so throughout the reform phase. Ou-yang even criticized his own friends and their actions.[22]

Pao Cheng observed that before the reform, "councillors who disliked other officials were apt to accuse them, whenever they spoke up, of being eager to make a name for themselves or of seeking promotion through agitation." The reversal of the situation was no improvement. "Whenever the policy critic-advisers and censors submitted memorials attacking alleged deficiencies and mistakes in court policies, the executive officials concerned were told either to report on the cases in detail or to be careful and do better henceforth." To Pao, criticisms tended to be exaggerated and excessive.[23] To avoid imbalance, critical power should be exercised, according to Han Ch'i, with restraint and consideration. When Han was a policy critic-adviser, he performed his duty without rancor. When he was made a councillor, he took criticism with grace. From his experience, he suggested the following:

> He who serves well as a policy critic-adviser resorts to neither hints nor denunciations. Those who use the technique of hinting speak gently around the subject and make delicate analogies in the futile hope that somehow the point will get across. They fail to realize that if they do not clearly analyze the matter at hand, their opinion is likely to be brushed aside or not listened to at all. Those who use the technique of denunciation speak emphatically and excitedly, even in alarming terms of grave dangers to the state, in the mistaken hope that fear will produce the response they desire. They fail to realize that exaggeration is likely to provoke resentment and hence rejection.... The proper way is to give utmost consideration to the general situation and the measures appropriate to it. It is to stress the reasonableness of a case and to present it in the most sincere terms.... If one knows that the time is not yet ripe for action, one should refrain from expressing what will merely look good on paper.[24]

Restraint could hardly prevail when factional feelings ran high. As a historian of many centuries later pointed out, from the time of the minor reform on, either the executive officials outmaneuvered their critics or the two sides were deadlocked. He went on to lament that "the emperor had no definite idea [about whom to trust]; the councillors had no assurance of long tenure in office; as confidence and distrust alternately came and went, the officials were tossed up and down as by the unpredictable waves of a drifting tide."[25]

The extraordinary influence Ou-yang and other critics had exercised at the time of the reform convinced many bureaucrats that the best way of achieving prominence was by making relentless attacks on others. Ou-yang himself soon admitted that critical officials were abusing their power:

> When one critical official receives a rapid promotion, many of his inferiors, eager for advancement, rush forward with their malicious tongues. Some effort must be made to stop this malpractice. Otherwise, how will it be possible to distinguish between the *chün-tzu* with his truth and the *hsiao-jen* with their pretensions?[26]

However, Ou-yang offered no specific remedies. Chang Fang-p'ing put the blame on him and other reform leaders for having worked to increase the critical officials' power:

> The institution of having critic-advisers and censors is for the purpose of securing careful deliberations and worthwhile suggestions to clear up various policy issues. It is not intended that these officials be allowed to agitate and swagger, as a shortcut to the advancement of their careers. Yet in recent years, these officials have increased in number; their promotions are extraordinarily rapid and the value of their opinions is overrated. Their preponderance produces factionalism, intimidates many good officials, and arouses many controversies. This is a perversion that defeats the purpose [of having critical officers].[27]

Liu K'ang, who was also sickened by the widespread malpractice, complained bitterly:

> Since the Ch'ing-li reform era, the policy critic-advisers and the censors have had their way. Any court decision or order, of value or not, will invariably run into their criticism, once made known. Moreover, they will persist in their criticism until their case is won.... Previous councillors, afraid of their adverse words, have

found it expedient to buy them off by having them promoted ahead of time.[28]

Malpractice aggravated by factionalism went on for decades after the reform. Many court officials felt reluctant to praise their colleagues for fear of being accused of factional favoritism. Equally hesitant to approve proposed actions, they took refuge in high-sounding platitudes and vague generalities, rarely coming to grips with the issues involved. However, they had no reservations about making negative judgments, feeling that such judgments would make them appear honest, frank, and impartial. Even minor officials tried to get their criticisms heard. When unsuccessful, they would pay frequent visits to policy critic-advisers, supplying information or fabricating misinformation in order to stir up controversies against men they disliked.[29]

The criticisms voiced soon degenerated into vicious slander. At the top appeared such allegations as high treason, disloyalty, disrespect to the emperor, and the like; at lower levels came accusations with respect to private conduct and domestic relations.[30] A number of Ou-yang's friends were victims of the former; Ou-yang himself, as will be discussed in the next chapter, suffered from the latter. In 1049 came belated recognition of the need for proper limits: an edict proclaimed that false accusations based on rumor and hearsay would be penalized, unless the case concerned serious misapplication of policy or extensive suffering among the people—an escape clause that made the edict less effective than intended.[31] When Han Ch'i, Ou-yang, and Fu Pi eventually returned to power, they caused three more edicts to be issued, between 1060 and 1061, confining criticism to official matters, and excluding alleged faults in private life and personal conduct. Unfortunately, these measures came too late, and were too weak to clear the air. Many bureaucrats continued to seek their own advancement by fault-finding tactics, at the expense of both their colleagues and the public interest.[32]

The bureaucrats' desire for an increase in critical power was basically a class interest. They did not want the lower classes to have any part in forming public opinion. A memorial Ou-yang submitted in 1055 reflected this class prejudice quite clearly:

> Printers have put on the market some twenty books with titles like "Prose of the [Sung] Dynasty." Their contents include a number of contemporary writings dealing with current affairs of state. . . . A scrutiny of the contents of these books clearly indicates that they should not be allowed to circulate.[33]

The memorial requested the burning of these books and a stricter enforcement of the existing law requiring that a publication be censored before being printed or sold.

The ideologically oriented neo-Confucianists cherished the conventional Confucian concept of hierarchical order, but they believed in the supremacy of moral authority as well, and assumed, in their excessive self-confidence, that they had more moral authority than anyone else. Consequently, they attempted to voice their opinions on all subjects they believed important as frequently as necessary. In their struggle to expand the critical power of the bureaucrats, they failed to give enough thought to the problem of that power's proper use. They did not realize that simply increasing the critical power, without strengthening the institutional framework for applying it, reviewing the results of its use, and correcting any mistakes or injustices that the reviews might discover, would inevitably throw the bureaucratic machinery of the Sung out of balance. They also did not realize that lack of unity within the bureaucratic class would inevitably result in the bureaucrats' turning their increased power against one another. Initially they were successful, getting rid of their opponents by criticizing their policies, but in the end the critical power was turned against them and they were turned out of power by accusations of a more personal nature, such as factionalism, disloyalty to the emperor,

and immoral conduct.[34] The only one who stood to gain from conflict within the bureaucracy was the emperor himself. Paradoxically, the abuse that the bureaucrats' critical power was above all
supposed to restrain—absolutism—was the only one strengthened
by its rise.[35]

CHAPTER SIX

LATE CAREER

AFTER THE MINOR REFORM, a slander caused Ou-yang to be relegated to local government posts for ten years. He was then reappointed to a prominent court position, and in another five years he finally reached the summit of his career, as a councillor in charge of state affairs, together with his old friends Han Ch'i and Fu Pi. By that time none of the three was interested in reform. Stability was their cardinal goal, and they were partially successful in attaining it. Ou-yang was eventually removed from court again, after another attack on his personal integrity. The last phase of his career, as a local administrator, was characterized by persistent objection to the policies of Wang An-shih. Soon after the major reform got under way, Ou-yang admitted that he was behind the times and requested retirement.

After putting an end to the minor reform, Ou-yang's opponents did not immediately find a weapon to get rid of him. With most reform leaders already dismissed, charges of factionalism and conspiracy were inapplicable. However, Ou-yang had previously attacked several officials on the grounds of immoral conduct in private life. Now it was his turn.[1] A widowed sister of his, Madame Chang, had come (or as the Chinese say, returned) to stay with his family some years earlier, bringing with her a daughter of her late husband by a previous marriage. The girl, though not related to the Ou-yang family by blood, was known as "niece Chang," and later married a distant member of Ou-yang's clan. In 1045, she was tried for adultery with a servant, and confessed not only to that charge but to having had intimate relations with Ou-yang before her marriage. Ou-yang soon found himself in prison, accused of incest.[2] Under investigation, Ou-yang denied the allegation: what niece Chang had supposedly confessed, he declared, was due either to a mistaken notion that she might draw a lighter penalty by involving him or to the malicious suggestion of someone else who had deliberately planted the story for the purpose of incriminating him.[3] Those who wished to ruin Ou-yang left no stone unturned. They supplied what purported to be circumstantial evidence, namely, some poems he had written years before. It seemed that he had indulged in loose conduct with courtesans in his younger days, betraying from time to time a dubious character and exhibiting his licentiousness in these poems. One poem pointedly involved a young maiden, who, his opponents declared, could very well be the woman in question. However, Ou-yang was hardly the only official to have composed suggestive lyrics. Moreover, as some scholars in later centuries pointed out, such lyrics were in most cases poetic allegories rather than treatments of realistic themes, let alone factual expressions of romantic feelings. Niece Chang's confession was simply a matter of her word against Ou-yang's. Consequently, the judge found her incrimination of Ou-yang to be inconclusive. He added, however, that Ou-yang was at fault on a separate count of negligence under the civil law, for a part of her dowry had been used to acquire some land that was falsely registered in the name of Ou-yang's family, apparently in order to apply Ou-yang's tax-exemption privilege to it.[4]

Not satisfied with the trial's outcome, Chia Ch'ang-ch'ao, the chief councillor, set up a retrial under another judge named Su An-shih, who was to be assisted by a palace eunuch, a customary way of showing the emperor's personal attention to a case and emphasizing its gravity. The eunuch, Wang Chao-ming, was said to have been chosen because Ou-yang had once blocked his appointment to a position he had wanted.[5] Presumably, he would now have a chance for revenge. However, Wang refused to exceed proper judicial limits. One account asserts that it was Judge Su who decided to uphold the original verdict, but two other accounts give the credit to Wang. According to the latter accounts, Judge Su suggested at one point during the trial that torture might be used to test Ou-yang's persistent denial, to which Wang retorted that he had been sent by the emperor to see justice done, and did not see how torture would be justifiable. Moreover, Wang reportedly added that the emperor mentioned Ou-yang daily, and that an arbitrary verdict based on insufficient evidence, though pleasing to some councillors at the time, might boomerang in the future under different political conditions. The statements about possible torture are unlikely to have been true, for the Sung policy of treating high officials well made torture at their trials almost unknown. On the other hand, some hint from the eunuch about Ou-yang's prestige might have been helpful in saving him from further harassment. In any event, the original verdict was upheld.[6]

However, resentment against Ou-yang was so deep that his enemies proposed yet a third investigation. At this point Chao Kai protested that while Ou-yang was no friend of his he felt it damaging to the dignity of the court to insist on punishing a high official, prominent scholar, and respected writer on such dubious grounds. Chang Fang-p'ing, in spite of his dislike of the reformers, was an experienced enough politician to see that a political storm was brewing. He advised Chia that since the antagonism between Ou-yang and him was well known, he was likely to be blamed for deliberately persecuting Ou-yang. Chia, thus made cautious, allowed the verdict to stand and the case to be closed.[7]

Ou-yang was thereupon demoted to prefect of Chuchow, a humble mountainous area, ostensibly for permitting the false registration of the Chang property under the name of his family. But what hurt him most, as his poems reveal, was the damage to his reputation.[8] He spent the next decade writing and studying, much to the advantage of his historical standing. At Chuchow he kept in good spirits, referring to himself as a "drunken elder," a name made immortal by his masterpiece of that title. In fact, he was only about forty years old. Three years after his demotion, in 1048, he was raised to the post of prefect of Yangchow, the metropolis at the junction of the Grand Canal and the Yangtze River. Within a year, he requested a transfer to a lesser place, for he was afraid that his enemies might become jealous and try to ruin him again. His next assignment was Yingchow, in the beautiful lake country where he settled his family permanently.[9]

According to the normal practice of the civil service, a man as highly qualified as Ou-yang would not be kept at humble local posts for long. But Ou-yang was not summoned to the capital again until 1054.[10] There he attended an imperial audience at which Jen-tsung was struck by Ou-yang's silver hairs, and asked him his age and the number of years he had been away. The incident immediately led to speculation that Ou-yang might come to power again. Within ten days his enemies moved once more. According to several sources, someone aroused the palace against him by circulating copies of a forged memorial, attributed to Ou-yang, containing a recommendation to reduce the number of palace eunuchs, beginning with those who had used their influence to enrich themselves. In response, one eunuch is reported to have warned the emperor that a man as excessively eager for fame as Ou-yang was would cause trouble, and might even interfere with the emperor's prerogatives.[11] Other sources tell of Ou-yang appearing at court before dawn, straight from a banquet that had lasted all night, and of some surprised eunuchs citing his act to the emperor as an example of how lightly he took his duties.[12]

In any event, Ou-yang was suddenly reassigned to another faraway prefecture. Wu Ch'ung, whose daughter had married Ou-yang's oldest son, protested that the reassignment was unfair, but his protest brought no response. Fortunately, the chief councillor, Liu K'ang, who disliked factional disputes and irresponsible allegations, and Fan Chen, another high minister and brilliant scholar, expressed themselves in favor of keeping Ou-yang at court. Through their intervention Ou-yang was assigned to the commission compiling the *New T'ang History*. Not long afterward, a promotion made him a Han-lin academician, a position of high prestige that also gave him some critical power.[13]

Ou-yang's years of self-cultivation and political quiescence were over. His ideological orientation and rather quick temper were as marked as ever; the self-restraint he had been cultivating had taken the bite out of his strong personality, but had not really mellowed it. Once back at court, he could neither stay away from politics nor hold his tongue. As always, he enjoyed company and conversation. He no longer desired to promote another reform, but he still wanted to see some improvements made. His realization of his past mistakes in provoking factional dispute did not mean that he would refrain from making criticisms or raising objections. In his capacity as an academician, with ready access to the emperor, he joined several policy critic-advisers in attacking the councillor Ch'en Chih-chung, and offered to resign when the attack proved ineffective. The court, wishing to keep him on and at the same time keep him out of trouble, decided to dispatch him on a mission to the Liao empire.[14] Shortly after his return from this mission, he clashed again with his old adversary Chia Ch'ang-ch'ao (then the military commissioner), first over an irrigation project and then on Chia's close contacts with eunuchs who were suspected to be bypassing certain regulations and playing favorites behind the scene. Under mounting criticism from Ou-yang and others, Chia was finally relieved of his post at court. Times were changing; soon the few surviving leaders of the minor reform, by virtue of their seniority and proven capability, would return to power.[15]

On the road back to power Ou-yang ran into some other obstacles. One involved the examination standards. The program of the minor reform had advocated an emphasis on interpretation of the classics and discussion of statecraft problems, for both of which ancient-style prose was better suited than the ornate current style. After the defeat of the reform, the old standards had been restored. In 1057, Ou-yang was appointed to take charge of the doctoral examinations. He made it known that he would pay attention to the substance of the examination papers, not their style. Among the successful candidates were a significant number of brilliant young scholars whose ideas, expressed in the ancient style, proved definitely superior. However, some bitterly disappointed candidates insulted Ou-yang personally, even reviving the slander of niece Chang.[16] Another obstacle was the eunuchs. In 1058, Ou-yang was appointed acting prefect of Kaifeng. At this post, he often received palace decrees or rescripts directly granting favors requested by eunuchs, without going through channels. Instead of honoring these rescripts, he denounced the men who had caused their issuance, saying that they should be penalized for doing so. The stand he took caused some resentment, but no retaliation, for by this time Ou-yang's influence was clearly growing. Besides, he had friends in the palace. The empress, who knew the family of his wife, now welcomed her back to the capital and occasionally invited her to visit.[17]

On the completion of the *New T'ang History* in 1060, Ou-yang was at long last given a high executive position, that of assistant military commissioner. The following year he was made an assistant councillor in charge of state affairs. Han Ch'i and Fu Pi were also given leading posts. The period from 1060 to 1066, when the three friends were generally in power (Fu soon ceased to cooperate closely), was recalled with nostalgia by many scholar-officials later in the Sung. Chinese historians in subsequent centuries also praised Han and Ou-yang for successfully managing two crises of imperial succession and achieving noteworthy stability between two turbulent periods of reform. The old reformers had changed. They had come to realize that their past errors had created crippling divisions in the bureaucracy. Now they were determined to have no more factionalism, but to cooperate with new talents and entrenched bureaucrats alike. After the minor reform Ou-yang and Fu Pi had discussed their roles in its failure at length. Both had agreed that they had been overanxious, overinsistent, and overconfident. True statesmanship, they concluded, called for thorough deliberation before action, so as to leave no cause for regret afterward. Ou-yang, on his return to power, was still in large measure quick, eager, and even impulsive, but intellectually he had been inclining toward a gradual approach to improvement for some time. Even before the minor reform, he had realized that too many changes would cause confusion and render government orders ineffectual. During the reform, he had stressed improvement of personnel rather than of legislation. Now he frankly opposed changing the laws unless the advantages of doing so were many and clear. He emphasized administration—making the existing laws work better.[18]

Does this mean that Ou-yang and his friends were no longer interested in progress? Not at all; what they had learned to value was orderly, gradual progress, which they felt would only be possible under stable conditions. And the improvements they achieved should not be underestimated. Let it suffice here to give a few illustrations. As assistant military commissioner, Ou-yang gathered information on the local garrisons, especially those along the borders, in a more systematic manner than before. As a councillor, he devoted his spare time to compiling a consolidated catalogue, with classified headings, of the laws and regulations, precedents and exceptions, discrepancies and contradictions that had been accumulating over the years in the separate offices of the Secretariat. When the emperor had a question about administration and Ou-yang was off duty, he would simply send a eunuch to the Secretariat to consult Ou-yang's catalogue.[19]

One of the measures adopted during the minor reform had been a reassessment of land for more equitable taxation. It was a case of a good idea carried out badly: the reassessment was made in haste, and was disturbing to many people and full of errors. Nor was the revised tax nearly as equitable as intended. When a similar policy was proposed in 1060, Ou-yang opposed it, realizing that to try to implement it would be overambitious. Instead, at his suggestion, local officials were simply directed to adjust existing tax rates by reducing those obviously in excess and raising those obviously too low. These officials also had the official power to grant exemptions or abolitions of taxes that had been unreasonably increased in recent years and those for which the justification had long since ceased to exist.[20]

All in all, Ou-yang and his colleagues distinguished themselves as conventional Confucian statesmen, improving the bureaucracy without upsetting it and acting in accordance with the belief that proper administrative conduct would go a long way toward solving the problems of the state.

To have an efficient but cautious administration, efficient but cautious officials were needed. Han and Fu found many who were competent in fiscal and judicial matters, but this achievement did not satisfy Ou-yang. His goal was to select and prepare young men talented enough to take over, eventually, the direction of state affairs. In 1065, he explained his plan to achieve this goal in an exclusive audience with Ying-tsung, Jen-tsung's successor. The normal road from doctoral degree to the highest positions went through three stages: service first at one of the three institutes, where young men became familiar with state affairs through such work as compiling historical documents, doing research, and composing documents for state occasions; second at the Bureau of Academicians or as a drafting official in the Secretariat; and third in the Chancellery or the Military Commission, the nerve centers of the entire government. In recent years, Ou-yang observed, only a few degree-holders ever got to even the first stage.[21] He recommended, and Ying-tsung agreed, that each of the highest ministers should recommend a few young men, making up a total of about twenty, who would be given qualifying tests for assignments at the first stage. Han Ch'i demurred: this number seemed to him larger than desirable, for it might lead to sharp competition, charges of favoritism, and serious controversies. But the emperor replied that if the candidates were truly talented the court could not have too many of them. Fu Pi objected that to lift a few young scholar-officials high over the heads of the others would cause friction in the bureaucracy.[22] Ou-yang's plan was pending final action when Ying-tsung died. Consequently, it was never implemented. On his own, Ou-yang recommended many talented young officials for promotion throughout the years he was in power, probably more than anyone else. Among his protégés were Wang An-shih and Lü Hui-ch'ing, the leaders of the major reform, and Ssu-ma Kuang and Lü Kung-chu, the leaders of its opposition.[23] The eventual conflict between the two sides was, of course, exactly what Han Ch'i had been afraid of. However, the fault did not lie with Ou-yang's recommendations; he recruited without reference to political opinion.

During Ou-yang's second term in power, the younger generation of scholar-officials was splitting once again into northern conservatives and southern reformers. They were divided, for example, over the issue of revising the examination standards. Ou-yang stood in the middle: having done much to change the standards in favor of ancient-style prose and interpretation of the classics, he no longer saw much room for improvement, and believed that the system would work fairly well so long as good officials were in charge of it. In 1060 Ssu-ma Kuang, reflecting the conservative view, complained that the emphasis Ou-yang had helped introduce put Ssu-ma's fellow northerners at a disadvantage, since they had been trained in the old way to adhere closely to the texts of the classics and the conventional commentaries. He submitted an alternative arrangement: grant an equal number of doctorates in every region, thus securing equitable regional representation.[24] Ou-yang disagreed, pointing out that if Ssu-ma's proposal were adopted, places with fewer candidates—i.e., the north—would have to lower their standards in order to fill the quota, whereas in places with more and better-educated candidates—the south—well-qualified candidates would be squeezed out. A uniform national standard, Ou-yang maintained, was the only fair formula.[25] Wang An-shih and the southerners, on the other hand, advocated weighting the examinations in favor of correct interpretations of the classics and application of such interpretations to the problems of statecraft, rather than simply emphasizing prose.[26] Ou-yang was against going that far. Who would decide what were the correct interpretations of the classics? Besides, he wished to recruit balanced and knowledgeable minds through the examinations, not experts of a particular persuasion.

The younger generation were by no means satisfied with Ou-yang's stand, and continued to argue among themselves for a long time after his death. It was Su Shih (Su Tung-p'o) from the southwest who raised the most basic question: could the examination standards ever be perfect? Highly stylized poetry and poetic prose, as Ou-yang had shown, had little bearing on statecraft. The prose style that Ou-yang had promoted facilitated the expression of academic opinions on state affairs, but whether such opinions were practically useful remained questionable. Interpreting the classics and attempting to apply them to government policies, examination standards that received great emphasis under Wang An-shih, were likewise of dubious practical value. In short, Su concluded, no examination standards can identify good administrators with any certainty.[27] After all, the real test was in deeds, not words. The debate over the examination standards reflected a dilemma of the neo-Confucianists. As their ideology developed, it produced a philosophical attitude that inquired into everything—looking beyond conventional precepts, suspecting popular and modish values, and objecting to conformity.[28] The examination system, however, had to be based on a uniform and definite set of standards. In retrospect, Ou-yang may be seen as quite perceptive in generally shifting his efforts, so long as the system was working

tolerably well, from proposals for further changes in it to the concrete task of finding and promoting capable men.

The efforts for stability and gradual improvements made by
Ou-yang, Han Ch'i, and others achieved only limited success. As
Yeh Shih, a leading Southern Sung scholar, observed, "The gradual approach was so gradual that in the end it could never reach
its objectives."[29] Sometimes, personality clashes marred an otherwise tranquil situation. Ou-yang, despite his realization of past
mistakes, failed to mend his habit of "arguing bluntly with colleagues ... and upbraiding them for their weak points right to
their faces."[30] Although "he would defend his own views to the
last ... he would jump on others even before they could open their
mouths."[31] Fortunately Han Ch'i understood his personality and
overlooked its defects.[32] But between Han Ch'i and Fu Pi friction
soon developed. Han was usually quick at decision-making, while
Fu was apt to ramble along without being able to make up his
mind. This difference was at least partly attributable to a difference
in policy. Han, in agreement with Ou-yang, wanted to carry out
general improvements, but Fu frequently had reservations about
even minor changes. Fu had been one of the most radical of the
leaders of the minor reform. Largely because of his views, he had
repeatedly been slandered as a traitor. The only reform leader to
be so denounced more than once, he now displayed not exactly a
conservative attitude, but rather a mind divided between the desire to take his original stand once more and the haunting fear of
political disgrace.[33] Once, over a matter of small concern, Fu's
indecision lasted for several days. Han, for once losing his pa-
tience, finally remarked: "Are you being fussy again?" It was
such an undignified colloquial expression that Fu blushed angrily
and muttered: "Fussy? What sort of language is that?" Fu offered
to resign as early as 1059, but was persuaded not to.[34]

Every high minister, because of his heavy responsibilities, was
exempt from the customary mourning leave of three years that
officials took on the death of each parent.[35] Han and Fu were

casually discussing customs and precedents one day, and Han indicated in a general way that he did not believe such exemptions justifiable. About a year later, Fu's mother died, and he declined the exemption and immediately went on leave, explaining that Han had long ago made his position quite clear. Though Han denied that his casual statement had been personal, Fu refused to believe that it could have been anything other than a broad hint. The two never regained their close relationship. When Fu returned to active duty in 1063, Han no longer came to him for private discussion of official business.[36] These incidents were like little wedges that drove a crack not only between these two old friends but also between Fu and Ou-yang, who generally sided with Han. It is a sad comment on relations between the scholar-officials that the best of them, in spite of all their Confucian virtues, still had trouble keeping their political team together and their private friendship intact.

A far more upsetting problem was that of the imperial succession. Jen-tsung, whose reign lasted for three decades, had thirteen daughters but no son. From 1056 on, his health declined, and many a minister gently urged him to designate an heir apparent. His response was silence or anger.[37] It was not until 1061, after long persuasion by Han Ch'i, Ou-yang Hsiu, and another minister named Tseng Kung-liang, that the emperor yielded. Even then, he only bestowed upon a nephew an honorary title implying a strong probability that he would make the young man his successor, but not making it explicit or definite.[38] The next year, Ou-yang took it on himself to make a last effort to get the line of succession established beyond doubt or dispute. He spoke his case in court, to the emperor's face. After he had finished, Jen-tsung stared silently at him for minutes, while Han Ch'i and the others in court held their breath in awed suspense. At last, the emperor agreed; the formal title of heir apparent was granted and announced.[39] In another year, Jen-tsung was gone, and Emperor Ying-tsung ascended the throne. Only a few days after the succession, however, the new emperor quite unexpectedly had an attack of mental illness, crying out hysterically that someone wanted to murder him. During his convalescence the empress dowager acted as regent. Some disharmony existed between them, and the divisive influence of the eunuchs, who took sides, made it worse. Ou-yang's wife was able to exert some good influence to persuade the empress dowager to be kind to her adopted nephew. She also conveyed the same wish from both Ou-yang and Han, who gave similarly calming advice to the emperor. These were no small contributions to the stability of the dynasty.[40]

Shortly after the recovery of the emperor, Han made a surprising and dramatic move. Catching the empress dowager off guard one day, Han got her to discuss giving up her regency. The moment she indicated a vague assent, Han immediately shouted at the attending eunuchs to remove the screen in front of her. The rigid custom of segregation of the sexes forbade an imperial lady to be seen in court by the ministers; hence, the screen was the very symbol of a female regency. Its sudden removal not only forced the dowager to withdraw in great haste, but signified in effect the end of her regency.[41]

Han had not mentioned his intentions to Fu beforehand, for he knew that Fu was rather sympathetic toward the empress dowager. This made Fu very bitter, for he felt that as a minister of equal rank and a colleague of many years he should have been consulted, or at least forewarned. In fact, he overreacted, suspecting that keeping him in the dark was a sinister maneuver to destroy his credit with the emperor. He resigned from court and retired soon afterward, breaking off his long friendship with Han and Ou-yang. The team that had worked for stability was itself partially wrecked.[42]

"One wave has not quite receded; another is already rushing up." Thus a common Chinese saying describes endless troubles. The new emperor hardly had time to make the acquaintance of his ministers before a violent dispute erupted over the issue of what posthumous honor should be given his true father without appearing ungrateful to Jen-tsung, his father by adoption. The details of this drawn-out controversy (known as *P'u-i*), with its elaborate arguments involving many of the more abstruse technicalities of Confucian rites, would probably be about as interesting to the Western reader as the arguments over how many angels can dance on the point of a pin would be to the average Chinese. It is important, however, to realize that the rituals concerned embodied the Confucianists' sense of hierarchy: of proper status, relationship, and order. On the other hand, disputes over ritual invariably had political implications. The new sovereign naturally wished to extend the title of emperor to his late father. But many officials objected to this idea persistently, even at the cost of their posts, on the grounds that the emperor should do nothing to lessen his gratitude to his predecessor, who had so graciously adopted him. The most appropriate honor for his own father, they contended, was the title of "imperial uncle." Ou-yang, with Han behind him, was the spokesman for the emperor's desire. They outmaneuvered the opposition by having the empress dowager take the initiative by giving her consent, while the emperor himself gracefully declined the full-fledged honor of sovereign status for his late father and decreed instead that he be given the posthumous title of "emperor," but not of "imperial parent," the latter honor being reserved as the symbol of his total gratitude to his predecessor. This hair-splitting solution did not end the political trouble, for the frustrated dissenters continued to seethe.[48] Several leading scholars of later centuries saw nothing wrong with the essence of the solution. The posthumous title of emperor, being merely honorary, did not confuse the line of imperial succession. These scholars thought little of the alternative title proposed by the opposition; it had no historical precedent in any comparable situation.

However, strenuous protests against the decision destroyed the bureaucratic stability that Han and Ou-yang had so carefully built up. A multitude of scholar-officials, unfortunately now including Fu Pi, denounced Ou-yang for shamelessly ingratiating himself with the new sovereign, permitting him to commit an unpardonable impropriety, concocting a wrong theory based on distorted interpretations of the ancient rites, maneuvering the empress dowager into erroneous acquiescence, and above all being utterly treacherous to the late emperor, who had kindly kept him in government service for three decades. Some of them branded Ou-yang a public enemy deserving of capital punishment. Ou-yang, disturbed and on the defensive, felt it necessary to write extensively on the subject in the hope of clarifying the issue for posterity. He understood quite well why the controversy had arisen. Most of the men denouncing him were conservatives. With no serious issue at hand, the best way to attack him and the others in power was to make an issue out of the problem of rites and propriety. After all, Fan Chung-yen had attained great fame by going against the wishes of his emperor; so would they go against the wishes of theirs. Ou-yang himself had been vehement in raising many issues; should they not be the same? He had refused to be deterred by demotion; their determination was no less resolute. In their case as well as his, the claim to ideological authority, the prestige of boldly expressing a difference of opinion, and the fame of making daring criticisms were ample compensation for temporary setbacks.[44]

Clearly, Ou-yang had won a battle but had lost the war. With so many enemies he could no longer be politically effective: to remain at the top of the government would merely serve to draw more attacks. However, his prompt and repeated resignations were refused. Then, from the least expected quarter, a Brutus came forth, back-stabbing him with a sword of slander that added insult to the injury it caused. Ou-yang had recommended that Chiang Chih-chi be made a censor, for Chiang in private discussion with him had supported the official solution during the ritual controversy. In 1067 Ying-tsung died. Although the new emperor,

Shen-tsung, refused Ou-yang's resignation once again, Chiang sensed that change was not far off, and decided to redeem himself in the eyes of the opposition group by betraying his patron. One day he suddenly appeared in court and asked that Ou-yang be put to death for incest, for it had been reported to him that Ou-yang had committed adultery with his oldest daughter-in-law. The accusation created a great stir: it was far more serious than the one that had brought Ou-yang down before. Ou-yang, feeling thoroughly humiliated, confined himself to his house to await a thorough investigation, which he requested with insistence.[45]

The case demonstrated again the lack of adequate rules of evidence and procedure of the Sung judicial system. When the young emperor asked for the source of the report, Chiang said he had heard it from another censor, P'eng Ssu-yung. P'eng claimed that, being old, he could not remember who had reported it to him. Moreover, he contended that regulations permitted censors to make charges without revealing their source. If such protection were not available, he argued, no one would ever dare expose a crime of any powerful minister. Therefore, out of loyalty to the emperor, he must decline to answer the question.[46] The regulations were ambiguous. As mentioned earlier, the edict of 1048 that forbade censors to rely on hearsay excepted matters concerning court policies or widespread suffering among the people.[47] Whether or not an allegation based on hearsay against a minister with policy responsibilities would fall under this clause of the edict was doubtful. By this time Ou-yang had few friends. In fact, no one rose to denounce the accusation as slanderous except Wu Ch'ung, the father of the lady allegedly involved. The young emperor, while inclined to consider the charge unsubstantiated, wanted to reward Chiang for being courageous enough to bring it up. He was advised, however, that mixing rejection and reward ambivalently was hardly a reasonable course of action. After some hesitation, he finally dismissed the charge, issued a public bulletin to that effect, had Chiang and P'eng demoted, and sent a special messenger to convey his imperial regards to the veteran statesman, who was nursing his hurt pride at home.[48]

Neither the two censors nor the political enemies of Ou-yang behind them ever expected to prove the accusation. Slander alone was enough to serve their purpose of ruining his reputation. A lame excuse for this malicious attack was later offered by Ch'eng Hao, famous in history as a founding father of neo-Confucianism. He contended that to find evidence for an offense so private in nature was impossible, whereas the very fact that the allegation was deemed credible by many people reflected a lack of confidence in Ou-yang's moral integrity. In other words, fire engines indicate fire. Ch'eng then curiously shifted his ground, stating that Ou-yang deserved to be removed from court because of his stand on the ritual controversy.[49] In other words, alleged error on one issue may justify politically motivated slander on another. It is amazing how the heat of politics apparently twisted the otherwise logical mind of a great philosopher.

In all probability, there was nothing behind the accusation. The slander was known to have originated, though it was never officially reported, with a second cousin of Ou-yang's wife, a minor official who shortly before the scandal had expected Ou-yang to save him from impeachment. But Ou-yang had refused to let a private relationship interfere with justice. Demolished hope turned into hatred, and the cousin began dropping hints in social circles. Ou-yang's wife maintained such strict discipline in her household, as those close to the family testified, that the alleged incest was hardly probable, even assuming Ou-yang's character to be suspect. Actually, few ever believed the slander. Almost a quarter of a century later, the censor Chiang was still generally despised for having made use of it.[50]

Even though Ou-yang was cleared, it was apparent to all that his position was isolated, his influence waning, his reputation damaged, and his effectiveness decidedly gone. As he himself pointed out, his continuing presence had become a liability to the court. On his renewed plea he was allowed to resign, and he never returned to power again. As a favor, he was made prefect of Pochow, near Yingchow, where his estate was located. There he enjoyed himself by going over his archaeological rubbings and writing anecdotes of his career. He wrote little else, not even much poetry. An active, creative, and turbulent life was quieting down; its end was not far away.[51]

Time moved along, and left Ou-yang behind. His resignation, followed by that of Han Ch'i a year later, left the door open for Wang An-shih. His gigantic reform soon began, in 1069. One of its measures was the farming loans, the so-called Young Shoots Money, extended by the government to the peasants during the sowing season, to be repaid by them with interest at harvest time. Ou-yang objected both to its principle and to the practice of imposing the loan on some peasants who were unwilling to accept it. When his objections brought no result, he resorted to the tactic of carrying it out in its first season and then, without first asking for authorization, ordering its cancellation for the next. Owing to his prestige, his defiance drew no penalty. He was simply instructed to rescind his unauthorized cancellation and get on with the program.[52] The next year, 1070, there were widespread complaints against the reform program. Emperor Shen-tsung, in appointing Ou-yang to Taiyüan, a metropolis in the north, had the idea of consulting him when he passed through the capital. Wang An-shih objected, remarking that Ou-yang was an obstinate man, and that though his prose remained the best, his failure to interpret the classics correctly had misguided many of the scholars of Wang's generation.[53] Times had indeed changed; the new wave was sweeping aside the earlier scholars, and Ou-yang had no intention of swimming against the tide. In six successive memorials, he declined to accept the prefecture of Taiyüan on the excuse of failing health, and sincerely pleaded for a lesser assignment closer to his home. The emperor agreed not to send him to Taiyüan, but still expressed an interest in seeing him, ordering him to come to Kaifeng for an audience as soon as his health would permit.[54] Again Ou-yang begged off, stating his frank objections to the major reform in these resigned words:

> While the time favors what is novel and unconventional, your servant alone wishes to keep his backwardness. When most people are actively taking up meritorious and useful tasks, your servant merely wants to follow the usual path.... It would be better for him, through his insistent begging, to be excused, for three reasons. First, in good conscience, he would not be comfortable in a position of any importance. Second, his energy has been exhausted. And third, the acts that he would be required to perform would not agree with what he has learned.[55]

To Ou-yang, the major reform was far too sweeping, unorthodox, and upsetting. He agreed with neither its interpretation of the classics nor its highly assertive mode of administration, and made it crystal clear that he wanted no part of it. Finally, the emperor granted Ou-yang's wish and transferred him to Tsaichow, still near his home.[56] Ou-yang was certainly wise in not going to the capital: soon many officials opposed to the reform found themselves on their way out. Among them, ironically, were several who had been bitter critics of Ou-yang during the ritual controversy. In the meantime, Ou-yang's health was failing fast. In the spring of 1071, at the age of sixty-four, he retired.[57] Death came the following year, ending a long career of hard struggle in politics and distinguished service in government.

Ou-yang's political career was beyond doubt outstanding. Still, like many another outstanding statesman, he could make but little progress toward solving the basic problems of bureaucratic government—how to select honest, capable officials; how to have just, effective laws; and above all, how to achieve a working consensus on these crucial matters among the leading bureaucrats. In any event, Ou-yang's political career alone would not be sufficient to earn for him the exalted place he holds in Chinese history. It was his political record in combination with his versatile contributions to several scholastic fields that made him one of the greatest neo-Confucianists.

CHAPTER SEVEN

CLASSICIST

CONFUCIAN SCHOLARSHIP covered many areas. Traditionally, it was divided into four major categories valued in descending order: the ancient classics, sometimes known as the Confucian Canons, and works related to them; histories of various kinds; works on other intellectual topics; and finally belles-lettres and miscellaneous works. A recognized classical scholar such as Ou-yang would be able to speak authoritatively in any of these fields, as well as on affairs of state.

In the field of the ancient classics there were many problems of textual criticism and interpretation. By the Sung, scholars laboring for centuries had produced a host of commentaries, textual critiques, critiques of variants, annotations with commentaries, supplementary commentaries, and the like. The disagreement among these works had been unimportant in earlier centuries to those studying for the civil service examinations. On the one hand, the examination system accepted only one text as official; on the other, with books hard to come by, many works on the classics were not generally available. The T'ang government, following earlier practice, had the official texts of the classics engraved on stone, so that interested scholars might make their own copies from them. The development of block printing in the T'ang also increased the availability of the *Correct Meanings,* the officially approved annotations and commentaries, though this work's distribution was still relatively limited by the early Sung.

In the early Sung, a candidate heading for the state examinations would somehow get hold of a copy of the official version of the classics and the *Correct Meanings* and then concentrate on memorizing them. Even members of wealthy families with extensive private libraries lacked the motivation to go beyond this conventional requirement. There was as yet no Sung learning as distinguished from that of the T'ang.[1] In fact, the attitude of the government at the time tended to discourage varying interpretations of the classics. Wang Tan, a much-venerated early Sung statesman, put it quite typically: "It would be inadvisable to allow scholars either to put aside the [approved] annotations and commentaries or to set forth different ideas, which might lead students astray and deprive them of the benefit of knowing for certain the proper basis on which their thinking should be anchored."[2]

The situation changed radically as economic prosperity grew and education spread, and particularly as printing developed. At first block printing spread to many large cities; later movable-type printing came into use. Not only the *Correct Meanings* and the official versions of the classics, but many other works became far more accessible than ever before. As Confucianism made unprecedented gains, a fundamental question began to be raised: what exactly did the classics mean? During the late T'ang, there had been a minor intellectual school of thought advocating the revival of Confucianism that had as one of its goals a purge of the many Buddhist and Taoist accretions in the annotations and commentaries, and a critical examination of the purified remainder in order to restore the original meanings of the classics. By the Sung, conditions were favorable for this school to develop into an energetic movement.[3]

Under these circumstances, the official version could no longer retain its monopoly. Yet Court lecturers merely repeated what was well-known, with trite elaborations, and added nothing significant to scholarship. They betrayed a narrow mentality that occasionally verged on absurdity. For example, they were usually afraid to touch on the apocryphal *wei* books (literally the "woofs"), which claimed to emulate as well as to complement the classics (the "warps"). However, these lecturers felt obliged to uphold those passages from the *wei* books that were included in the official annotations and commentaries as being definitely valid and beyond challenge.[4]

The learned scholars who checked into the other sources that were becoming increasingly available to them found many apparent shortcomings in the official versions, such as dubious texts of non-Confucian origin, misleading interpretations, and possible textual errors, all beclouding the real meanings of the classics. Those who dedicated themselves to the revival of Confucianism soon put forward their own interpretations through writing and tutoring. In time, their scholarship gained in influence, and their superior qualities had to be recognized. Their study of the classics was much more than an academic undertaking. They viewed the correct meanings of the ancient texts as a basis for proper action. They wanted not just to send better-educated men to the government, but to instill in all the literate people of the country their own zeal to master Confucian principles and apply them to remolding society after their Confucian vision. They wanted to realize a utopian moral society in which everyone, led by the scholars, would live a virtuous life. The Confucian belief was secular; but the visionary spirit of these scholars, who concerned themselves with everything, was comparable to religious zeal. Confucianism was truly being born anew.[5]

The minor reform was but a political expression of this invigorating neo-Confucian movement. Its policy of government support of schools, for example, aimed not only at a quantitative increase in the number of schools but also at their qualitative improvement. The hope was not merely promotion of practical education, but Confucian permeation of the entire society. Though the reform program lasted only a year, this particular policy, owing to its justification on Confucian grounds that no one could possibly dispute, long survived in principle. It added considerable impetus to the further spread of education and Confucianism.

The political defeat of the reformers did not cost them their intellectual leadership. About a decade after the minor reform, two leading private neo-Confucian scholars who had been sympathetic to it, Hu Yüan and Sun Fu, were appointed to lecture at the Directorate of Education and the National University. Their prestige was greatly enhanced; many students became converted to their views; and the official annotations and commentaries of the classics gradually lost their hold. Other private scholars in various parts of the country, much encouraged, began to raise their voices to question and reinterpret. The body of thought that developed came to be honored as "the learning of the Ch'ing-li reign," the very beginning of Sung learning itself. These innovations in scholarship and interpretation were no less than the first major change in the study of the classics since the Han period (206 B.C.–A.D. 222), nearly a thousand years before.[6]

Ou-yang Hsiu was a key figure in this change. He helped both Hu and Sun, though he seemed more inclined toward Hu. According to Ou-yang, "Hu had a large number of students. His school in Huchow was attended by hundreds, who in turn taught the classics to others elsewhere. His approach in teaching, being the most comprehensive ... came to be adopted by the National University in 1044." But it was not until 1056 that Hu himself was appointed there, on Ou-yang's recommendation. "Then so many students came from distant places that the National University, having no room to accommodate them, had to take over other government houses nearby and convert them into school buildings. Among those successful in the civil service examinations usually four or five out of ten had studied under Hu."[7] However, though Hu's teaching methods were highly praised in his time, only their basic points were remembered a few decades later. We know only that he stressed both the broad meanings of the classics and their practical applications to current affairs; that his approach was general but solid; that the terms he used were never intangible, but always readily understandable; and that his attitude was balanced and fair.[8] These characteristics are quite similar to those of Ou-yang's own scholarship.

Ou-yang also praised Sun Fu. In the order appointing him, Ou-yang wrote that "Sun follows neither misleading commentaries nor arbitrary theories that would confuse the meanings of the classics. His own words are simple and clear." In his specialty, the classical chronicle known as the *Spring and Autumn Annals,* "Sun established with clarity the respective merits and demerits of the ancient feudal rulers and their officials, thereby assessing how the time prospered or declined, and inferred how orderliness resulted from the kingly way or chaos from the lack of it, thus ascertaining much of the classic's original meaning."[9] But Ou-yang, who was an authority on this classic himself, sent his oldest son to study under Hu rather than Sun.[10] Hu and Sun were unable to get along at the National University, and often avoided each other—a sad commentary on Confucianism in practice. Sun, it appeared, had a strong personality, quite different from Hu's gentle temperament.[11] He also had some radical ideas that drew much criticism from conventional scholars, whereas Hu's ideas were usually so well put that they found ready acceptance. For example, Sun went to the extremity of advocating a thorough revision of all the classical texts, as well as the official annotations and commentaries. Ou-yang himself merely called for the elimination of superstitious prognostics and dubious *wei* passages.[12] Sun's overzealous attitude was reflected by his leading disciple, Shih Chieh. Ou-yang, though a good friend of Shih, chid him in these sharp words: "Your self-esteem seems too inordinate, your criticism of the current conditions too excessive . . . as if you deliberately set out to be different just for the sake of claiming superiority."[13] This frank criticism might to some extent be applicable to Sun as well. Though in favor of new opinions, Ou-yang refused to be attracted simply by their novelty. In fact, he explicitly stated that he disliked what might appear to "extol the strange and praise the unusual." What really mattered should be an interpretation's soundness.

Ou-yang's approach to the classics was particularly noteworthy. His experience as a self-made man led him to emphasize the importance of primary sources. "Having had no master to guide me," he said, "I have gained by self-education the boldness to stand on my own and hold with conviction the conclusions I myself arrive at. This is possible because the classics left by the sages are available for direct confrontation and verification."[14] He also put it another way: "When there is no master to be found, scholars should take the very text of the classics as their master. This means an independent search for the classics' meanings."[15]

According to Ou-yang, great scholars reached for the meanings in the texts through careful reasoning. "Seven or eight times out of ten, the classics can be understood without resorting to the commentaries. But five or six times out of ten their meanings become confused just because of what the commentaries have inadvertently asserted." Reasoning of course had its limitations. As Ou-yang explained, "Many remote events that happened long ago have since become quite obscure. However, it is not really essential for us to know them. Ignorance of them does not prevent one from becoming a *chün-tzu.*" One should be satisfied with "grasping the essentials without necessarily understanding the rest of the details, which might as well be left in doubt."[16]

The logical corollary of the principle of reasoning was continuous research and discussion. In Ou-yang's words, "some meanings of the six classics, lost through failures in transmission, can no longer be ascertained.... Let various scholars present their respective contributions and let the enlightened ones choose the best.... By gradually gathering the best ideas from the many, most of the lost meanings could be closely approached."[17] Throwing modesty aside, Ou-yang proclaimed his faith in the usefulness of scholarly discussion through the ages: "Two thousand years after the death of Confucius, there appears a certain Ou-yang Hsiu who asserts a particular interpretation. Given another two thousand years, who could deny the possibility that there might appear yet another scholar who would assert the same.... When that interpretation comes to be shared by an increasing number of scholars, it will overcome and supersede what the present majority has mistakenly considered to be correct."[18] Through careful study, discerning discussion, and eventual verification, the best interpretation would stand.

Ou-yang believed that study of the classics should be vigorously and strictly disciplined.

> I cannot believe it possible for any scholar to propose an interpretation without having looked at the theories proposed by scholars in the ages intervening between the ancient times and the present. Unless after exhaustive research these theories are found to be inconsistent, unless when subjected to the sayings of the sages they appear very much contrary to reason and to the texts of the classics themselves, unless there is no alternative but to replace them, what justification could one possibly have in bringing up yet another different interpretation, which would merely cause more disputes? ... Only when all arguments are exhausted and a particular theory is still found to be unconvincing have I ever endeavored to correct its mistake. Far be it from me to be fond of asserting variant opinions.[19]

Classical studies, Ou-yang sighed, were already full of mud; why throw in more? These characteristics of Ou-yang's scholarship were well evaluated in the *Sung Standard History*: "He directed his main attention to the broad meanings. He neither stressed [the minute problems in] textual criticism nor deliberately differed with other scholars."[20]

Ou-yang thought his approach to classical studies superior for yet another reason. Only by working on the classics rigorously, reflecting on them thoroughly, and thinking through all their implications exhaustively could scholars really be sure of what their truths were. The very process of such study, the neo-Confucianists generally believed, would infuse scholars with Confucian zeal to serve the state and society.

At the core of Ou-yang's approach to the classics, and to all scholarship, was the concept of *li*—reason, rationality, or a rational principle of order. Anything rational, according to Ou-yang, should meet three criteria: it should be readily understandable; it should be capable of being practiced; and it should agree with common human feelings, or at least should not lie far beyond them.[21] Ou-yang described his rationalistic, pragmatic, and humanistic thinking in these words: "It is incorrect to describe the way of the sages in lofty words of little factual substance.... The way of the sages is to be manifested in one's personal conduct, carried out in one's practical affairs, and expressed in one's writings, thereby bearing witness for the benefit of succeeding generations.... Their way is easy to understand as well as to follow ... for it is applicable in reality."[22]

The classics themselves were rational, Ou-yang contended. "Their language is simple and straightforward; it is the commentaries that make novel and unusual points. Simpleness and straightforwardness are not particularly pleasing to the ear, whereas novelty and unusualness have many appealing qualities. This is why many scholars have liked the commentaries, and have sometimes become confused by them."[23] The trouble had begun long before, in the Han period. On its establishment as the state cult, Confucianism had absorbed certain beliefs of the Taoist cosmologists and magicians. Many other non-Confucian elements crept in from then on—"the chart floating down the Yellow River and the writing found in the Lo River," for example. To Ou-yang, these elements were simply superstition.[24] The prophetic and *wei* passages incorporated into the *Correct Meanings* during the T'ang fell into the same category: in 1059 he proposed to have all such passages expunged. Jen-tsung ordered that all the passages in question be copied and submitted to his personal review, but the matter went no further, for the leading councillors would not support any revision of the official version.[25]

Ou-yang subjected all the classics to his rational analysis. He found the *Classic of Songs* full of human feelings, an opinion that was eventually used as a basis for personal attacks on him. He was rather skeptical of the *Rituals of Chou,* doubting its textual authenticity and also whether the multitude of institutions it described could ever have actually existed.[26] His study of this classic led him to emphasize administrative improvement, as opposed to Wang An-shih, who believed in the *Rituals of Chou* and stressed institutional reform. Like many another scholar with reservations about the *Rituals of Chou,* Ou-yang was particularly attracted to the *Spring and Autumn Annals.*

The most complex and difficult of all classical textual problems were those relating to the *Classic of Change.* According to modern scholars, this classic is probably an amalgamation of ancient omens and interpretive messages with later, more sophisticated auguristic texts. If the classic were regarded strictly as an oracle, there would be little trouble. But some unknown philosophers, long after Confucius and very likely as late as the early Han, added to it appendices claiming that it contained profound cosmological and metaphysical principles that formed the ultimate basis of the Confucian ethical system. Supporting this claim was a passage in the *Analects* in which Confucius himself said that, given more years of life, he would devote them to the study of the classic of change. This quotation, we are now rather sure, was a subsequent textual corruption falsely attributed to Confucius, but during the Sung no one questioned the tradition that Confucius had respected this classic as the most profound of all. What made things especially confusing was that Confucianists and non-Confucianists alike—Confucian scholars, Taoists, magicians, and fortune-tellers—constantly used the work for auguristic purposes and other superstitious practices.

Ou-yang was among the few Sung scholars to raise serious doubts about this classic. Understandably, under the limitations of their time, these pioneering neo-Confucianists did not go so far as to question the authenticity of the text, its date, or Confucius' alleged wish to study it, but they did question the authenticity, validity, and reliability of the appendices. Ou-yang also tried to dissociate Confucius from the dubious parts of this book by contending that his purpose in studying it would have been to clarify its cosmology and metaphysics so that it would not be used to support superstition.[27] To Ou-yang, everything Confucianism stood for must be rational, and Confucianism must rid itself and society of everything that appeared irrational. This, by the standards of his time, was a bold as well as a refreshing interpretation.

Ou-yang's rationalism went farther than that of his contemporaries. He insisted that even principles he regarded as rational, valid, and acceptable must not be relied on blindly or superstitiously. To the question of whether goodness would eventually defeat evil, for example, an overwhelming majority of Confucianists would answer emphatically in the affirmative. But Ou-yang courageously pointed out that good would not necessarily triumph:

> It is not that heaven does not prefer what is good; heaven probably cannot always prevail on human beings, mixed as they are. This is the rational meaning of the cardinal principle that governs the relationship between heaven and human beings.... Knowing this principle, one understands rather than feels surprised by the fortune or misfortune, the success or failure, that the sages and the good people in history may or may not encounter.[28]

Ou-yang's contributions to the study of all the classics received a mixed evaluation by the philosophers of the Southern Sung. His pioneering efforts were acknowledged and his brilliance respected, but his views were generally thought to be excessively simple and his scholarship to lack profundity. To some of his critics, his reliance upon the texts of the classics was too heavy. More than once

Ou-yang affirmed that he believed in what was written in the classics, but would hesitate to accept anything that was not there.[29] To his critics, this belief was unduly restrictive, and it seemed unreasonable in terms of his own rationalism, since the classics contained so many obscure details and complications that their meaning was hardly self-evident. Many scholars felt that the extant annotations and commentaries, despite their errors and limited reliability, were nevertheless helpful and should not be categorically ignored. As Yeh Shih pointed out, Ou-yang himself went to other sources than the classics. The high praise he showered on the Han and T'ang empires, especially the good reign of T'ang T'ai-tsung (whom he almost equated with the sagacious rulers of ancient legend), conflicted with his proposition that the principles in the classics were entirely sufficient as guides to virtue.[30]

The main weakness of Ou-yang's rationalism can best be seen against the historical background of Confucian thought. As originally formulated, Confucianism failed to give men a philosophical basis for explaining the natural world. Hence superstitious non-Confucian elements—magic and augury—were gradually incorporated into the classics, their commentaries, and the many other works that came under the umbrella of Confucianism. These elements, however, had little appeal compared with the profound speculative philosophies of neo-Taoism and Buddhism, which gained a vast following even among the best-educated in the half-millennium before the Sung, and which continued to claim significant support during the Sung itself. Ou-yang's rationalism was too narrow in scope to compete successfully with these philosophies. It was confined almost exclusively to human affairs. Ou-yang himself had little knowledge of natural phenomena or interest in them. When he could not give a rational explanation of magnetism, for example, he merely offered the lame excuse that even the sages would have declined to discuss what reasoning could not penetrate.[31] He and enlightened scholar-officials like him attacked the superstitious practices of the court, but offered nothing in their place. It is hardly surprising that the attacks of the rationalists brought little improvement.[32] Tseng Kung, who of all the neo-Confucianists of the early Sung stood closest to Ou-yang in scholarship, was well aware of the inadequacy of Ou-yang's brand of rationalism. "Is it not overreaching," he asked, "to assert that heaven, earth, the million things between them, and all their changes involve nothing more than what man can observe merely by his ears and eyes?"[33] Ou-yang would have been hard put to it to answer.

Ou-yang was concerned so exclusively with human affairs themselves that he could not even understand the interest others took in the basic philosophical problems that human affairs give rise to. As he said: "Disturbed by scholars nowadays who are fond of discussing the nature of man, I constantly express the opinion that it is not an urgent problem for scholars, just as it was not with Confucius himself." As he observed, none of the classics ever discussed this problem; none of the disciples of Confucius ever asked him about it, and Confucius himself touched on it only once. Many Sung scholars interested in the problem of man's nature usually took as their point of departure a famous passage in the classic titled *The Doctrine of the Mean*. Ou-yang argued that the passage in question was not meant to direct men's attention toward the metaphysical, speculative, and meditative realms; on the contrary, it emphasized the importance of cultivating Confucian virtue, and declared that studying was the only way to do so. His argument continued:

> Scholars who like to discuss the nature of man ... have been misled by the many biased theories that have been proposed since ancient times. The discussions of these scholars have produced only useless verbiage.... To be a *chün-tzu* requires no more than self-cultivation and the ability to govern other people. It is not necessary to determine whether man's nature is good or bad. If human nature is good, self-cultivation is still necessary, as is the ability to govern other people. If it is bad, these requirements are even more imperative.[34]

Ou-yang felt his opinion supported by the great philosophers of ancient times. Mencius had claimed that men were basically good, but still had to be educated. Hsün-tzu had held that men were basically bad, yet would not give up attempting to educate them. Yang Hsiung thought man's nature to be mixed, but he too thought men should be educated. Ou-yang concluded that speculation on human nature without an emphasis on education was bound to be fruitless and wasted. Instead of confronting the question, he brushed it aside as being of little practical consequence. Whatever his other distinctions, Ou-yang was certainly no philosopher.

Does a man who was not a philosopher deserve to be rated as a great Confucian master? The neo-Confucian philosophers of the Southern Sung thought not. They were much more inclined to the metaphysical than their forebears. They conceived *li*, for example, as a universal principle, transcendental and metaphysical. Under their leadership, neo-Confucian classical scholarship acquired new depth and came to be known as "the study of *hsin li*," a compound term meaning human nature and universal principle. By the standards of Southern Sung scholarship, Ou-yang, though respected as a pioneer, was too superficial a pragmatist to be honored as one of the great masters.[35]

The moral standards of the Southern Sung were far stricter and more rigid than those of the Northern Sung—or of Victorian England, for that matter. This increased austerity also had an adverse effect on Ou-yang's historical standing. For example, Ou-yang had defended certain romantic verses in the *Classic of Songs* against the contention of several scholars that the verses bordered on impropriety. Ou-yang, in his belief that the rational principle is never far removed from human feelings, did not find the verses to be particularly objectionable. His comments were: "They are indulgent without being licentious; they are joyous without being lewd. As such, they are in the final analysis essentially proper."[36] This defense found little acceptance. To many high-minded classicists of the Southern Sung, it may have reflected a trace of impropriety in Ou-yang's own conduct.

The scholar-officials of the Northern Sung, following the T'ang style of life, were not in the least ascetic. Fan Chung-yen was said to have been in love with a young courtesan. Ssu-ma Kuang, who was much respected for his upright conduct, did not refrain from writing *tz'u* on the theme of love. Ou-yang, more than any of them, open-heartedly partook of all life's pleasures.[37] Chu Hsi criticized Ou-yang harshly for this attitude, saying that he "cultivated his literary works but made no effort to cultivate his personality. All day long he sang songs, drank wine, and sought to enjoy himself." Such conduct, Chu Hsi opined, betrayed a lack of profundity in Ou-yang's philosophy that could only be attributable to the superficiality of his scholarship.[38] Thus Ou-yang could not be regarded as a great Confucianist.

Neither Ou-yang nor his critics dealt with the basic difficulty of Confucianism's evolution: the conflict between increasing pressures to establish an orthodox interpretation of the classics and increasingly numerous and diverse individual interpretations. Ou-yang disagreed on many points with the orthodoxy of his time, and sought to promote his own interpretations. He was certain of the correctness of his own ideas, and other scholars were equally certain of the correctness of theirs.[39] As a pioneer, Ou-yang helped break the hold of the official version of the classics in order to promote discussion, through which, he believed, truth would eventually prevail. What he did not foresee was the considerable friction that would exist when diverse opinions arose. When Wang An-shih justified the major reform by invoking the particular interpretations of his own New School, and then imposed those interpretations on the country as a new orthodoxy, the problem became no longer an academic dispute or intellectual controversy, but an inseparable part of a political power struggle.[40]

The conflict between orthodoxy and diversity was bound to occur at a time when Confucianism was seeking a response to changing times. Su Ch'e, Su Tung-p'o's younger brother and also a protégé of Ou-yang, realized at the time of the major reform that the only means of saving Confucianism from internal conflict would be the toleration of diversity among contending schools under a broadly constructed orthodoxy. Such pluralism would allow a scholar to choose freely among a variety of interpretations, or to reach independent conclusions of his own.[41] But no one else took Su's suggestion up, and it was lost in the turmoil of factional politics.

Would it have been possible, had there been no factional dispute, for Confucianism to have accommodated a diversity of interpretations within a general orthodoxy? It is doubtful. Pressures toward diversity were strong. They were the products of changing political, economic, and social conditions, and arose when many ideologically oriented scholars (those from non-bureaucratic origins in particular) found the existing orthodoxy to fall short of their vision of what Confucianism should be. But the need to have an orthodoxy was overwhelming. The majority of scholars, who were not ideologically oriented, wanted to see the state examination system adopt an undisputed, unconfusing set of standards. The bureaucratic machine strove for uniformity, as bureaucratic machines usually do. The emperor preferred an orthodoxy: it would provide a means of strengthening his control over the scholar-officials. To the emperor, the bureaucracy, and most of the scholars, diversity was only upsetting.[42]

The evolution of neo-Confucianism eventually culminated in the choice of the School of the True Way as the new orthodoxy. Diverse opinions among individual scholars were permissible only within strictly prescribed limits. The bold pioneering spirit of Ou-yang and his contemporaries was to be respected from a distance, but not to be tolerated if it showed any signs of reappearing. Neo-Confucianism was aging; its growth had slowed down.

CHAPTER EIGHT

HISTORIAN

"THE SIX CLASSICS are all histories." So declared Chang Hsüeh-ch'eng, a great historian of the eighteenth century.[1] Chang's statement became so famous that an almost identical statement made by Wang Yang-ming at the dawn of the sixteenth century was nearly forgotten.[2] Chang based his statement on the grounds that "ancient men never talked about principles without illustrating them with facts" such as "the ancient ruler's accomplishments, institutions, codes, and customs."[3] It echoed what Ou-yang had stated long before: "To learn the way [of the sages], one must study antiquity.... What is meant here by antiquity are such things as the sovereigns and their officials, their systems of governing and the people they governed, their rites and their music, their penal codes and their laws."[4]

Among the classics, the *Spring and Autumn Annals* was Ou-yang's favorite. It recorded information of practical value in a "precise and concise" style, thereby reflecting its author's sound methodology.[5] Its laconic style appealed to him most. He was not interested in its study of ancient history as such; he did not think it contained enough data. Accompanying it and covering roughly the same period were two exegetical works known as the *Tradition of Kung-yang* and the *Tradition of Ku-liang,* and an elaborate account of political events with some imaginative reconstruction of detail known as the *Tradition of Tso.* These three books were usually viewed either as commentaries on the main classic or as lesser classics. Ou-yang considered them commentaries, and not very reliable ones, for his research discovered that they had obvious defects. (For example, a person referred to as a man in the first two Traditions was referred to as a woman in the *Tradition of Tso*.)[6] The lack of detail in the *Spring and Autumn Annals* itself did not bother him. Confucius, he said, was "cautious on what was not definitely known" and "would refrain from speaking on remote antiquity, on which available evidence is even more scanty." To Ou-yang, filling in details without being sure of their authenticity was a serious error. He considered the Han scholars bad historians, for they incorporated into their historical works "curious compilations and strange versions," sometimes drawing on hearsay or even their own imaginations. The monumental *Records of the Grand Historian* compiled by Ssu-ma Ch'ien also came under Ou-yang's criticism: "Ssu-ma, learned in many ways and inclined toward the curious, tried to make himself appear well-informed by gathering all the versions available, without being selective at all. It almost seems as if he were afraid that otherwise he might have missed something."[7]

History, to Ou-yang, must rely on evidence. His dislike of previous works stemmed from their lack of it. He was much interested in archaeology, eagerly looking for bronzes, stones, and other artifacts, "the material remains from the mid-Chou period down to the eve of the Sung, which are scattered all over the country, in the mountains and around the lakes, on precarious cliffs and inaccessible gorges, in wild forests and abandoned tombs." Since copying might result in errors, he had rubbings made, filed, catalogued, and annotated. The result, totaling about 1,000 portfolios, was his renowned *Collection of Ancient Inscriptions*.[8] He insisted that the gathering of evidence, the first step in the study of history, should be exhaustive. Discoveries should be recorded as soon as made. Not ready himself to move on to the next step of writing on early history, he preferred to "leave the scholars of subsequent generations a wealth of information that may help fill the gaps and rectify the mistakes in written documents."[9] Whether an item was allegedly connected with spirits, immortals, ghosts, or demons, or whether it was by a Buddhist or a Taoist, made no difference; he saved every discovery for whatever research value it might have.

Ou-yang cared for historical evidence in two other fields: bibliography and the preservation of contemporary sources. From 1034 until his dismissal from court with Fan Chung-yen in 1036, he participated in the compilation of *Ch'ung-wen tsung mu,* a catalogue of the imperial library covering 3,445 titles. This catalogue surpassed earlier catalogues by its new approach of having "annotations under each title." These descriptive notes, "clear and comprehensive," set a model for later bibliographies.[10] Though a junior member of the project, Ou-yang probably contributed a larger share than his status would indicate. It was he who wrote the essay that explained the nature of the annotations and the method by which they were composed. After the project ended in 1041, he continued to be interested in its emendation. As he later pointed out, there had been "on the one hand some duplications in it and on the other some titles omitted that should have been included."[11] Also, the compilers had not been given access to "books on military affairs and astronomy classified as secret." After Ou-yang became a councillor, he made a special request (in 1062) for permission to release these books, as well as a number of rare books that had previously been withheld. All of them were then copied, examined, and included in the catalogue. Only then was the famous compilation complete.[12]

Ou-yang was equally industrious in preserving contemporary source materials for the benefit of future historians. In 1059, when he was working on the *New T'ang History* at the Bureau of History, he found some of the Bureau's procedures to be less than satisfactory. The Sung government, like that of previous dynasties, had official historians gather key government records and prepare a State History (sometimes translated as National History). While these documents were occasionally used for reference on specific precedents, their main purpose was for posterity, when the succeeding dynasty would follow the time-honored tradition of assigning a commission to use them in preparing the Standard History of the dynasty's predecessor.[13] Ou-yang discovered that an official formerly in charge of the State History had submitted what had been completed of it to the emperor and destroyed all drafts. In Ou-yang's opinion both steps were undesirable. Drafts should be preserved for reference, and the finished version should not be submitted to the emperor, for the knowledge that the emperor would see it might inhibit the official historians. Ou-yang submitted to the emperor a memorial on the subject, which reads as follows:

> Nowadays the Records of Current Government ... do not record (as they should) the statements and actions of the emperor on some debatable issues, nor what the imperial orders were, nor what the officials stated, orally or in writing. They merely record such items as announcements of appointments, of imperial audiences, of grants to officials of leaves from court, and the like. The Diary of Activities and Repose [of the emperor] is not any better. It hardly differs in substance from the routine reports made by various offices.... The Daily Records [for the most part based on the two records just mentioned] are equally unsatisfactory.... Official historians wishing to make the records more complete have been unable to do so. There was an ancient tradition by which emperors refrained from looking at the accounts of their own reigns. Current practice is different. Once work is completed, the records are submitted to Your Majesty. Accordingly, when it comes to happenings that some consider best left unmentioned [literally "avoided"], even if the official historians want to write it up, they hesitate to do so.... It is hereby requested that henceforth these records not be submitted to Your Majesty.[14]

本紀第四五定本淨本並已付第六
已下如未取得速取之恐行魿弟書目
局中相見也

儁書

As to the portion of the State History already submitted, Ou-yang asked that a copy be made and sent back to the Bureau of History to be available for reference.[15] The request was only partially successful. The court agreed that the early drafts should not be destroyed and that the Bureau should keep a copy of the finished version, but Ou-yang's objection to its submission to the emperor was merely noted without being sustained. Consequently, the practice continued.

Ou-yang realized that the independence of historians was not always respected by the government, and that official recordings invariably suffered from many limitations and inhibitions. Private accounts were from this standpoint highly valuable. A number of scholar-officials in the Sung period were fond of jotting down their experiences, as well as interesting information they came across, in private notebooks. These random recollections skipped from serious subjects to gossip to ghost stories, often incongruously following one another without discernible sequence or organization.[16] However, it was occasionally an author's deliberate intention to bury the politically sensitive among the inconsequential. Many private notebooks preserved a wealth of historical data. Owing to their uneven nature, traditional bibliographies would not honor them as works of history proper. They were classified at best under "miscellaneous histories," "miscellaneous writings," and sometimes under "stories," along with fiction. Ou-yang left a work of this kind, titled *Notes on Returning to the Farm*. In his words, "it includes court anecdotes worth noting, incidents the official historians have not recorded, and excerpts from the enjoyable conversations of scholar-officials."[17]

Ou-yang's lasting fame in the field of history is due mainly to his *New History of the Five Dynasties* and to his part in compiling the *New T'ang History*. These two works did not attain their goal

---

The calligraphy opposite is a note written by Ou-yang Hsiu while working on the *New T'ang History*. (From the Palace Museum collection.)

of superseding the old histories, but did have enough merit of their own to be included among the Standard Histories. The *Old T'ang History* of the early Sung was little more than a compilation of official records. It met with increasing criticism as the quality of Sung scholarship advanced, and finally another commission was appointed to make a new effort. Sung Chi was responsible from the very beginning for compiling the biographies. Ou-yang probably also worked on some of the biographies, but in deference to Sung's seniority claimed no credit for his work on them. His chief responsibility was the rest of the History: accounts of the emperors' reigns, a host of tables, and treatises on various institutions. Ou-yang devoted much attention to the way institutions functioned, the difficulties they encountered in achieving their purposes, and the ways in which they changed.[18]

Ou-yang's interest in the Five Dynasties, the period of disunity and instability immediately preceding the Sung, began early and lasted throughout his life. In his younger days, when he had little time for history, he proposed to write an account of the Five Dynasties as a joint undertaking with his friend Yin Shu, who was also a leading writer of ancient-style prose and a great admirer of the *Spring and Autumn Annals*. Yin unfortunately died in the prime of life, having written only about four thousand words on the Five Dynasties. In 1036, when Ou-yang was banished to I-ling, where he had little of interest to do, he decided to go on by himself.[19] Throughout his career, whenever he was assigned to a relatively inactive local post he would devote himself to research. Occasionally he sent drafts to his friend Mei Yao-ch'en for consultation. Ou-yang confided to Mei that he was proud of the principles he adopted, the judgments he reached, and the unconventional classifications he developed in his work. However, he said he would only discuss them with a few good friends—other people, he felt, would not be able to understand them.[20] That he was working on a history of the Five Dynasties was of course not unknown. In 1060, after his return to political prominence, he was asked as an honor to present his manuscript to the court. He chose to decline, excusing himself on the grounds that it was not yet satisfactory or even complete, since in remote places it had been hard to collect data and check references, and since his recent work on the *New T'ang History* left no time for private research.[21] His reluctance to reveal his manuscript persisted throughout his life, for he believed that many prominent scholar-officials, his political adversaries in particular, would disapprove of it. Shortly after his death, however, the court ordered his family to relinquish it, for the purpose of having it officially published as a posthumous honor to Ou-yang. As Ou-yang no doubt foresaw, it was held up by the objection of Wang An-shih, who disagreed with many of its interpretations. Five years went by before it was published and Ou-yang's place among the great historians of the ages was recognized.[22]

An elegant laconism characterized both the *New T'ang History* and the *History of the Five Dynasties,* especially the latter. Their excellent literary style won them great popularity among the readers of the Standard Histories. As historical works, however, they were open to criticism. Concise to a fault, they often provided little more than bare summations.[23] This defect was the major reason why they could not replace the old histories, as had been intended.

When the *New T'ang History* was presented to the court for approval, its compilers claimed that on the one hand "it achieved an economy of words" and on the other "it dealt with more events" than its predecessor.[24] Many historians in later centuries disagreed on both points. The *New T'ang History* could have been a far more useful reference work than it was if its compilers, in their insistence on brevity, had not chosen to ignore the vast amount of detailed information that was available to them in the *Veritable Records* of the T'ang, which were forever lost when the Northern Sung came to an end. Though the new history is more readable than the old one, it is not nearly as informative, and it does not satisfy those interested in historical data. For example, the biographies in the *New T'ang History* usually made no reference, as other Standard Histories did, to the family background of the men discussed. (This idea did not originate with Ou-yang: it was probably due to the influence of Liu Chih-chi, a great T'ang historiographer.)[25] The elimination of this information greatly handicapped scholars who tried to trace the social origins of the men whose biographies were included. Another fault resulted from Ou-yang's literary taste. Most of the T'ang documents had been written in the ornamental, allusive style of parallel prose, which Ou-yang did not like. Accordingly, he either threw out the T'ang documents altogether or cut and edited them to his own liking.[26] In doing so, scholars of later centuries felt, he destroyed much of historical value.

Ou-yang and his colleagues put into the new history information they obtained from sources the old history had not used. It appeared, however, that they did not check the authenticity of their information carefully enough. Some critics even suggested that they used sources they knew to be dubious. At any rate, the *New T'ang History* contained many mistakes: one later historian classified its defects into twenty categories. Some dissatisfaction was already felt at the time of its publication.[27] Ssu-ma Kuang, in compiling his monumental *Comprehensive Mirror for Aid in Government,* chose to rely on the *Old T'ang History* as being more faithful in preserving the contents of the original sources.

Although the ruling houses rose and fell in rapid succession during the Five Dynasties period, traditional respect for history was great enough so that most of their records were kept intact. The *Old History of the Five Dynasties,* like its T'ang counterpart, simply followed these records without attempting to interpret them.[28] This was exactly what displeased Ou-yang and a few other scholars who wished to see it rewritten. Ou-yang's new history was chiefly interpretive. He paid little attention to events, many of which he dismissed as being inconsequential occurrences of a chaotic period or undesirable results of Buddhist influence, and as having little meaning or value. Instead, he concentrated on developing and applying the didactic concept of presenting facts selectively to support a moral judgment. Usually at the end of a chapter in his history, Ou-yang discussed the principles by which he had selected and arranged the information. Commentaries on the chapter's moral message followed. Some critics complained that these discussions and commentaries went too far in decrying the evils of the period. Ou-yang, in his own defense, maintained that the period was so utterly chaotic that only exclamations seemed called for.[29]

At the core of the didactic interpretation of history was the principle of praise and blame established by the *Spring and Autumn Annals*. For centuries, historians had accepted the idea that their calling obliged them to uphold political morality by judiciously evaluating historical figures. However, Ou-yang was the first historian to apply the idea systematically. Carrying on the spirit of his favorite classic with great zeal, he developed new categories in which to classify biographies, such as "martyrs to political integrity" (literally, to chastity) and "martyrs to duty." In glorifying men who resolutely lived up to a high standard of political morality in corrupt and decadent times, Ou-yang endeavored to drive home the lesson that loyal Confucianists should follow the correct way at all times, valuing their virtue more than their lives.[30]

Ou-yang blamed as well as praised. Feng Tao, chief councillor of five different dynasties under a royal house of eight different surnames, was singled out as a symbol of degeneracy, lacking both loyalty and a sense of honor. Feng had been highly regarded by his contemporaries as a conscientious Confucian, but according to the strict and rigorous creed of the Sung neo-Confucianists, he was no Confucian at all.[31] Ou-yang's biography of him is filled with moral indignation.

Ou-yang's evaluations were not always so explicit: some were conveyed by subtle historiographic techniques. A technique used by many historians was to make implicit evaluations through careful weighing and deliberate choice of every word. Another technique, which Ou-yang originated, may be described as "compensation by alternate suppression and expression." In writing the biography of a generally worthy man, Ou-yang would stress his major achievements and not mention his minor shortcomings—which, however, were fully noted elsewhere in the history, in connection with a relevant subject. Chao I, a great historiographer of the eighteenth century, praised this technique as generous and wise, to be recommended for all historical writings. It would serve to encourage morality by making the deeds of a worthy man all the more inspiring, but still would keep the record truthful.[32] Ou-yang's development of this technique shows his compassion and personal warmth as well as his concern with history as a means to moral instruction. The moral standards of his history, though rigorous, were not to be applied harshly or inconsiderately.

Ou-yang attributed the commentaries in the *New History of the Five Dynasties* to his relative and disciple Hsü Wu-tang, but modern scholars believe them to be Ou-yang's own work.[33] Ou-yang was probably afraid that his moral judgments on political behavior, though concerned strictly with the past, might supply additional fuel to the factional controversies then ablaze. Hsü, however, had nothing to do with politics. (By coincidence, his surname connotes "gradually," and his given name, "Wu-tang," "no faction" or "without partisan bias.") Attributing the didactic commentaries to him removed much of their sting.

Although his technique and style were admired by historians of later centuries, Ou-yang's vigorous moral evaluation of the men he studied was generally felt to have been overzealous. Chang Hsüeh-ch'eng felt that Ou-yang went too far in viewing history only didactically.[34] Interpretive history was acceptable, but Ou-yang's was too charged with emotional argument. Consequently, most historians continued to use the *Old History of the Five Dynasties* as a substantive reference. Ssu-ma Kuang was considered a better historian than Ou-yang. His *Comprehensive Mirror for*

Aid in Government, a sequel to the *Spring and Autumn Annals* that chronicled the period from 403 B.C. to A.D. 959, was also written in a laconic style and for didactic purposes, but was neither as insistent nor as argumentative as Ou-yang's work. Accordingly, scholars interested in history more than literature generally turned to the *Comprehensive Mirror* or its various short versions rather than to Ou-yang's work.[35]

Ou-yang had his own ideas about dynastic legitimacy, an important concern of Confucian historiography. The conventional view was of a continuous succession of legitimate dynasties, each owing its legitimacy to the cyclic operation of the mystical five elements, to its virtuous reign, to its descent from previous legitimate rulers, or to some combination of these factors. To Ou-yang, the theory of the five elements lacked rational validity. Claims that legitimacy was based on descent were often politically motivated, and ignored the reality that some regimes, viewed as legitimate dynasties by descent, had controlled only small corners of the country, while other regimes, viewed as illegitimate usurpers, had unified large areas and lasted for a long time. As Ou-yang explained, the term for legitimacy, *cheng-t'ung,* involved two separate elements: *cheng,* the moral right to succession, and *t'ung,* the fact of unified political control.

At times, these two elements simply did not coincide. Though a moralist, Ou-yang pointed out that a regime's lack of virtue did not nullify the fact of unification.[36] Indeed, he maintained that a dynasty lacking moral right at its beginning might, through stable rule, acquire legitimacy as time went on. He also disagreed with the concept of continuous succession. "The scholars who have discussed dynastic legitimacy conceive it to be ever-present, without interruption. In the case of a major political disruption, they have arbitrarily assigned some regime legitimacy as if the line still continued. This is where their theories go wrong."[37] According to Ou-yang's theory, dynastic legitimacy simply lapsed in periods of disunity—in the past, the Three Kingdoms period after the legitimate Han, the Northern and Southern Dynasties after the legitimate Ch'in, and the Five Dynasties after the legitimate T'ang. This was a noteworthy and reasonable contribution, but it did not find general acceptance.[38] The idea of the legitimate line of succession having breaks in it, and that of *fait accompli* unification granting legitimacy, were hard for the conventional Confucian mentality to accept. Many historians continued to search for formulas that would somehow reaffirm the old belief that only virtue led to legitimacy and that only a legitimate regime would be able to unify China. Centuries later, the efforts of such historians were further complicated by the need to explain the existence of two dynasties of conquest, the Mongol and the Manchu.

Ou-yang also made a major contribution to a minor branch of history: genealogy. Members of the emergent scholar-official class of the Sung were envious of the extensive records of illustrious forefathers and paternal relatives kept by the aristocrats of bygone centuries, and tried to emulate them. Of course, those who attempted to raise their prestige by tracing their families back to distinguished origins often did not find enough solid facts to substantiate their claims.[39] But interest in genealogy rose considerably. The aristocrats in their heyday had maintained very large *tsu* (clan organizations, roughly). Their genealogies followed the primogenitary paternal line of descent and recorded all clan members, including those many times removed. In the Sung the term *tsu* came to mean a much smaller kinship group, mainly a family's relatively close branches.[40] With increased social mobility, distant relatives no longer lived near one another. Thus the old method of compiling genealogies became far too cumbersome and confusing. Ou-yang Hsiu and Su Hsün, the father of Su Tung-p'o, independently arrived at new methods, only to discover to their mutual delight that their methods were essentially the same.[41] From that time until the early decades of the present century, all genealogies followed the principle of their methods. The direct line of descent was followed, primogenitary or not, as the trunk of the kinship tree. Only descendants less than three generations removed from the direct line were recorded. It was assumed that more distant branches would have separate genealogies of their own. Genealogies were not without sociological significance: they served to reinforce family solidarity, a Confucian ideal.[42]

Despite some criticism of his craftsmanship, Ou-yang deserves to be honored as an outstanding historian. Joint compiler of one standard history, private author of another, pioneer of archaeology, great bibliographer, preserver of contemporary records, original thinker, and noteworthy contributor to various branches of historiography—he far surpassed all but a very few of his predecessors, his contemporaries, and his successors.

CHAPTER NINE

POLITICAL THEORIST

OU-YANG'S ORIGINAL CONTRIBUTIONS to Confucian political thought are contained chiefly in his two famous essays "On Factions" and "On Fundamentals." "On Fundamentals" advocated revitalization of Confucian social institutions to cut down the influence of Buddhism.[1] Strictly speaking, both essays dealt with applied statecraft rather than political philosophy. Ou-yang was pragmatically oriented, and was never much interested in abstract theories with little bearing on issues immediately at hand. In this respect he was a fairly typical Confucian scholar-official.

His change from reformer to exponent of stability to opponent of reform has intrigued many historians. Did he go through the commonly observed cycle of starting out as a radical but converting to conservatism? Or was it rather a natural change in outlook that came with increasing age?[2] Both theories have had their supporters, and both contain some truth. But neither has taken into account an essential point: the difference between the kind of reform Ou-yang supported and the kind of reform he opposed. Even in his early career Ou-yang was never a drastic reformer who demanded large-scale institutional changes. Although he ceased to advocate reform later in his career, he did not become a conservative. In fact, it was the conservative elements who attacked him in the ritual controversy and drove him from power. In old age he opposed the major reform of Wang An-shih, but his opposition was not active, and he did not join the anti-reformers. Perhaps he can best be described as a gradualist, at first in favor of a reform of limited scope to correct certain defects within the existing system, later working hard to improve but above all to stabilize the existing system, and ultimately refusing to go along with a gigantic reform that introduced a different system altogether. In other words, throughout his career he tried consistently to make the existing system work better. Admittedly, his stand as a young critic was not identical with that he took as an elder statesman. The difference, however, was not fundamental—it was rather a shift in emphasis from ideally desirable goals to realistically feasible ones.

Nothing demonstrates his gradualism better than his essay "On Fundamentals." He saw no possibility of eliminating the influence of Buddhism within a short time. Even given the intensification of "rites and righteousness" he advocated, it would still take a very long time to replace Buddhist practices.[3] His gradualism manifested itself in another way. He believed that neither good institutions by themselves nor virtuous men on their own would be sufficient; for good government, both were needed. While he fully recognized that institutions had all-embracing effects, he refused to believe that everything depended on them. Elaborate institutions might have tremendous intellectual appeal; but were they workable?

Ou-yang's general attitude toward institutions is best illustrated by his comments on the *Rituals of Chou:*

> Every time I read the *Rituals of Chou* and come upon their methods of educating people, establishing schools, selecting talents, and recruiting *chün-tzu* for government service, I invariably cannot help pausing and exclaiming in admiration.... In early life, the characters of the *chün-tzu* were gradually molded by education and cultivation. Once in government, there were the rewards of rank and income. Were they less than careful, there would be shameful punishments, such as dismissal, deportation, permanent disqualification [for office], and decapita-

tion. Placed in between these inducements and penalties, the *chün-tzu* could hardly resist...becoming good officials. Oh, if only human relations were so well organized now, all the *chün-tzu* in the country could be made to behave well. But if such good organization of human relations should deteriorate, even *chün-tzu* to whom heaven has given many fine qualities would be influenced for the worse.[4]

Though greatly impressed, Ou-yang remained skeptical. As a classicist, he was not sure of the authenticity of the text of the *Rituals of Chou*. It did not become available until late antiquity, and some portions of it might well have been written in the Warring States period and retroactively attributed to ancient times.[5] As a pragmatist, Ou-yang also asked whether the enormous amount of institutional activity this work describes was practical —it seemed to him that no one would have the time to be that active. As a historian, he doubted that such institutions had ever functioned to the extent described.[6] Even assuming that they had, under ancient feudalism, were they applicable under the system of centralized empire that had existed since the Ch'in? One should recall, Ou-yang asserted, that Wang Mang's attempt to partially revive such institutions in the middle of the Han period had been unsuccessful. Ou-yang's skepticism on these points long preceded the rise of Wang An-shih, who used the *Rituals of Chou* as the ideological justification for his reform. It was not that Ou-yang underestimated the importance of institutions; to him, Wang erred in overrating institutions at the expense of other considerations.[7]

When Ou-yang was a reformer, he did not pin his hopes entirely on institutional change. He advocated some minor improvements on the existing administrative system, but he was increasingly aware that much depended on how well these improvements were implemented by the administrators. His experience as an administrator of a backward subprefecture after his demotion in 1036 opened his eyes to the realities of bureaucratic practice. As his biography in the *Sung Standard History* reported:

On his demotion to the minor post of I-ling he had little to do. Reading old files in the office over and over again, he noticed innumerable injustices and mistakes. Thereupon, looking up to the sky, he said with a deep sigh "When such a small, desolate, and remote subprefecture turns out to be like this, one can easily imagine what goes on in the rest of the country." From then on ... when friends called, Ou-yang would discuss nothing but administrative matters.[8]

For efficient administration, frequent and sudden changes were undesirable. In 1040, a few years before the minor reform, Ou-yang wrote an essay "On the Origins of Malpractice," which realistically portrayed how "the more officials changed laws for minor advantages, the more worn-out the laws and the more deplorable the conditions became."[9] In an official letter written at about that time he raised the same criticism: "Sometimes, a single change in the law causes a loss of several millions a year.... When one change comes after another, seemingly without end, the losses become much larger."[10] One of his poems contained this verse: "If one starts changing in a hurry, one merely adds much chaos and misery."[11]

In 1042, on the eve of the minor reform, in response to an edict calling on all court-rank officials to present their views on various matters, Ou-yang submitted a memorial that repeated his warning against excessive changes by vividly describing how such changes affected administrative conditions for the worse:

If the words of the government change often, they are not convincing. If orders are frequently amended, they are hard to carry out. Nowadays, orders are issued without being carefully deliberated first, and are enforced for only a short while before being revised. This amounts to the use of unconvincing words in the futile hope of enforcing orders that are hardly followed. Thus, whenever the court decides on a certain measure, the local government anticipates that the decision is not yet final. Some officials tell one another not to carry it out, since it may well be changed before long. Yet other officials say, "Let us just go through the formalities of complying with it by issuing a few directives to our subordinates." Overnight, their anticipation comes true; there is indeed another change! This goes on excessively. Officials are continually being transferred all over the country. Those who greet them on their arrival only to soon send them off again feel quite exhausted; and with documents flying in all directions, neither high-ranking officials nor their subordinates can possibly carry out their orders.[12]

During the same year, Ou-yang wrote an essay "On the Difficulties of Being Emperor."[13] It dealt not with reform, but with how the autocrat should function as chief administrator. Its thesis was similar to the opinions Fan Chung-yen had expressed previously in a famous series of four essays. On the one hand, Fan and Ou-yang upheld loyalty to the emperor; on the other, as loyal servitors they insisted on moral and ideological autonomy. Even in theory, their loyalty as officials was not absolute insofar as their ideological authority was concerned.[14] In concrete terms, they usually asked for assurances on two issues. The first was their privilege of presenting frank criticism, which the emperor should listen to without prejudice. Even if a criticism displeased him, he should not penalize its proponents, for he should understand that their motives were beyond reproach. This privilege may be termed "the privilege of loyal criticism," though it should not be confused at all with the democratic right of loyal opposition. The second issue was the delegation of power—not the emperor's sovereign power, but executive power commensurate with administrative responsibilities. For the scholar-officials to do their jobs properly, Ou-yang said, "their responsibility must be exclusive and the confidence placed in them must be earnest."[15]

When the reformers held power in 1043-44, Ou-yang more than anyone else emphasized the importance of selecting good administrators. His advocacy of the appointment of intendant-inspectors to review the qualifications and performance of local government officials, and his personal inspection of the Ho-tung region, are two examples of his concern with efficient administration.[16]

After the minor reform was abandoned, Ou-yang confessed to friends the difficulty of making changes. "It is very easy," he said, "to make proposals on what should be done, what should be eliminated, and how the laws and institutions should be changed. It is really hard, however, to make sure that these proposals are implemented without being blocked by obstacles or revised beyond recognition." He explained his gradualism in these words: "to be gradual is to proceed slowly and to take enough time to make the effects far-reaching." When he came back to power late in life, his gradualism became even more deliberate. He quoted the common saying that "a law should not be changed unless there are a hundred advantages to be gained by doing so," and complained that "nowadays, some officials in policy discussions seize on one particular aspect [of a subject] and promptly proceed to propose changes." Opposed to such rash and premature opinions, he said he preferred to "assist the emperor in keeping the time-tested laws originally set up by the imperial ancestors."[17]

Although Ou-yang's gradualism lost much momentum as the years went by, it remained his basic belief that the need to improve institutions and the need for good administrators were interdependent. He had said in his younger days:

To provide enough for the country, nothing is more important than financing. To maintain the security of the country, nothing is more important than defense.... To economize on state finance and to have effective defense, nothing is more important than setting up proper institutions. Once these institutions have been adequately established ... nothing is more important than entrusting [them to good] officials.... These two requirements are complementary.[18]

Ou-yang's actions on the issue of land reassessment for equitable taxation provide a good illustration of this principle. When Ou-yang advocated a reassessment during the minor reform, he foresaw the difficulties that would be involved in its implementation. Many local officials "did not know how the reassessment should be made," and there was also danger that "before the tax could be made more equitable, the people might first suffer a great deal of disturbance." Quite possibly, the reassessment might be made carelessly or even corruptly, in which case the arbitrary distribution of the tax burden would get worse rather than better. Ou-yang therefore suggested that several officials who had been successful in experimenting with similar measures should be sent to the Finance Commission in order to work out a sound procedure in detail.[19] Since the minor reform ended soon afterward, the reassessment came to nothing. Almost two decades later, in 1060, the government adopted a similar policy and set up a special bureau to make a reassessment. Without being at all against the principle of the policy, Ou-yang severely criticized its implementation. Without trustworthy and knowledgeable men in charge, he pointed out, the policy did far more harm than good. "The population was greatly disturbed; many by false alarms.... Thousands of them converged on the Finance Commission with their grievances."[20]

How would he choose the administrators whose importance he stressed so much? He made several negative observations. For example, he considered it a mistake "to regard someone who dissents from the majority as being particularly enlightened, to regard someone who refuses other people's advice as being not easily misled, or to regard someone who acts impulsively on bias as being resolute and decisive." He would not choose those who "misconstrue fault-finding as strictness in supervision, and rudeness as straightforwardness." Nor did he like "those who create sensations and those who challenge convention merely to make a name for themselves as fast as they can." He also had a dim view of those "who appear clever and dramatic in argument" and "newcomers who like to give the impression of being courageous and sharp." He felt that such men probably talked much better than they acted, for "their superficial opinions have no substance and little practical value." To Ou-yang, the good administrator would be "refined, gentle, deliberate, proper, well-informed, and understanding of the broad principles"—in modern terms, a mature, experienced, well-balanced man, a man of sound judgment.[21] Quoting his friend Fu Pi, Ou-yang explained how such a man would arrive at a decision: "In order to make sure that something is workable, one has to give the matter thorough consideration, so as to leave neither room for improvement nor cause for regret later on."[22]

How would such good administrators perform? In other words, what did Ou-yang believe to be the ideal mode of administration? When he was acting metropolitan prefect of Kaifeng, a revealing discussion took place:

His predecessor Pao Cheng [the renowned Judge Pao of Chinese fiction], by imposing stern control over his subordinates, had established an awesome reputation all over the city. Ou-yang's administration was simple, relaxed, and lenient. It seemed that he did not particularly care to achieve a reputation for himself. When someone urged him to follow Pao's example, he responded: "Capability and temperament vary with individuals. ... If I should strain to try what I could not do well, I would inevitably fall short. As a matter of fact, I am pursuing what I happen to be good at."[23]

Simple, relaxed, and reasonable administration characterized his excellent record in local government service. According to one epitaph, "During his entire career, in which he governed seven

POLITICAL THEORIST

different prefectures, he exercised attentive supervision without being harsh and practiced magnanimity without being lax. In Chuchow and Yangchow his subordinates and the people liked his administration so well that they put up a shrine in his honor while he was still alive."[24] Another famous conversation was recorded in his biography in the *Sung Standard History*:

> Someone asked Ou-yang: "How is it possible for a magnanimous and simple administration not to be lax and neglectful?" Ou-yang replied: "If one misconstrues magnanimity as leaving things adrift and simplicity as carelessness, indeed laxity would result, important matters would be left unattended, and the people would suffer. What I mean by magnanimity is to avoid being deliberately harsh. What I mean by simplicity is to avoid getting entangled in excessive details."[25]

Although his own approach differed from that of Pao Cheng, Ou-yang certainly would not have criticized a stern administration that was effective. On the contrary, he was critical of most local officials for not being strict enough. He complained: "When court policies, whether important or not, came down as instructions, the prefectural and subprefectural officials merely made a formal pretense of following them."[26] To him, such conduct bordered on irresponsibility. One of his poems reads in part:

> Peace in the country has lasted so long,
> That bureaucrats only care to go on.
> Enjoying their pleasures, they claim excellence;
> Laxness they excuse by *jen* or benevolence.
> Today, minor matters are given up;
> For all say they really do not matter.
> Tomorrow, important things break down;
> Beyond them to repair, so they mutter.[27]

He concluded the poem by emphasizing that "severity and magnanimity are mutually complementary principles, according to the

teachings of the classics." Strictness was just as necessary as leniency; but both should be exercised in balance, with discretion, in accordance with circumstances. There could be no good administration without sound judgment.

Ou-yang never wrote extensively on his theory of administration. However, we may reconstruct it by drawing on what he
described, in the tomb inscriptions and epitaphs he wrote in memory of numerous officials, as good administrative actions. These
compositions are more laudatory than factual, but nevertheless
reflect his own ideals. When so reconstructed, his principles of
magnanimity and simplicity are readily understandable. They
involve in practice three related policies: on communication with
the people, on serious troubles, and on administrative routine.

For the people to understand the government's policies and
its goals, according to Ou-yang, statements on policy must be
convincing, and those about goals must be clearly expressed.
Wang Tan, a great statesman shortly before Ou-yang's time, was
said by Ou-yang "to speak and smile only sparingly. His words,
though simple, conveyed a compelling logic." Ou-yang also
praised Ming Kao as another official who "used few words to express all possible arguments quite exhaustively." From the cases
of these men Ou-yang generalized that "as a rule, one who is
simple and dignified will command awesome respect." He said
of Hsüeh Liang-ju, who had once been administrator of Chin-
chow, an area in which there were several non-Chinese (or non-
Han) minorities, that Hsüeh "simplified the laws and regulations
to ensure that they would be fairly enforced. Consequently, he
was both respected and liked by the minority peoples." What Ou-
yang wrote about Chang Hsi casts more light on Ou-yang's views
on the desirability of communication with the people:

Chang's predecessor often closed the gates of the office building
and put screens in the halls. These barriers resulted in an undesirable administration. When Chang arrived, he threw the

gates open and had the screens removed. To the people, he declared: "My administration wants to achieve three objectives. I would give first priority to the punishment of all these abusive elements: the strong ones who abuse their power, the wealthy ones who use money to get around the law, and the offenders who evade punishment by paying fines in redemption." And this was what the people said of him: "His words are so straight he must mean them. His way of enforcing the law is so simple, it would certainly be strict." Consequently, the powerful and influential elements were more careful, whereas the good but humble people had their grievances heard.[28]

In dealing with serious troubles, it was essential in Ou-yang's mode of administration to punish the key offenders with severity, and be magnanimous toward the rest. A common and firmly entrenched evil in local government was corruption among the clerks. One official, Wang Chih, Ou-yang praised for making sure he would be "feared by the clerks but loved by the people." When Wu Yü took over the administration of Kaifeng "it took him only a few days," Ou-yang said, "to expose a leading corrupt clerk and have him exiled beyond the mountain ranges of Kwangtung. The entire prefectural office was given a rude awakening." At a minor post,

Wang Tai-shu, temporarily appointed acting subprefectural administrator, let it be known that he intended to take a simple action that would greatly benefit the people. This was to arrest a senior clerk, enumerate his past wrongdoings to the prefectural office, and have him flogged. All the abusive elements in that subprefecture began to restrain themselves in both words and deeds. They even warned one another that it would be dangerous to violate the laws while Wang was administrator. Wang himself commented: "If I could serve as administrator for just one year, not only would the good people no longer need to fear the bad elements, but the bad elements themselves could be made to do some good."[29]

Another evil common in local government was interference with justice by influential elements. Kaifeng was particularly notorious. However, Ou-yang recorded that when Tu Yen was the administrator there, "even high-ranking officials dared not interfere," and that he governed it "like any other place." Changan (Sian), the ancient capital of the Han and T'ang dynasties, had the same problem. But there, Ou-yang said, Liu Ch'ang discovered and punished offenses committed by a family of great prestige, paying no regard whatsoever to its influence and access to power.[30] Ou-yang admitted that a good official ran the risk of being defeated by the combined forces of influential elements who abused their power and corrupt clerks. He gave the case of Ti Li as a frustrating example:

Teng and Ku were two wealthy subprefectures on the Han River. The officials in charge of appointments in the Ministry of Personnel frequently gave these posts to candidates who paid them large bribes. As long as whispers in the Ministry rated these appointments as the most coveted, the people of these subprefectures could hardly ever expect to have honest officials govern them. The corrupt and influential elements in these communities were in turn proud of their adroitness in bribing the dishonest administrators. When Ti Li went there, he restrained all bad elements by strict enforcement of the law. The corrupt citizens and bad clerks, in resentment, often went to his superiors with charges against him. However, no investigation ordered from above could change his decisions. In fact, when he received orders from the prefectural office that were not in proper order, he invariably declined to follow them and simply sent them back. The clerks in the prefectural office, grinding their teeth, tried hard to find fault with him in revenge, but in vain. Ti Li became even more upright than ever before. Eventually, however, he made a wrong decision in a property dispute. When the injured party appealed, Ti was censured and removed.[31]

Ti Li's case might also be used to underscore the point that strictness alone would not suffice. The need to balance severity toward key offenders with leniency toward the rest was dramatically demonstrated in several other cases in the writings of Ou-yang. These cases concerned mutinies and potential threats to security. The same Hsüeh Ch'ang-ju mentioned earlier was in Hanchow when the following event took place:

> Several hundred prefectural soldiers killed their officer and burned their barracks.... Hsüeh gathered the mutineers, explained that the choice between life and death rested with themselves, and asked those who admitted to be genuine rebels to stand apart to the left and those who had joined the mutiny under duress to stand apart to the right. Several hundred moved to the right, leaving only thirteen ringleaders, who immediately took flight. The prefecture regained peace.[32]

Hsü Yuan was said by Ou-yang to have had much the same experience in Taichow. A band of mutinous soldiers from a neighboring area suddenly descended on the prefecture. The administrator did not know what to do. Hsü, a military judge, demanded of the soldiers their reason for coming. "Two or three fellows in the group stood out to answer his questions. Suddenly he ordered his guards to arrest them, declaring them to be the agitators and assuring the rest that they would be sent back without punishment." The incident ended peacefully. Ou-yang also described how Wang Shu prevented a mutiny. "He arrested one or two and put them to death, without even interrogating the rest, who immediately realized how dangerous such conspiracy was." According to Ou-yang, the same technique was used by Hsieh Chiang in curbing an unlawful religious group in Tengchow, which for nearly a decade had been holding meetings day and night, with hundreds of men and women. Hsieh executed a few leaders and let their followers go free. "The followers, realizing how severe his law enforcement could be, appreciated his kindness all the more."[33]

According to many Confucianists, magnanimity had an immediate moral effect. Ou-yang mentioned Ts'ai Ch'i, a vice-administrator at Weichow prefecture, as an example:

It was discovered that someone had forged the seals used on tax receipts for over ten years. In tracing the entangled cases, several hundred individuals were implicated.... Ts'ai was most lenient in conducting the investigation. A dozen men, who would normally have been liable for the death penalty, received reduced sentences; all the rest were acquitted. The people of Weichow said to themselves: "He did us a kind deed in hopes that we might become good people." From then on, the social order was much improved.[34]

In Kaifeng, young men with records of delinquency had long been put into protective custody during the Lantern Festival, which occurred at the first full moon of the lunar year. Ou-yang recorded that Ch'en Yao-tso acted differently: "Summoning these youths, he told them: 'Previous administrators regarded you as bad; how then could you possibly become good? I am treating you as good fellows instead; are you going to misbehave yourselves?' Every one of them was set free. During the five evenings [of the festival], none of them violated the law."[35]

According to Ou-yang's account, Hsü Ti governed Yangchow in much the same manner:

Many officials who had served in this southern metropolis took up residence there. Many families of those who had died in office did likewise. Some of the sons and younger brothers [of these officials and these families], taking advantage of their connections and their privilege of avoiding punishment for wrongdoings by paying a fine, often went about committing crimes. ...Hsü arrested a few notorious offenders, flogged them, and explained to them that this was not so much an administrative measure as one intended to be disciplinary on behalf of their own fathers and elder brothers [to protect the welfare of their families]. The humiliated youths, and some others, began to repent; some of them even turned to studies and behaved well.[36]

With respect to administrative routine, Ou-yang's theory held that the best administration was the one that bothered the people the least. A magnanimous policy would make the life of the people much simpler. This applied particularly to tax collections. Ou-yang said that Wang Yao-ch'en, while serving as Acting Finance Commissioner, made a thorough reappraisal of the empire's system of taxation, "deciding which revenues were essential and which were not, assigning them respective priorities, eliminating causes of corruption and loopholes in the system, abolishing miscellaneous taxes that were not only unjustified but actually harmful, and finally compiling a clearly itemized list of all taxes." Thus, Ou-yang concluded, Wang was able to obtain adequate revenue without raising the tax rates. The same Tu Yen mentioned earlier explained to the people in his prefecture that although he could neither exempt nor reduce their tax burden, he would make it as easy as possible by taking into consideration, in the words of Ou-yang, "the present availability of requisitioned commodities, their current prices, the distance involved in shipping them, and the possibilities of extending the time granted for their delivery." One result was an orderly distribution of goods, which prevented prices from rising. Another was the prevention of influence-peddling by the clerks of the prefecture, since the details of the tax-collecting procedures were made clear to all.[37]

Where did Ou-yang's theory of administration stand between the Confucian theory of rule by moral influence and the Legalist theory of rule by strict law enforcement? The difference between these two schools of thought has been much exaggerated. It is true that in philosophical terms they are basically contradictory. However, when translated into action, they are often complementary.

The Chinese empire by its very nature had a Confucian orientation but a Legalist structure. Magnanimity, for example, was a Confucian virtue, while severity was a Legalist value; yet the two often complemented each other in practice, as Ou-yang himself explained.[38] Several of the examples just given demonstrate how strict law enforcement also exerted a kind of moral influence by preventing potential violations. For centuries there was a common saying: "To kill one is to warn a hundred." Execution could only be regarded as a Legalist action, but the effect it had was desirable in Confucian terms. Ou-yang reaffirmed the Confucian tradition by adapting Legalist means to conform with Confucian ideals. A good Confucian should be considerate and sparing in enforcing the laws, assuring himself that he was thus setting an example for all others to see. Ou-yang thought such action both moral, practical, and in accordance with his concept of simplicity. In modern terms, we might call it efficient and effective.

Chinese thought on administrative methods had been greatly influenced by historiography ever since Ssu-ma Ch'ien's *Records of the Grand Historian* had set up two contrasting types: "oppressive officials" and "principled officials" (sometimes translated as "harsh officials" and "reasonable officials"). Harsh officials were useful in putting an end to chaotic conditions and establishing order, though they would be condemned as excessively cruel under normal circumstances. Ou-yang was definitely in favor of reasonable officials, who stood for Confucian principles. The essential quality of reasonable officials was enunciated in a commentary in the *Standard History of the Former Han*: "to be reasonable in applying the law from above and in considering the feelings of the people below." Reasonableness, however, would not preclude severity if circumstances required it.[39] By Ou-yang's theory, these contrasting types of officials may be interpreted as representing two complementary modes of administration, each with its proper sphere of application.

Ou-yang was by no means alone in advocating this administrative theory, but he did articulate it more eloquently than other officials. Generally speaking, the Confucian scholar-officials regarded themselves more as scholarly generalists than as practical-minded officials, and were little concerned with developing administrative theory as a specialized body of knowledge. In fact, many a scholar-official regarded administrative matters as mundane, and discussions on them as of little intellectual, moral, or social value. This shortcoming in the Confucian outlook was neither remedied nor given much attention in the centuries that followed Ou-yang's time, and his contribution to administrative theory accordingly aroused little interest.

CHAPTER TEN

MASTER OF
SUNG LITERATURE

OU-YANG'S GREATIST ACHIEVEMENTS, in modern eyes, were in literature. This evaluation is based on his writings alone: the evaluations of past critics varied, usually in accordance with the critics'
opinions of Ou-yang's public life and private morals. Today Ou-
yang's writing is respected perhaps more highly than ever before,
both in the West, where his poems in particular are meeting with
increased appreciation, and in China, where despite a revolutionary decline in interest in much traditional writing, appreciation of
his poems has not diminished at all.[1]

In the evolution of *shih,* the leading form of Chinese poetry, in
which all lines are usually of equal length, Ou-yang played an
important role. He helped bring about the downfall of the dominant school of his time and then set out on a new path, blazing
the way for many other outstanding poets, and thus heralding the
rise of Sung poetry. The Hsi-k'un School, which had dominated
the early Sung, took the late T'ang poet Li Shang-yin as its model.
The style of this school is full of charm; delicate and subtle feelings are conveyed by carefully chosen, matched expressions. However, this style does tend toward "preciosity, over-defined techniques, elaborate allusions, and stereotyped themes," and is characteristically lacking in breadth and boldness.[2] Ou-yang and his
literary comrades Su Shun-ch'in and Mei Yao-ch'en rejected it,
and worked out a different style that permitted more freedom to
develop techniques for expressing strong feelings. They claimed

to be stylistic descendants of Han Yü; their style was known as the ancient style, and they themselves as the Ch'ang-li School, after Han's native place. Their style, however, is neither imitative nor derivative, but fresh and innovating in the true spirit of the eleventh century. Strictly speaking, neither these Sung poets nor those who came just after them constitute a particular school. Their contribution was in making a drastic break with the artificiality of the Hsi-k'un style and setting the next generation of poets free to experiment.[3] Only with that generation did Sung poetry come into its own.

Praise of Ou-yang's poetry began with his contemporaries. Su Tung-p'o compared him to Li Po, the T'ang genius. Wang An-shih, a great poet himself, thought Ou-yang had excelled Li Po.[4] Since both Wang and Su had received much encouragement from Ou-yang, their comments were understandably laudatory, and perhaps exaggerated. However, all the standard histories of Chinese literature agree that many of Ou-yang's poems rank with the best. Some Western readers regard them as poetic equivalents of the masterpieces of Chinese painting. Let a few translations speak for themselves:

Fisherman

The wind blows the line out from his fishing pole.
In a straw hat and grass cape the fisherman
Is invisible in the long reeds.
In the fine spring rain it is impossible to see very far
And the mist rising from the water has hidden the hills.[5]

In the Evening I Walk by the River

The frozen river is drifted deep with snow.
For days, only a few spots near the bank have stayed open.
In the evening when everyone has gone home,
The cormorants roost on the boats of the fishermen.[6]

His imagery is always vivid. Poems of monochrome tranquillity alternate with poems rich in color, filled with serene joy in life.

"The Spring Walk to the Pavilion of Good Crops and Peace,"
for example:

> The trees are brilliant with flowers
> And the hills are green.
> The sun is about to set.
> Over the immense plain
> A green carpet of grass
> Stretches to infinity.
> The passersby do not care
> That Spring is about to end.
> Carelessly they come and go
> Before the pavilion,
> Trampling the fallen flowers.[7]

He sometimes wove a skillful combination of lively spirit and
tranquil mood, as in "Green Jade Plum Trees in Spring":

> Spring comes early to the gardens
> Of the South, with dancing flowers.
> The gentle breeze carries the sound
> Of horses whinnying. The blue
> Green plums are already as large
> As beans. The willow leaves are long,
> And really are curved like a girl's
> Eyebrows. Butterflies whirl in the
> Long sunlight. In the evening the
> Mist lies heavy on the flowers.
> The grass is covered with dew.
> Girls in their transparent dresses,
> Indolent and lascivious,
> Lounge in their hammocks. Swallows, two
> By two, nest under the painted eaves.[8]

Or he would let a cheerful scene fade into a delicate and somber
mood, as in "East Wind":

The burgeoning trees are thick with leaves.
The birds are singing on all the hills.
The east wind blows softly.
The birds sing, the flowers dance.
This minor magistrate is drunk.
Tomorrow when he wakes up,
Spring will no longer be new.[9]

In a beautiful *tz'u* called "Spring Days on Jade Pavilion" Ou-yang describes charming scenes and enchanting feelings, then shifts his tone and ends on a melancholy note, again alluding to the east wind:

A slight touch of leisurely sadness creeps into my heart.
I realize, the gentle east wind will not make it go away.[10]

In numerous instances he reverses this technique and evokes from a melancholy setting a high spirit, a supreme rapture, a care-free enjoyment, a gentle calmness, or sometimes "a kind of insubstantial dream life."[11]

One cannot fully understand Ou-yang the poet without a knowledge of the theoretical contributions in his book *Liu-i shih-hua*. *Liu-i*, or "Six Ones," was a pen name he gave himself, referring to one library, one archaeological collection, one musical instrument, one chess set, one pot of wine, and himself, one old fellow who enjoyed their company.[12] *Shih-hua* means literally "talk on poetry." A rare genre in previous times, it began to develop among these pioneering Sung poets, who were fond of discussing their craft and their colleagues. Works in this genre, though they often contain considerable amounts of literary criticism, also include such material as "notes, letters, reported conversations, prefaces to anthologies," anecdotes, and gossip—information related more to poets than to poetry. *Shih-hua* are neither organized nor formal, but are meant, in their leisurely fashion, to entertain. They are, perhaps, close to the vernacular literature of the professional storytellers who flourished during the Sung, and whose stories were also described as *hua* ("talks").[13]

There are two major difficulties in discussing Ou-yang's theories of poetry—in fact, about discussing all traditional Chinese theories of literature. Traditional writers on literature seldom define their terms; they attempt to communicate with their readers, accomplished poets themselves, by evoking feelings and impressions. In attempting to translate either their terms or the points they make, one inevitably imposes one's own views and interpretations, which may not necessarily reflect what the poems originally meant to the traditional Chinese themselves.[14]

Ou-yang's criteria for good poetry may be seen in his comments on the work of two fellow poets, Su Shun-ch'in and Mei Yao-ch'en. Su, he said, wrote "forcefully to an unrivaled degree." His poetry "rises far above, excels, and definitely surpasses" the works of many others.[15] Su complained, however, that Ou-yang was even more favorable to Mei. For Mei, Ou-yang wrote an epitaph and compiled an anthology of poetry, which he introduced with a preface full of praise. He credited Mei with "giving deep thought" to every nuance of meaning, "with minuteness and precision," and described Mei's works as being "profound and far-reaching" (*shen* and *yüan*) in meaning as well as "leisurely and nonchalant" (*hsien* and *tan*) in expression. He admired Mei for "being good at describing both scenery and human feelings" in verses "profound as well as far-reaching in both implications and derivations."[16] The repeated use of "profound and far-reaching" reflected Ou-yang's appreciation of a simple and concise style that drew the maximum of meaning from the minimum of words. The admiration was mutual. Mei reportedly said of Ou-yang: "Even if I should work for decades, I could never equal his best verses."[17] On one theoretical point, Ou-yang quoted Mei:

Poets like to follow their inspirations. The difficulty they encounter is in finding the right expressions. One does well when one can skillfully express new ideas, setting forth what has never been said by anyone. But to really qualify as the best, one must be able to portray a scene that is hard to describe, to make it come alive, as if it stood immediately before one's eyes, and moreover, to imply in it meanings infinitely beyond explicit words.[18]

This was a standard not always met by even the best poets, Mei included. Ou-yang did not consider Mei's poetry faultless: he said that "Mei occasionally goes too far in polishing and contriving, so as to make his verses deliberately strange or obviously clever." He also mentioned that Mei, who had been frustrated in his career, sometimes burst into "abusive sarcasm and bitter satire."[19] In Ou-yang's opinion these were minor, understandable defects in an otherwise great poet.

Ou-yang was also influential in the evolution of the *tz'u*.[20] A form of song, the *tz'u* is "characterized by lines of unequal length, and by prescribed rhyme and tonal sequences occurring in a large number of variant patterns, each of which bears the name of a musical air." It first appeared during the T'ang as an informal and playful kind of poetry, and at the beginning of the Sung was dominated by the Hua-chien School, literally "the school among the flowers." Many of the lyrical themes of this school center on love. The school's works are generally "subtle, voluptuous, and suggestive; their weakness is an overrefinement that implies shallowness of feeling."[21] During the Sung, a great transformation took place. The *tz'u* absorbed a colloquial vocabulary not commonly admissible in formal poetry, and gained much in richness of content as well as popular appeal. Much of the best Sung poetry was written in this form. The best-known Sung writer of *tz'u* was Liu Yung, who spent a great deal of his time with singing courtesans.[22] Ou-yang did the same: early in his career, at Lo-yang, he learned the songs of the courtesans and borrowed many colloquial expressions from them. What he took over he refined into poetry—not necessarily as songs, although some of the songs he wrote were adopted in turn by the courtesans. This particular literary activity of his was said to be unknown to many, as is shown by an amusing story whose accuracy is open to question. On his return from a mission to the Liao empire in 1055, Ou-yang was reportedly entertained by Chia Ch'ang-ch'ao, who ordered some courtesans to put on a special program. The courtesans apparently made no special preparations, which puzzled Chia. He was all the more bewildered when at the banquet held in Ou-yang's honor he found Ou-yang listening very attentively to the songs of the courtesans, emptying his wine cup after each. Only afterward did Chia discover that all the songs were *tz'u* composed by Ou-yang himself.[23]

These popular works, many on themes of love, got Ou-yang into considerable trouble. As mentioned in a previous chapter, his political adversaries cited some of them to cast doubt on his moral character when he was charged with amorous scandals. He was not, however, without defenders, who contended that women, wine, and song had not harmed Li Po, the genius of T'ang poetry, and would not harm Ou-yang either. But this defense tended to fall on deaf ears in subsequent generations, when standards of conduct became much stricter than ever before. The *tz'u,* their literary worth having been proven, especially by the work of Su Tung-p'o, ceased to be limited to lyric subjects (let alone erotic ones) or associated with music (let alone courtesans). Moreover, having courtesans at formal banquets ceased to be an accepted custom. Under these changed conditions, the critics of the Southern Sung denounced some of Ou-yang's poems as "vulgar." Even those who admired his poetry in general found it advisable to reject some of his *tz'u,* asserting that these were not actually Ou-yang's own work but had been composed by others and attributed to him. One anthology thus deleted some seventy-three pieces from Ou-yang's works.[24]

Whether women, wine, and song inspired Ou-yang the poet,

as they had many T'ang literati, or disqualified him as a moral Confucianist, as was sometimes believed, has little to do with the quality of his poetry. Moreover, for centuries critics simply missed or chose to ignore the argument that the love themes in his poetry may have been allegorical. Chang Hui-yen, who compiled a well-known anthology of *tz'u,* was one of the few exceptions. He pointed out that many love-making verses in the *Classic of Songs* are actually allegorical descriptions of something else. Chang saw the romantic themes in the poetry of many scholar-officials as political allegory. As he explained: "The joy and sorrow in many love themes are thus used as allegories to convey the private lingering feelings deep in the hearts of those [politically oriented] *chün-tzu* who could not express themselves in any better way." Chang cited Ou-yang as a leading example: his portrayal of a merciless storm that tore lovers apart might well have meant a political disaster. His description of pretty girls in flight, like flowers scattered by wind and rain, might well have referred to the sudden banishment of many officials at the end of the minor reform.[25] But to the highly moralistic philosophers who dominated Southern Sung neo-Confucian thought, romantic feelings, even in imagination, were unworthy of a Confucian *chün-tzu.* That they themselves did not produce moving poetry (to us, perhaps, poetic justice) was completely irrelevant to them.

No sharp distinction existed in traditional Chinese literature between what Westerners term poetry and prose. Instead, they formed a continuum, at the middle of which was the intermediary form of *fu* or prose-poetry, which partook of some of the characteristics of both. It had originated in ancient times as a poetic form with a prescribed rhyme pattern and strict parallelism. This form had been required in civil-service examinations since the T'ang period. From then on, a modification appeared "with the introduction of a large element of prose, and the more or less haphazard use of rhyme." In the hands of the great Sung poets, Ou-yang Hsiu and Su Tung-p'o in particular, the transformation into a prose genre was completed. Acknowledged as *wen-fu,* literally, prose-poetry, it took on the expository and narrative functions of prose, while retaining some rhyme, a lyric tone, occasional parallelism, and a poetic air.[26]

Ou-yang's famous composition "The Sound of Autumn" is an excellent illustration of this genre—it has invariably been included in authoritative selections of Chinese literature. After a calm opening sentence, it rises immediately to a powerful climax, which is followed by a gentle pause:

> One night when I was reading I heard a sound coming from the southwest. I listened in alarm and said:
> "Strange! At first it was a patter of drops, a rustle in the air; all at once it is hooves stampeding, breakers on a shore; it is as though huge waves were rising startled in the night, in a sudden downpour of wind and rain. When it collides with something it clatters and clangs, gold and iron ring together; and then it is as though soldiers were advancing against an enemy, running swiftly with the gag between their teeth, and you hear no voiced command, only the tramping of men and horses."
> I said to the boy, "What is this sound? Go out and look."
> The boy returned and told me:
> "The moon and stars gleam white and pure, the bright river is in the sky, nowhere is there any sound of man; the sound is over among the trees."

Then Ou-yang turns to philosophical reflection on the punitive and destructive nature of autumn, then to a feeling of profound sorrow:

> "Alas! The plants and trees feel nothing, whirling and scattering when their time comes; but mankind has consciousness, the noblest of all intelligences. A hundred cares move his heart, a myriad tasks weary his body; the least motion within him is sure to make his spirit waver, and how much more when he thinks of that which is beyond the reach of his endeavor, wor-

ries over that which his wisdom is powerless to alter! It is natural that his glossy crimson changes to withered wood, that his ebony black is soon flecked with stars! What use is it for man, who is not of the substance of metal and stone, to wish to vie for glory with the grass and trees? But remembering who it is who commits this violence against us, why should we complain against the sound of autumn?"

Instead of concluding on this serious note, Ou-yang ends with a light poetic touch:

The boy did not answer, had dropped his head and fallen asleep. I heard only the sound of the insects chirping from the four walls, as though to make a chorus for my sighs.[27]

Although this translation is in prose form, *wen-fu* may also be translated as verse. "The Cicada," an equally famous piece by Ou-yang in the same genre, has been admirably rendered into English verse:

Some old trees grew amid the grass
Of the deserted court. Here was a thing that cried
Upon a treetop, sucking the shrill wind
To wail it back in a long whistling note—
That clasping in its arms
A tapering twig perpetually sighed,
Now shrill as flute, now soft as mandolin;
Sometimes a piercing cry
Choked at its very uttering, sometimes a cold tune
Dwindled to silence, then suddenly flowed again,
A single note, wandering in strange keys,
An air, yet fraught
With undertone of hidden harmony.
"What creature can this be?" "Cicada is its name."
"Are you not he, cicada,
Of whom I have heard told you can transform
Your body, magically molding it

To new estate? Are you not he who, born
Upon the dungheap, coveted the sky,
The clean and open air;
Found wings to mount the wind, yet skyward sailing
Upon a leafy tree-top checked your flight,
Pleased with its trim retreat? Are you not he
Who with the dew for drink, the wind for food,
Grows never old nor languid; who with looped locks
Frames womanish beauty?
Again your voice, cicada!
Not grave; not gay; part Lydian,
Part Dorian your tune that, suddenly begun,
Suddenly ceases."
Long since have I marveled
How of ten thousand creatures there is not one
But has its tune; how, as each season takes its turn,
A hundred new birds sing, each weather wakes
A hundred insects from their sleep.[28]

The beauty of Chinese prose-poetry lies in the fact that it is poetry, though it reads like prose, and *vice versa*. The versatile Ou-yang, at home in prose or poetry, produced many masterpieces that inspired not only many generations in China, but, through translations, those who love literature elsewhere in the world.

As a literary innovator, it was in prose that Ou-yang made his strongest impact. It was largely through his efforts that the ancient style came to dominate Chinese prose for the next thousand years.[29] Replacing parallel prose was no mean achievement; by Ou-yang's time it had been the preferred style of the aristocratic class for centuries. To Ou-yang it was a decadent, excessively ornamental style: its rigid form left little room for freedom of expression, and it could not be used for effective communication. During the Yüan-ho era of the mid-T'ang, Han Yü, in his attempt at a Confucian revival, had urged the application of Confucian principles to literature, arguing that "prose should convey the Confucian way" in its didactic function. For inspiration, Han drew on the pre-Han models of expository prose and narrative accounts—hence the name "ancient style." Though traditional in aim and spirit, the style Han Yü developed represented not a return to the archaic, but a vehicle of new enrichment. It contained no arbitrary rules; the writer was free to include whatever rhythms or constructions he pleased, as long as he felt them to be natural rather than contrived. It afforded maximum scope to individual expression, absorption of current vocabulary, and development of new syntax. Its other master in the T'ang was Liu Tsung-yüan. Neither he nor Han had a large following, and their writings were not widely circulated in the early Sung.[30] Parallel prose continued to be dominant: after some relaxation and modification of its rigid rules, it came to be known as the "current style," and was used in the examinations.

Before Ou-yang, only a handful of writers preferred the ancient style. Wang Yü-ch'eng, a prominent official, was one. He in turn encouraged Sun Ho and Ting Wei, praising them as worthy successors of Han Yü and Liu Tsung-yüan and their works as truly following the path of the "six classics." But Sun and Ting were hardly listened to.[31] Liu K'ai was another pioneer. He devoted his life to studying the works of Han Yü, and considered his own prolific writings in the ancient style to be the best writing of his time. To others, who disliked his fanaticism and conceit, he was an oddity.[32] The next pioneer, Mu Hsiu, fared little better. Like Liu K'ai, he was fanatically devoted to the T'ang masters of the ancient style. He carried Han Yü's works with him wherever he went, and continually searched for better copies. Only after twenty years did he manage to put together a nearly complete set. But few others seemed interested in it. In his old age, much elated by the discovery of a good copy of Liu Tsung-yüan's works, he printed hundreds of sets, went to the Hsiang-kuo-ssu, the leading temple and marketplace of Kaifeng, and set up a store there to sell them himself. To attract attention, he offered to give a set away to anyone who could read a selection from it without making a single mistake, for Chinese books traditionally contained no punctuation. This promotional effort was singularly unrewarding. Sometimes for a whole year not a single set could be either sold or given away.[33] Most scholars simply refused to appreciate the ancient style; they regarded it as having little aesthetic value.

When Ou-yang was a young man, the works of Han Yü were largely unknown. Thirty years later they were universally hailed as the best models. Ou-yang, their prime promoter, told his own story in these words:

My youth was spent in the region east of the Han River, a region much isolated and culturally rather backward, where there were no learned scholars. My family, being poor, had no collection of books. However, a wealthy family named Li in the southern part of the district had a son, Yao-fu, who was fond of learning. As his boyhood companion, I often visited his home. One day, noticing a broken storage basket of old books behind a partition, I looked and found six volumes of Han Yü's works. Some parts were missing, others out of order. I asked the Li family to let me take them home. On studying the words of Han, I was struck by their profundity, richness, boldness, and breadth. Although young and as yet unable to understand their full meaning, I was already attracted by their tremendous, almost boundless spirit. At that time, scholars...followed the current style. Those good at it got degrees, achieved fame, and received many honors. No one ever talked about Han's prose. Preparing for the examination of doctorate in letters, I likewise devoted myself to poetry and prose-poetry according to the standards set by the Board of Rites. When I was seventeen, I took the district examination, but failed. Once again, I turned to my copy of Han's works. Re-reading it, I sighed and said: "Scholars should go as far as that before they stop [making efforts to improve their literary skill]." Though I marveled at how misguided the present generation was, I myself did not have the time to go on studying Han's writings. However, the hope of being able to do so eventually always remained close to my heart. It was necessary for me to devote my time to preparation for the doctoral examination, so that I could become an official and support my parent. But I resolved that once I had the income of an official I would make the utmost effort to learn to write in Han's style, and thus fulfill my long-cherished desire. Seven years later, I obtained my degree and was assigned to Loyang, where I joined Yin Shu and other friends who wrote in the ancient style. I also managed to fill in the missing parts and correct the errors in my old copy of Han's works by referring to some better editions I had discovered. Later on, scholars gradually turned to the ancient style and Han's prose circulated throughout the country. Some thirty-odd years have passed since my initial discovery, and nowadays scholars wish only to study Han Yü. Oh, how marvelous it is![34]

The beginning of the ancient style's rise came when three men met: Ch'ien Wei-yen, an influential patron; Yin Shu, one of the pioneers of the ancient style; and Ou-yang, the bright talent who responded to the stimulation Yin provided. Ch'ien was no ordinary official, but a grandson of the former Prince of Wu. He was originally from the lower reaches of the Yangtze River, the region that led the nation in cultural refinement. Related to the Sung imperial house by marriage, Ch'ien occupied at one time or another almost every high position in the Sung civil service, save for the key post of state councillor. When he served at Loyang, the cultural center of the north, he had on his staff many talents from both the north and the south. The time was peaceful and prosperous, the patron an accomplished man of letters, the company distinguished, and the interaction exhilarating.[35] On the occasion of the remodeling of Ch'ien's official residence and the adding to it of a new mansion and garden, Ch'ien assigned both Yin and Ou-yang to write celebratory essays. Ou-yang finished first, with an essay of about a thousand words. Yin said he could do better in five hundred. When Yin's essay was completed, Ou-yang had to admit that it was superior to his own, especially by virtue of its simplicity. But he refused to give up the competition, and began to call on Yin often, bringing wine with him, staying all day, learning and discussing Yin's views on literature. He was particularly impressed by one remark Yin made: that many writers, attempting to strengthen their compositions, used emphatic expressions; but that if the framework was feeble, no such effort would help. On the contrary, Yin said, excessive verbiage would only weaken a composition. Ou-yang soon volunteered to write another essay, this time in the ancient style. This essay was even shorter than Yin's, and compelled the master's admiration for the young writer who had learned so well and so rapidly.[36]

Another factor aiding the rise of the ancient style was the advancement in technical skill of its practitioners. The work of the early Sung pioneers mentioned above had been "abrupt, diffused, awkward, and crude."[37] In the hands of Yin, the ancient style became at once concise and elegant. Ou-yang often praised Yin profusely. However, when he wrote Yin's epitaph he merely stated that Yin's prose was "simple as well as exemplary." The extraordinary shortness of his tribute aroused speculation that Ou-yang had deliberately withheld laudatory expressions out of jealousy. This Ou-yang denied. He said that he had paid Yin the highest possible tribute. Even among the classics, only the *Spring and Autumn Annals* deserved the description of "simple as well as exemplary"; the others, not written by Confucius himself, were not as concise. "Only the ignorant people in the world," Ou-yang retorted, "...would mistakenly measure a tribute by counting the number of words in it."[38] However, Ou-yang did not regard Yin as the very best. For example, when Ou-yang met Su Hsün he made the observation: "I have read the compositions of many people and have only liked the works of Yin Shu and Shih Chieh. Still, I have not felt completely satisfied. Reading your works makes me thoroughly gratified."[39] Though he had initially learned from Yin, he did not consider his own work in any way inferior to Yin's. In a poem he sent Mei Yao-ch'en recalling their days together in Loyang, he wrote: "At a meeting on prose, the championship is luckily mine. When it is a contest of poetry, the prize goes to you."⁴⁰ Ou-yang's claim to have excelled Yin was confirmed by history: Ou-yang became honored as one of the eight great prose masters of the T'ang and Sung periods, and Yin did not.

Since it is hard to discuss the fine qualities of Ou-yang's prose in English, I shall cite just one sample without comment, in the hope that some of its flavor may come through even in translation. A famous piece, invariably included in Chinese anthologies of Sung literature, it is titled "The Pavilion of the Old Drunkard." The old drunkard is a man who "delights less in drinking than in the hills and streams, taking pleasure in them and expressing the feelings in his heart through drinking." And he enjoys being with people. This is how the scene at the pavilion is described:

The local people may be seen making their way there and back in an endless stream, the old and infirm as well as infants in arms, men carrying burdens who sing as they go, passersby stopping to rest beneath the trees, those in front calling out and those behind answering. There the governor gives a feast with a variety of dishes before him, mostly wild vegetables and other mountain produce. The fish are freshly caught from the stream, and since the stream is deep the fish are fat; the wine is brewed with spring water, and since the spring is sweet the wine is superb. There they feast and drink merrily with no accompaniment of strings or flutes; when someone wins a game of cottabus or chess, when they mark up their scores in drinking games together, or raise a cheerful din sitting or standing, it can be seen that the guests are enjoying themselves. The elderly man with white hair in the middle, who sits utterly relaxed and at his ease, is the governor, already half drunk. Then the sun sinks toward the hills, men's shadows begin to flit about and scatter; and now the governor leaves, followed by his guests. In the shades of the woods birds chirp above and below, showing that the men have gone and the birds are at peace. But although the birds enjoy the hills and forests, they cannot understand men's pleasure in them; and although men enjoy accompanying the governor there, they cannot understand his pleasure either. The governor is able to share his enjoyment with others when he is in his cups, and sober again can write an essay about it. Who is this governor? Ou-yang Hsiu of Luling.[41]

Various literary critics in history agree that Ou-yang developed ancient-style prose into a supreme art. He used nothing more than the ordinary vocabulary, but what he turned out is marvelous and elegant. In his hands ordinary words convey something extraordinary: delicate feeling, profound thought, grand spectacle, or novel idea. Yet it all seems effortless.[42] This is an innovation, not the rediscovery "ancient style" would seem to imply. For instance, in the original, the sample just given uses the ordinary particle *yeh* twenty-one times, each at the end of a sentence to signify a delightful, rhythmic pause. No one else had ever dreamed of such a technique. It is extraordinary; yet it reads completely naturally, with a simple, lingering charm.[43] Such rhetorical skill did not come from brilliance alone; it took a great deal of disciplined practice. As Ou-yang explained, one should "compress one's robust inspirations into studious thoughts." Even for a short informal note, Ou-yang would usually make a first draft. For a formal composition, "he would always compose a draft, post it on the wall, read it over and over again, while he was sitting around or lying down. Not until revisions had made it perfect would he show it to people."[44] Another anecdote illustrates his perfectionism. When Han Ch'i retired, Ou-yang sent him a piece written to celebrate the occasion, which fully captured Han's feelings on returning to his native place in full glory. A few days later another version arrived, with the request that the previous one be replaced. The only change Ou-yang had made was in its first sentence, where he had twice added an identical conjunction to each of two parallel clauses. The change makes a remarkable difference in the delicacy of feeling conveyed.[45]

These technical points may interest modern students of literature, but they were not half as significant to the pioneering authors themselves as the Confucian principle underlying their advocacy of the ancient style. It was to them not merely a stylistic reform, but part of a moral regeneration. To Ou-yang and his friends, writing was itself a discipline in self-cultivation; or conversely, only profound self-cultivation made a man's writing meaningful and worthy. This was why Han Yü had said "prose should convey the Confucian way." For the same reason, Ou-yang and his friends advocated "the use of prose to comment on state affairs." But prose would not be much used to serve the noble cause unless the current style could be deprived of the grip it held on public taste—a grip given it by its establishment as the only style that could be used in the state examinations. The examination standards, Ou-yang and his friends decided, would have to be changed; and they could only be changed by long, hard political struggle.[46]

Earlier, in 1029, the court had considered the criticism that the state examination papers were full of literary exaggerations and ornamental diversions, with little bearing on the art of government. Owing to general inertia and lack of consensus, no formal change was made.[47] The next year, Yen Shu was in charge of the doctoral examination. Believing in the didactic function of prose, he took the opportunity to support a suggestion previously made by Fan Chung-yen, who at the time was under his patronage. Fan's suggestion was that a section on the problems of statecraft should be added to the examinations, in which the candidates would express their opinions in prose. The recommendation was rejected on the technical and typically bureaucratic ground that statecraft was outside the field in which the candidates customarily prepared themselves. Nevertheless, in administering the examination Yen gave less weight to form than was usual, and paid more attention to content: interpretations of the classics and opinions on statecraft. By these standards, the highest honor went to a candidate named Ou-yang Hsiu. It was this much-coveted honor that sent him to Loyang.[48]

From Loyang his fame spread. But promotion of the ancient style still had a long way to go. After his demotion in 1036, Ou-yang's historical research and writing greatly improved his prose, in form as well as content. In 1043–44, when Fan Chung-yen led the minor reform, Ou-yang and several others jointly proposed a change in the examination system on the following grounds:

> To emphasize discussion of the problems of statecraft will turn the attention of men of letters to the study of political well-being and troubles. To simplify certain regulations on the form of the examination papers will permit bold-spirited and broad-minded candidates to express their ideas fully and freely. To test the candidates on interpreting the classics will free them during their preparation from concentrating on mere memory work.[49]

This recommendation was approved, and Ou-yang was assigned to draft the edict announcing the new standards.[50]

It was only a fleeting moment of triumph. Soon the reformers were out of power, their program was abruptly ended, and this particular change in the examination system was rescinded. Moreover, the conservatives counterattacked, claiming that regulations on phonetics and rhymes, to which poetry and prose-poetry must conform, provided an objective basis for fair grading. This would not be true of prose essays on statecraft problems. On the contrary, prose would permit so many diverse opinions that grading could not help being influenced by subjective views. This argument was coupled with a malicious charge that the change had been ill-considered and uncalled-for, inasmuch as the old system had served well under the previous emperor.[51] The insinuation was that those who had dared to criticize the established system were being disrespectful to the imperial ancestors. Implicit in the charge was a clever point: had not the reformers themselves come up through the old system? Were they not themselves evidence that their agitation was groundless?

In 1046, Chang Fang-p'ing, who had agreed with the reformers in recommending a change, was appointed to take charge of the doctoral examination, and promptly reversed his original position. He wrote a memorial arguing that the emphasis upon statecraft problems had led to an undesirable fad: many candidates, in the mistaken belief that the best way to succeed was to have unusual ideas, did not hesitate to indulge in unorthodox and even bizarre assertions. The argument won the day; Chang's memorial was posted in huge characters in front of the examination hall as an admonition to the candidates to abide not only by the orthodox style, but by orthodox ideas as well.[52] Although the examinations reverted to the old standards, many students in the National University, admiring the aspirations of the reformers, continued to express themselves in ancient-style prose. But the conservatives kept up their attack. The battle ended in 1048, when an edict formally reprimanded the students for their allegedly mistaken notions.[53]

Ou-yang's frustrating years out of power in no way altered his convictions, or his eagerness to promote the ancient style. Wherever he went, he sought talented writers, befriending and encouraging them. He was quietly gathering a new army. In about a decade, the dust of the battle over the minor reform gradually settled, and the wind of politics shifted to a favorable quarter. In 1057, Ou-yang, again in power, was assigned to administer the doctoral examination. Without asking for a change in policy, he chose examination topics that naturally emphasized interpretation of the classics and opinions on statecraft.[54] The battle was joined then and there, right in the examination hall. Many candidates, not accustomed to writing on such topics, asked for clarification, as was their privilege. Welcoming the opportunity, Ou-yang responded to their questions throughout the day in the hope of dispelling their doubts, conveying his ideas, and converting some of them. He did not quite succeed. Toward evening, a number of them were still standing around the hall, arguing and complaining.[55] The results of the examination were greeted by a storm of angry protest. Some candidates, who had been judged promising beforehand but did not get their degrees, formed a mob outside the court. When Ou-yang came out, he was stopped, surrounded, and openly cursed. The furor was so great that the guards had a hard time stopping it. That was not all. Someone sent a funeral ode in mockery to Ou-yang's residence, and others wrote and circulated lewd *tz'u*, reviving and intensifying the slanderous attacks on Ou-yang's private life.[56]

These debased attacks by their very nature indicated the weakness of the disappointed candidates. They dared not challenge Ou-yang on theoretical grounds, and they could not manage to discredit him politically, for his position at the time was secure. Above all, the results of the examination spoke for themselves. Among the successful candidates, Tseng Kung, the famous Su brothers, and many others were brilliant beyond dispute. Once they had won their degrees, more people read their works and found them definitely superior.[57] Ou-yang's long and strenuous efforts, made at the cost of personal embarrassment, had won a decisive victory for the ancient style. On this point, the historical records compiled shortly afterward were in unanimous agreement, though they varied somewhat in the way they described it. The original draft of the *Veritable Record* is the most objective, saying that "the disappointed candidates were at first angry, complaining, cursing, and sarcastic; gradually, they were convinced and even converted; and as time went on, more people changed their mind in favor of the ancient style." The revised draft of the *Veritable Record,* compiled by the followers of Wang An-shih, who were in favor of the ancient style and the emphasis on statecraft discussions, overstates the case, claiming that "a great change toward the ancient style soon followed." The *State History,* being a compilation based on both drafts, takes a middle position: "the style used in the examinations changed from then on." The *Sung Standard History* uses this exact wording. More exact details are found in the biographical data appended to Ou-yang's works: "in about five to six years [after this examination] prose writing gradually turned to the ancient style." The prose style Ou-yang had been introduced to by a boyhood discovery in a broken basket finally became, largely through his incessant promotion, the established style for the next thousand years![58]

The victory was followed by some disappointment. Once the ancient style became popular, it was imitated by hacks and incompetents who relied on countless clichés, and put little thought and care into their writing. The ancient style became debased, as had happened to the current style. Ou-yang himself sighed in his old age that too many people had seen prose writing as "a vehicle to secure reputation and a tool to attain prestige."[59] An anecdote illustrates the difficulty of distinguishing between genuine dedication to principle and mere imitation of form. Liu Chi had enjoyed literary fame for a long time, but failed at the examination of 1057, which made him extremely bitter. It was Liu, according to this story, who turned out licentious *tz'u* and libelously attributed them to Ou-yang. This cunning talent soon mastered the ancient style. A few years later, Ou-yang was administering another examination, and was most impressed by a paper by one Liu Hui, to whom he accordingly awarded first place. Then someone told him the author's identity: it was the same old Liu Chi, who had changed his name. Ou-yang was stunned, but there was nothing he could do.[60] This story may not be true, but it makes a significant point. The ancient style meant a great deal to its first struggling advocates, but as a required form that had to be conformed to it inevitably degenerated into an empty shell of triteness. This was, however, a product of the way the examination system was set up, and not a defect of the style itself. With its freedom of construction and its inherent promotion of Confucian principles, the ancient style did represent a step forward.

Subsequent centuries bestowed on Ou-yang the crowning position in prose. Of the eight great masters of the T'ang and Sung— Han Yü and Liu Tsung-yüan in the T'ang, and Ou-yang, Tseng Kung, Wang An-shih, Su Hsün, Su Shih (Tung-p'o), and Su Ch'e in the Sung—Ou-yang was the central figure: he perfected the style of his two forerunners, and encouraged and promoted his five contemporaries. Tseng, closest to Ou-yang in scholarship, was probably not as talented or versatile as the others. He ranked with the rest in prose, but fell short in poetry. Besides literature, Tseng was interested in the study of the classics and in probing their metaphysical dimensions, an anticipation of the trend of the Southern Sung that was later recognized by Chu Hsi himself.[61] Each of the other four was as versatile as Ou-yang. Wang An-shih was also a great poet, and a leading scholar in classics, but was best known for his gigantic reform. Su Hsün and his two sons, all of them poets, also distinguished themselves in political theory and practice, winning much admiration by their brilliant arguments.

It was Tseng, however, who introduced Wang An-shih to Ou-yang, and who initially acted as intermediary in their correspondence. In 1044, he wrote to Ou-yang:

My friend Wang An-shih is as good in ancient-style prose as he is in conduct. Though he has a doctoral degree, he is known to but few people. He feels that he does not particularly care to become well known among those who are unable to appreciate him. He has told me that only someone like you, Sir, would understand him.[62]

Not long afterward, Tseng wrote another letter, reporting back to Wang:

The Honorable Ou-yang read your writings, liked them very much, and had them copied. . . . He hopes he may have the opportunity of meeting you someday.... He wishes that you would write more expansively, without contrived constructions or imitations of what the forerunners have composed.... As he remarks: "The works of Mencius and Han Yü are tremendous; yet one does not have to write the way they did. It is better to be natural."[63]

Thereafter, Ou-yang and Wang corresponded and exchanged poems. Ou-yang recommended Wang for promotion in 1055 and again in 1056, without as yet having met him in person. (One of the memorials that recommended Wang, the great reformer, also recommended Lü I-chien's son Lü Kung-chu, who subsequently became a leading conservative.)[64] The political disagreement between Wang and Ou-yang never erased their friendship, as is shown in the funeral ode Wang wrote for Ou-yang: "Everyone in the country, whether worthy or unworthy, burst into tears and cried in sorrow. This is especially true of those serving at court, who had had the privilege of Ou-yang's company and friendship in the past." In his own heart, Wang wrote, he had always felt "great admiration, respect, and affinity" for Ou-yang.[65]

Ou-yang was also introduced to Su Hsün by others. As was previously mentioned, he considered Su's prose better than anyone's. In a letter to the poet Mei Yao-ch'en, his praise of Su ended with repeated exclamations: "Most delightful! Most delightful!" Of Su's two sons, Ou-yang correctly put Tung-p'o ahead. He told many people that from then on he would have to defer to this new genius. To Tung-p'o himself, he said: "I am old and will soon be retiring. The leadership in prose writing is now yours."[66]

Ou-yang could retire with the gratifying feeling of success in a great mission. The great Southern Sung philosopher Chu Hsi, critical of Ou-yang with regard to scholarship and personal conduct, had nothing but praise for his poetry and prose. They are, as Chu said, "perfect."[67]

CHAPTER ELEVEN

RATIONALISM AND RELIGION

Ou-yang's essay "On Fundamentals" gave most historians the impression that he was an agnostic.[1] This, however, was not exactly the case. To begin with, no scholar-official could possibly escape the pervasive influence of religious beliefs and practices in Sung China. Buddhism had been the dominant religion for several centuries. Taoism continued to compete with it as a poor second, while a rather bewildering assortment of folk cults interpenetrated both of them. Some of these cults were popular in the same form throughout the country, while others had regional variations.

Scholar-officials were often called on from both above and below to compose religious documents. They were obliged to render this service to the court, imperial clan members, and maternal relatives of the imperial house, Buddhists and Taoists alike.[2] It was also their duty to perform whatever religious rites might be desired by the common people who were under their jurisdiction as local governors. In the collected works of Ou-yang are about 400 odes of invocation. About one-fourth of them were composed during his days at court.[3] These were the *ch'ing-tz'u,* literally "green prayers," so called because they were written in red ink on green paper (which was probably closer to gray) and burned during the ceremony of invocation. All the odes, according to custom, were written in the style of parallel prose, much to Ou-yang's distaste. They were addressed to a large variety of deities and spirits. Among them were, for example, the gods of the Five Dragons, the Nine Dragons, the Eastern Sacred Mountain, the Northern Sacred Mountain, the river, the city, and so on. There was also an incongruous assortment of historical figures, such as the first Han emperor; one of his successors, Emperor Ching; and Chang Fei, a ferocious general of the Three Kingdoms period at the end of the Han who was a popular figure in legends and operas.[4]

Ou-yang complied with the formality of composing these odes with ill-concealed skepticism and a trace of annoyance.[5] As he explained, many of them were unavoidable responses to natural calamities. According to custom, "an official, though realizing that human power is of little help, has no alternative but to put forth his best effort."[6] On several occasions, Ou-yang followed a precedent set by Han Yü by putting into the odes a rationalistic plea reminding the supernatural beings that it was their responsibility to save the people from suffering. Ou-yang wrote, for example: "Flood and drought cause disasters. The officials, who bear no responsibility for these happenings, have no choice but to report them to the gods." In another religious ode, he reasoned: "Officials know only human affairs. They do not know about rains.... However, they will do their utmost within their realm of responsibility. Beyond that, may the deities by their spiritual power extend protection to the people. May the two sides, on earth and in heaven, carry out their respective duties without letting the people down." Elsewhere, he wrote in a similar vein: "To save the people from unseasonable flood and drought and from epidemics resulting from famine is beyond the reach of human power. That is the function of the deities." The concept of functional deities, which Han Yü, Ou-yang Hsiu, and many other rational-minded Confucianists accepted at least outwardly, was characteristic of the religions of traditional China. The scholar-officials' acceptance of this concept reflected their own bureaucratic frame of mind, as if the deities themselves maintained a bureaucracy to take care of the world of nature and beyond.

Confucianism, though based on its own rational and secular

principles, contained some anomalous religious and nonrational beliefs of non-Confucian origin. The concept of *yin* and *yang* and the theory of the five elements, for example, had been accepted since the early Han. Confucianism was thus driven into the anomalous position of upholding the belief that the heavenly order and human events do interact. By this belief, both sympathetic magic and moral conduct *would* help bring good fortune. However, sympathetic magic received little emphasis from rational-minded Confucianists. They believed that moral conduct served the purpose better, for heaven would reward the upright man. Natural disasters and unusual omens were customarily interpreted as warning signs by which heaven expressed its disapproval of human conduct at court—sins of either omission or commission. Hence, it was generally held more important for the emperor to take rectifying steps than to resort to prayer. This was the stand Ou-yang took. On the occasion of a great flood, he submitted a memorial invoking this conventional belief to urge Emperor Jen-tsung to adopt an heir apparent, since his august wish to have a son had gone unfulfilled for years. Privately, Ou-yang confessed that the matter had been on his mind for some time, and that he "merely took advantage of the great flood as an opportune moment."[7] He was essentially faithful to Confucian rationalism, but was willing to make necessary compromises with prevailing nonrational beliefs, or to use them to serve rational ends, without really believing in them.

Rationalism made Ou-yang iconoclastic. He justified his views by invoking precedents set by the sages: "All things have some ordinarily understandable reasons. As to things that cannot be understood, even the sages would decline to comment."[8] From this standpoint he often cast doubt on Taoism. In one of his poems he said: "No one could ever visit the world inhabited by the immortals; who can tell then whether they really exist?" Another poem reads: "Deities and immortals perform many a strange deed. So the tales about them time and again repeat; whether truly or falsely, no one knows."[9] In pursuing his historiographical studies,

Ou-yang came across a Taoist work titled *The Classics of the Yellow Court*, a work probably written in the second or third century A.D. that deals with the control of nerves in connection with a sexual regimen believed to be helpful for longevity. To this book he added a critical preface that reads in part as follows:

> Since ancient times there has existed the Way, but not immortals. People through the ages knew that the Way existed but did not know what it was. However, without realizing that immortals do not exist, they mistakenly tried to learn a method of becoming immortal. . . . The Way is no other than the way of nature. Life is inevitably followed by death; that is a natural principle. . . . Through the centuries, people who coveted life turned to exercises alleged to prolong it. They stopped at nothing. Some chewed herbs, some swallowed metals and stones, and yet others claimed to inhale the essences of sunshine and moonlight. Still others contended that all these actions would not help. They said that it is internal hygiene that counts. Hence they put thoughts to rest, suppressed desires, worked on the alleged essence of life within the body, and practiced breathing exercises diligently. . . . *The Classics of the Yellow Court* is a book on hygiene by the Taoists of the Wei and Chin period. It deals with internal techniques, and contains many strange theories.[10]

This preface was signed "Wu-hsien-tzu," literally "The Master Who Negates Immortals."

Taoism, by its very nature, emphasized withdrawal from the world, seclusion, non-activity, quietness, and tranquillity. Its believers generally kept its mysteries and techniques to themselves. It had little disruptive influence on society. The historical fact, as Ou-yang observed, was that "unless it was especially favored by some ruler, Taoism was unable to gather much momentum on its own."[11]

Buddhism was different. It had entered Chinese society, or conquered it, as is sometimes said, in about the third century A.D., and since then had become a vital, integral part of Chinese life. By the T'ang it had reached flourishing maturity. Temples were everywhere; magnificent ones in the hearts of cities, exquisite ones nestled in foothills, famous ones halfway up scenic mountains, and small ones in even the remotest villages. In them took place activities in numerous spheres: intellectual, educational, artistic, economic, and social. They received support from all segments of the population; shared the position and influence of imperial and aristocratic families; owned land exempt from taxation; engaged in commerce; produced learned monks who consorted with scholars; accommodated students who had no other libraries available; gave relief to the needy, and sanctuary to all in times of trouble; spread Buddhist religious teachings and philosophical ideas alike through lectures, discussions, tales, plays, and other popular media; entertained crowds during festivals; maintained close relations with the common people, among them many pious laymen; in short, acted as cultural and social centers for the entire populace. Buddhism was more than a religion; it was much of the Chinese way of life.[12]

During the Sung, Buddhism declined somewhat in popularity, but only as compared with its heyday during the T'ang. From the standpoint of many scholar-officials dedicated to the cause of Confucian revival it still had too much influence. Part of their complaint was directed against its numerous secular activities, which they regarded as highly objectionable, especially in their capacity as administrators. Buddhism represented a powerful social force, with a strong grip on the masses that the Confucian state found troublesome and hard to control. As Ou-yang put it, "Buddhism, playing on human emotions, is capable of stirring up the people by the theme of fortunes and misfortunes. Those who turn to it are large in number and intense in belief.... It would not take much effort for Buddhism to cause various kinds of disturbances and undesirable activities."[13]

According to an account given by Ou-yang, his uncle Ou-yang

Tsai had encountered a social tragedy caused by the blind belief ignorant people placed in a Buddhist malpractice:

> There had been a drought in the area near the capital. A Buddhist monk, praying for rain, cut off his own arm. His action aroused so much attention that the government built a temple for him on Tortoise Hill, along the Huai River. Many noblemen and high-ranking officials in the capital treated him with courtesy, which made him quite influential throughout the region. He had a way of inducing ignorant people to drown themselves in the Huai River, claiming it to be a canonical way [of salvation] in Buddhism. Actually, he made material gains from such self-sacrifices. The number of victims reached several hundred in a year. Before the act of drowning, the monk had his disciples, chanting, push the victims toward the river. Some victims began to regret, tried to get away, and cried out loud. But they could no longer escape the stampede. On hearing of this, Ou-yang Tsai exclaimed: "What harm could be greater!" He had all the disciples arrested, uncovered among them some criminals, sentenced a few of these to death, sent the rest back to their native places, and ordered the temple destroyed.[14]

Cases as serious as this were rare, probably exceptional. But it was by no means unusual, as Ou-yang mentioned, for Buddhists to "induce several hundred men and women to hold meetings day and night" in mixed company and "to make profits by gathering a crowd for religious ceremonies."[15] From the Confucian viewpoint these were immoral customs that should be stopped.

Some Buddhist activities, though leading to neither public disorder nor immoral conduct, were nevertheless wasteful, and therefore objectionable to the Confucianists on economic grounds. At the cultural center of Loyang, leading Buddhist temples long received generous gifts and land endowments. The architecture of those in the best areas of the city rivaled that of the great mansions. From the early Sung on, some families of aristocratic origin and a number of wealthy merchants gradually moved away, and the support given Buddhism in Loyang decreased. But elsewhere in the north Buddhism continued to enjoy the support of the wealthy. Whatever it might have lost in the north was more than compensated for in the south, especially in the beautiful city of Hangchow and in several cities in Fukien. In Hangchow, later made famous by Marco Polo as the leading city in Cathay, thousands of families burned exquisite incense from morning till night. The walls of the Buddhist temples had shining, richly colored decorations; the halls glittered with golden splendor; the furniture was of the most expensive kind; and the meals were elaborately prepared vegetarian delicacies. Sometimes a feast would cost a thousand pieces of silver. The cities in Fukien were even worse for conspicuous consumption. For funerals and other Buddhist ceremonies, people would spend the largest amount they could possibly afford; otherwise they would feel socially disgraced. From the standpoint of Confucian frugality, such extravagance was unjustifiable. From the standpoint of the good of society, it was wasteful and unproductive. Many Confucianists resented Buddhist temples as being parasites: attracting wealth and enjoying it under the privilege of tax exemption, but contributing little to public welfare beyond their occasional acts of charity.[16]

At times, some outstanding bureaucrat would try to do something to rectify the situation. Ou-yang told the story of how another uncle of his, named Hua, forced a Buddhist temple to contribute to famine relief:

The Fiscal Intendant suspected that a large temple with plenty of money and commodities might have been engaged in profiteering. Ou-yang Hua was sent there to investigate. The head monk presented him with a gift, one thousand taels of silver. Declining it with a smile, he said: "What use have I for this? However, would you listen to my advice? This is a year of great famine. You have in storage some sixty to seventy thousand piculs of grain, would you donate them to famine relief? If so, I will not impound them." The head monk complied, and many hungry people were thus saved.[17]

During Fan Chung-yen's term as administrator of Hangchow, that usually affluent metropolis paradoxically suffered a famine. Fan devised a rather modern policy: stimulating the general economy by an increase in government and private spending. He asked the Buddhist temples for charitable donations, and also persuaded them to start construction projects in their temples, projects that provided employment and income for the poor.[18]

Another Confucian complaint was that Buddhists interfered with government administration. Buddhists patronized by palace ladies and befriended by eunuchs would often seek special favors from the government. An official who refused to grant them might run the risk of incurring the imperial displeasure, if the Buddhists' friends were influential enough. The court generally supported officials who abided by regular procedures and standards against such influence, but occasionally there was trouble. Another area of friction was the appointment of priests. In theory, recommendations on whom to appoint were made to the court by the Secretarial Department, after due screening of qualified candidates. However, influential Buddhist monks were sometimes appointed directly, by palace decree or rescript, thus bypassing the normal procedure. "Such interference with administration through the manipulation of palace attendants," Ou-yang pointed out, "should not be allowed to happen."[19]

These criticisms of Buddhist practices reinforced the basic philosophical objections that the pioneering neo-Confucianists had against Buddhism. It was their zealous resolve not only to revitalize Confucianism in education and state affairs, but to restore its dominance over all aspects of society, that Buddhism, in their view, had unjustifiably and unfortunately been allowed to usurp. In this zealous spirit Ou-yang launched his theoretical attack on Buddhism. His theory was based on an interpretation of history that gave primary emphasis to social customs, particularly the customs collectively known in Confucian terminology as the rites, or rites and music. In his study of the *Rituals of Chou*, as discussed earlier, he gave high praise to the ancient scheme for regulating human behavior. In the introduction to his "Treatise on Rites and Music" in the *New T'ang History*, he repeated the same theme with much greater force. What had rites and music meant in his utopian society of antiquity? By no means merely empty ceremonies! They expressed the society's consciousness of its own identity and regulated, in an all-pervasive way, every need, every detail, indeed everything in human life, in accordance with a meaningful, aesthetic, harmonious, and satisfying moral and philosophical order. Since the legendary Three Dynasties of remote antiquity, and especially since the Ch'in empire had swept away the ancient institutions, no government had grasped the deep significance of these customs or given them the attention they were due. In degeneration, the rites and music failed to meet the needs of the people and became "expressions without reality": empty, lifeless, mere formalities. This vacuum of unmet needs had been filled by Buddhism. In order to rectify the situation, there could be no solution other than the reinvigoration of Confucianism, and with it the restoration of the ancient customs. Together, good teachings and good customs would have the moral force to make Buddhism or any other religion unnecessary and unwanted.[20]

This theory found its full expression in his famous essay "On Fundamentals," which promptly replaced Han Yü's "What Is the True Way?" as the guiding light of the Confucian revival. Han Yü had called for open persecution of the Buddhists: "Let their priests be turned into ordinary men again, their books be burned, and their temples be converted into homes!" This was more emotional than reasonable, and hardly a feasible solution. Shih Chieh faithfully followed Han Yü, and attacked Buddhism with vehemence.[21] Ou-yang disagreed. As he saw it, the popularity of Buddhism was a reality that had to be recognized. Outright suppression would be not only futile, but impossible. It was necessary to go deeper, to identify the underlying causes of Buddhism's appeal. Only when these causes were removed would its popularity be undermined. Hence, Ou-yang called for a positive program of reform, not a negative persecution. Moreover, the Confucianists must realize that personal moral reform would not be adequate to solve a social problem. A fundamental renovation of social customs would be necessary.[22]

"On Fundamentals" used a medical analogy. Buddhism was a disease that had taken advantage of Confucianism's run-down condition to infect China:

> When kingly rule ceased, and rites and righteousness were neglected, Buddhism came to China. It is clear that Buddhism took advantage of this time of decay and neglect to come and plague us. This was how the illness was first contracted. And if we will but remedy this decay, revive what has fallen into disuse, and restore once again to the land kingly rule in its brilliance and rites and righteousness in their fullness, then although Buddhism continues to exist, it will have no hold upon our people.[23]

What was Ou-yang's prescription? He had no use for Han Yü's strong medicine of forcible suppression for yet another reason. The defeat of Buddhism depended on rites and righteousness, which had to be gently introduced, with the cooperation of the patients.[24] There would be no immediate cure, but in time these gentle medicines would take effect. As Ou-yang argued:

> People have flocked to Buddhism, for Buddhism claims to do good deeds. Oh! If only people can be made to understand how to do good deeds through rites and righteousness, is there any doubt that they will flock back to Confucianism and follow it? ... For a long time, Buddhist theories familiar to the ears have

captured the hearts of the people. But rites and righteousness have not been much seen or heard. If people should be told that Buddhism is prohibited and rites and righteousness are hereby imposed, they would be scared away. There is no better way than to introduce them gradually, so that the people will take them up without realizing it.[25]

This statement again shows Ou-yang's preference for gradual improvement over drastic reform. His gradualism demanded a fine balance between idealistic zeal and realistic appraisal. Its approach was also reasonable, in line with his belief in rationalism.

Ou-yang's attack on Buddhism, so well put and so well known, was confined to theory: in practice, even he himself did not rigorously follow his own preaching. To abide strictly by Confucian tradition, he and his family should have cared for the grave of his parents themselves, and personally performed the ancestral rites. But his bureaucratic calling interfered. Custom gave high-ranking bureaucrats the privilege of having the government arrange for a local temple to look after these rites. In most cases it was a Buddhist temple, so Ou-yang did not apply for this privilege for some time. Eventually, his friend Han Ch'i persuaded him to have an arrangement made with a local Taoist temple, and thereafter Taoist priests performed the annual memorial rites "as if they were the descendants" of the Ou-yang family.[26]

Nor did Ou-yang's denunciation of Buddhism keep him from the company of learned monks. While at Loyang, some friends prevailed upon him (he was initially reluctant) to go along on a visit to a secluded and scholarly monk. It turned out that this monk was so well-versed in Buddhist scriptures, so articulate, soft-spoken, and brilliant in countering questions, that Ou-yang could not help admiring him. Later, he was much impressed by Chien-yü, another monk, for whose book on phonetics he wrote a preface in which he conceded that no Confucian scholar could rival Chien-yü in discovering and correcting mistakes in earlier works. But Ou-yang mentioned that Chien-yü was originally from a scholarly family and had mastered the *Classic of Change*—implying that he was a Confucianist at heart.[27] Ou-yang also befriended monks who were accomplished poets. He expressed his regret that a collection of the poems by nine Buddhist monks of the early Sung was not generally available. Through the friend of his youth mentioned earlier, Shih Man-ch'ing, Ou-yang came to know two poet-monks, Pi-yen and Wei-yen, for whose works he also wrote prefaces.[28] He took care to mention something in these prefaces about the Confucian qualifications of both monks. Of Pi-yen he said:

> In stature and countenance Pi-yen is of heroic mold, and there is a greatness in his bosom. Devoting himself to Buddhism he has found no practical application for his gifts. Only his practice of poetry might carry his name before the world, but again he is too idle to care. Now, an old man, he has opened his bundle and brought out some three or four hundred pieces, all of them charming.[29]

As to Wei-yen, according to Ou-yang, he was as learned in Confucianism as in Buddhism. He lived for fifteen years without ever leaving the Hsiang-kuo-ssu, the leading temple of Kaifeng, receiving visitors there and having long discussions with them on current problems of the country.[30]

All these learned monks, well-educated by Confucian standards, were regarded by Ou-yang as "lost talents." Now and then, he would try to induce them to return to secular life. One of his verses, presented to a poet-monk, reads:

> You are a Buddhist, and I a Confucianist;
> We are like different wheels; no common tracks exist.
>
> . . . .
>
> If only you would be to our fold returning;
> The way is always there for a new beginning.

One of the most long-standing of Ou-yang's friendships with monks was with Hui-ch'in, who often came up to Kaifeng from

Hangchow. Ou-yang would complain to him about the luxurious self-indulgence and other social malpractices of the Buddhist temples in the south, adding other arguments in the hope of weakening his religious belief so that he might eventually turn back to Confucianism. It seems that occasionally Ou-yang tried to apply the gradual social approach outlined in "On Fundamentals" to his own dealings with some Buddhists. However, he never converted anyone.[31]

Basically, the Confucian rationalism Ou-yang upheld had definite limitations. It had little to say, for example, on why people in danger, as if by instinct, would cry out to the deities for help—as he confessed he himself had done many times on a precarious voyage up the Yangtze during his banishment from court.[32] Destiny was another puzzle for which Confucianism had no good explanation. As Ou-yang commented:

It has been said that a *chün-tzu* understands destiny. Can this so-called destiny really be understood? ... Some people have good fortune, while others run into misfortune. Sometimes things ought to be one way, yet they turn out to be the contrary. Since no one really knows the reason why things happen the way they do, the reason is attributed to heaven and called destiny. The saying that a *chün-tzu* understands destiny thus means that he really knows nothing more than that.[33]

As a rationalist, Ou-yang did not hesitate to be iconoclastic. He questioned some of the common sayings and beliefs of Confucianism itself, even the assumed wisdom of the master. The following paragraph shows his reasoned skepticism at its best:

It has been said that a benevolent [*jen*] person will enjoy longevity. Actually, this is no more than a hope on the part of his friends. Can we claim that goodness inevitably results in good fortune? Is this not tantamount to projecting man's wishes onto heaven? Disasters and blessings, good luck and bad, these are extremely difficult to fathom. Even the master called it destiny and seldom commented on it. Was this not because he himself, when it came to such questions, had no good answer to offer?[34]

Ou-yang could only conclude that "destiny is so hard to understand that one might as well give up searching for its reasons."[35] If the question of destiny puzzled Ou-yang, fortune-telling made his puzzlement worse. Physiognomy, he noted, was very strange; its predictions often turned out to be accurate. He told Su Tung-p'o, for example, that in his youth a physiognomist had predicted that he would enjoy great fame, for his ears were lighter in color than his face; but that he would suffer unfounded slanders, for his lips did not quite cover his teeth. In his parents' burial ode, Ou-yang recorded that a fortune-teller had correctly predicted the year in which his father would pass away. These experiences led him to ask: "Is so-called destiny really predestined? And can one really know one's own predestination?"[36]

The Buddhist view—that a being comes into existence in a reincarnation predetermined by his previous life or lives—was difficult to reconcile with the Confucian tenet on venerating ancestral spirits that was strongly adhered to by the Chinese. That ancestors would appear through rebirth as perfect strangers was a revolting concept to the Confucian mind. The most widely and firmly held view of destiny was native to China: the belief in moral retribution, or, more concretely, the idea that a man's good or bad fortune depends on the moral merits or demerits of his ancestors. This generally seemed the most reasonable view to the family-oriented and ethically minded Chinese. As Ou-yang stated in his parents' funeral ode: "No goodness will fail to bring reward, either sooner or later as the case may be. My ancestors and parents, through accumulated goodness and well-cultivated virtues, ought to enjoy rewards. Though they were unable to attain such rewards during their own lifetimes, they have now been awarded posthumous honors and titles by government order." In numerous epitaphs composed for other families, he expressed the same conviction.[37]

The trouble with believing in moral retribution was that it did not always seem to work. Exemplary conduct of their ancestors notwithstanding, many families simply did not prosper. Ou-yang was forced to explain away the obvious divergence between belief and reality by contending that it took a long time to accumulate sufficient moral merit, that the reward to be expected might well be slow in coming.[38] But the last straw was the tragedy that happened to the family of Ou-yang's wife. Her father, a virtuous, well-known scholar-official, had only one son, who was often ill and died young. There was no grandson at all, though the son had married twice. The paternal lineage of the Hsüeh family thus came to a sad end. The tragedy was too close to home for Ou-yang to deny that "moral retribution sometimes misses."[39] In distress, he sought comfort in the philosophical concept of social immortality. As he said, "The virtuous persons and the *chün-tzu* who have lived since ancient times have not always had male offspring. Their merits, their virtue, and their fame have nonetheless come down through the ages and attained wide renown, not by being transmitted by their descendants...but by being transmitted by the entire society."[40] This philosophy had first been expressed in the *Tradition of Tso* (sometimes regarded as one of the lesser classics), which advised that one should seek to establish lasting social merit by virtue, good deeds, and good words. To this Ou-yang added his own interpretation: "Cultivating virtues, carrying them out in deeds, and expressing them in good words are the three accomplishments that are immortal and everlasting."[41] (The same view was reiterated in early-twentieth-century China by the pragmatic philosopher Hu Shih, who combined his Western training with the rationalistic outlook of traditional China.)[42]

The philosophical concept of social immortality, no matter how rational it may be, could not take the place of religion. By the time Ou-yang was driven to that position, he had exhausted all the logical alternatives available to Confucian rationalism and still could not find peace of mind in his confrontation with the mystery of destiny. Did he remain in this rather unstable position? According to a friend of his sons, he did consider turning to Buddhism shortly before his death. Having heard that his good friend Fu Pi, for whose integrity and cautiousness he had much respect, had been converted to Buddhism, he could not help wondering if perhaps there were not something in it after all. Reportedly, he called on a leading monk nearby and began to read Buddhist scriptures. But he probably reached no definite conclusion, for he soon passed away.[43] Han Yü, Ou-yang's forerunner in the denunciation of Buddhism, was also alleged to have gone in his old age to study with a Buddhist monk. Likewise, Yin Shu, who had joined Ou-yang in attacking Buddhism in their younger days, later became interested in its teachings.[44] The story about Ou-yang, true or not, seems to fall in with the common tendency to fill the vacuum in Confucian rationalism with Buddhism, which, despite the social ills it fostered, had the strongest intellectual appeal of all the religions of traditional China. It was Ou-yang's protégé Su Ch'e, the brother of Su Tung-p'o, who openly declared that "when one has gone through a great deal of hardship in the world, the realization comes that one can turn to the Buddhist canon."[45]

It should further be noted that while Ou-yang himself was a Confucian agnostic, his wife believed in Buddhism and made the rest of the family follow suit.[46] It was natural for her to do so, coming from the unfortunate Hsüeh family. There is a witty anecdote that throws some light on Ou-yang's family life:

> Ou-yang's youngest son was nicknamed "Monk." Some friend asked why, since Ou-yang disliked Buddhism and opposed the monks, his child had such a nickname. Ou-yang replied: "This is disparagement, just as some people call their children 'Bull' or 'Donkey.'" Everyone who heard this had a good laugh, and admired Ou-yang for his clever argument.[47]

Hidden in that last phrase is the clue: more likely than not, it was Ou-yang's wife who had nicknamed the child. Ou-yang could neither change nor deny the name, and had no way of escaping from the dilemma of apparent inconsistency between public and private life except through humor.

The neo-Confucian philosophers who succeeded Ou-yang hardly noticed his alleged interest in Buddhism, or his family's conversion to it. But they did feel that the views he expressed in "On Fundamentals" and other writings did not go to the heart of the problem. While agreeing that promotion of Confucian social customs would help to cut down Buddhist influence on the social level, they felt that the only tool that would completely root out Buddhism's appeal was philosophy. Yang Shih, a leading Confucianist of the late Northern Sung, commented that Han Yü, Ou-yang, and other pioneers had failed to make their opposition to Buddhism effective primarily because they did not go beyond the level of human affairs.[48] How to challenge the Buddhist outlook on life? Confucianism had to reach a higher plane. Just as Confucian social customs would repel Buddhist ones, so would a better developed Confucian metaphysical system replace Buddhist thinking.

This approach reached its highest point in the Southern Sung with Chu Hsi, the great synthesizer, and his School of the True Way, which set out to construct a comprehensive, all-pervasive doctrine that would provide a metaphysical underpinning for moral self-cultivation and Confucian social improvement as well. For example, *li*, the rational principle in Ou-yang's thinking, was expanded by these philosophers into an eternal principle equated with the reality of the whole universe, a principle that formed the basis for man, his mind, his nature, and everything else. Ou-yang had merely identified *li* with reasoning, the thinking process. These philosophers contended that to understand *li* required a conceptual investigation of everything in the universe, which in turn required constant discipline in concentration. The discipline consisted of banishing all desires and emotional fluctuations and cultivating a profound, perceptive, pure, and spiritual tranquillity.

This was the synthesis: a Confucian metaphysical system with a mode of philosophical contemplation obviously influenced by Buddhism. Once developed, it turned to challenge Buddhism.[49] Life is meaningful—not empty. Man is mortal—but his realization of the universal principle is lasting. The universe is reality, this world and the metaphysical reality together—beyond it there is no other-world. The enlightened Confucian mind is at one with reality—with the universe and everything in it, not the transcendental, mystically experienced reality that was the Buddhist delusion.

This neo-Confucian philosophy surpassed all earlier thought.[50] Did it replace Buddhism? Perhaps for a minority of leading thinkers; but Buddhism was still the leading religion among the vast majority of the people. Even Chu Hsi admitted that the persistent appeal of Buddhism would be very hard to resist. A good Confucian might refuse to honor Buddhism during his lifetime; his children might follow; but the third generation probably would not.[51] This was an ultimate admission that the Confucian philosophy, even with Buddhist admixtures, was no substitute for religion. The anomalous coexistence of Confucian rationalism and a multitude of religions endured. All the efforts of the neo-Confucianists could neither uproot Buddhism nor create a purely Confucian society after their own vision.

CHAPTER TWELVE

EPILOGUE

FAME HURTS REALITY—so the philosophical Taoists say. Whether this be whimsical coincidence or profound paradox, it certainly applies to Ou-yang Hsiu. Who would suspect that he, who is well known in history and highly spoken of as a rule, has been in some measure underestimated and in some ways misunderstood?

That Ou-yang should be underestimated is perhaps natural, for his greatness spread over so many different areas that past accounts of him (though most were favorable and some were even laudatory) were unable, from their limited viewpoints, to present a picture of the whole man. In any of the particular areas in which he worked, Ou-yang did not necessarily overshadow his contemporaries. But he was a pioneer; he influenced and helped these other talents, sometimes discovering them in the first place. In political histories, Ou-yang has been overshadowed by both Fan Chung-yen and Wang An-shih. Forgotten is Ou-yang's extensive influence on both of them, let alone the help he gave many others throughout the span of his career. It was Ou-yang who paved the way for the minor reform and who vigorously defended it when it faced defeat. It was he who discovered and promoted the talent of Wang An-shih. He was also responsible for recommending yet other talents, who eventually led the opposition to Wang's reform.[1] Indeed, he never tired of searching for first-rate scholar-official material. Nor did he blame any of his protégés for turning against him afterward, merely saying: "It has been my fault rather than theirs."[2] Vigorous and self-confident, he felt no need for their gratitude.

A number of intellectual histories have been misleading, over-praising Ou-yang in some ways and downgrading him in others. A standard survey of intellectual developments honors him as the founder of a school of Confucian scholarship named the Luling School, after his ancestral home.[3] Actually, he had few disciples other than Tseng Kung, and neither Tseng nor the others regarded themselves as members of a school at all. The label merely reflects the narrow outlook of the later neo-Confucianists, who insisted on classifying everyone by school. In doing so, they missed the whole point of Ou-yang's greatness: widespread influence over all the different schools. The downgrading of Ou-yang started with Chu Hsi and his School of the True Way, who reserved their highest praise for their own forerunners, the few philosophers who chiefly excelled in metaphysics and related moral teachings, such as Ch'eng Hao and his brother Ch'eng I. This school respected Ou-yang as a pioneer, but disapproved of him in some respects, and did not regard him as being among the great. After it became the orthodoxy, its position tended to color historical evaluations. True, Ou-yang was no philosopher. But that need not disqualify him as a great Confucian.[4]

Ou-yang was overpraised for his two famous essays. "On Fundamentals" won him credit as a meritorious champion of the neo-Confucian cause, upholding rites and righteousness as the only means of realizing the ideals of a moral and purely Confucian society. The fact that religion did not diminish in strength as a result of this essay was ignored; the fact that Buddhism was strong even in Ou-yang's own family was rarely noted. "On Factions" was considered an original contribution to political thought. But the circumstances that led Ou-yang to formulate this ingenious lawyer-like defense of factions were underplayed. That Ou-yang himself did not believe the essay's argument was hardly mentioned.

To rank Ou-yang's achievements by specific fields, literature was foremost. The timeless quality of his literary work speaks for itself. Historically speaking, his greatest influence was on prose. In the short span of two decades he established the ancient style as dominant, won a recognition as its respected master that has lasted until the present century, and brought several protégés up to his own towering height. His achievements in historical studies come next. Besides his lasting contributions in such specialized fields as archaeology and genealogy, he introduced new methods in the compilation of general histories, though his rigorous application of neo-Confucian precepts in interpretation and his insistence on using nothing but ancient-style prose were open to criticism. His classical studies, and by extension his theoretical contributions to the revival and further development of Confucianism, form a third category of intellectual achievement, though they are achievements in historical study as well. What he established in this field had an awakening effect on later scholars; so inspired, they went on to new heights, making greater contributions than Ou-yang's own. To be overtaken by subsequent generations is a not unusual fate for pioneers. Finally, the administrative theory he developed from his experience and observation deserves credit, although little ever came of it. Ou-yang's inability to develop his theory beyond broad propositions to specific methods and formulas was perhaps an inevitable product of his environment. The overwhelming majority of neo-Confucianists went nowhere near as far as Ou-yang, for they valued the classics, philosophy, literature, and history far more than mere administrative matters.

Ou-yang's temperament was more suitable for a pure scholar than an important official. The very fact that his foremost accomplishments are in literature suggests that he was more artistically inclined than practically oriented toward politics. His brilliance came through in both his private and his public life, but in strikingly contrasting ways. Among his nonpolitical writings were many charming pieces. In private life he was delightful company, and an exhilarating conversationalist. When it came to government affairs, he appeared to be more argumentative than eloquent—sharp and cutting, forceful to the point of being implacable, certainly not an easy colleague to get along with. Ever eager to win all points and reluctant to yield any, he often gave vent to a belligerency that was politically self-defeating. One would expect a statesman with as much to say and as great a talent for making enemies as Ou-yang to have little staying power.[5] Only the enormous political, literary, and scholarly prestige he accumulated over the years enabled him to remain in the political arena as long as he did.

Ou-yang's career throws a great deal of light on the political complexities of the Sung. With better education and rising prestige, with new-found energy and great zeal, the scholar-officials asserted their ideological authority more than ever before, demanding a larger share in the power of the state. Their growing clamor could not help but be heard, but the problem of how to cope with it presented considerable difficulties. On the one hand, they were dissatisfied with convention. On the other hand, they disagreed with one another. Mutual interference drowned out much of the meaning in their claims and counterclaims. Absolutism and factionalism compounded the difficulties. They developed their political thought, but they did not develop it sufficiently in the direction of building or remodeling an institutional framework to accommodate their growing power in an orderly manner that would produce progress. In the meantime, though there were many and better scholars to be chosen as officials, excellent scholars did not necessarily make good administrators. The problem of making the machinery of government work better had no easy solution.

The neo-Confucianist scholar-officials advanced haltingly. They pressed on, but also pressed hard against one another. They fought for their common cause, but they also quarreled among themselves. But, following their pioneering precursors, they marched on with remarkable momentum. Harassed and handicapped politically, they turned toward new fronts: social reconstruction, self-cultivation, and above all, philosophical formulation. What they did not lack was boundless vitality.

Of vitality, the pioneering Ou-yang Hsiu had plenty. It is his tremendous versatility that sets him above his contemporaries, the incredible diversity of his achievements that makes him the finest product of his time. This searching mind and restless soul, ever surging ahead in new directions and dimensions, in one field after another, embodies the early spirit of neo-Confucianism. From dawn to the high noon of his career, from noon to golden sunset, he blazed in the intellectual firmament of the Sung with a brilliance that, beclouded though it sometimes was, outshone all others still.[6]

NOTES

NOTES

Abbreviations composed of capital letters indicate a primary source; those composed of authors' names and publication dates indicate a secondary source. Full titles and publication data are given in the Bibliography, pages 207–19. For convenient reference, primary and secondary sources are listed separately in the Bibliography, in alphabetical order by abbreviation.

CHAPTER ONE

1. Reischauer and Fairbank (1960), 235.
2. CTCS, 59:4; CTWC, 12:447.
3. Nivison (1959a), 226–27.
4. Locke (1951). For translations of Ou-yang's works into Western languages, see the listing in Davidson (1957), 437–40. This is no longer up to date; see, for instance, Birch (1965) and Rexroth (1955).
5. K. C. Huang (1958).
6. Twitchett (1961); Twitchett (1962); and J. Liu (1963a).
7. OYNP (Hu); OYNP (Hua); OYNP (Yang); the one by Hua is the best.
8. For formal works, see mainly CCTY, HCP, HCPM, MCYHL, SHY: CK, SHY:HC, SS, and WHTK. For informal sources, it is most convenient to begin with SJYS and Saeki's indexes of 1954 and 1960.

CHAPTER TWO

1. Kracke (1955); Reischauer and Fairbank (1960), 183–88.
2. J. Liu (1964).
3. See Kracke (1953), 8–27, for the best summary of the historical setting.
4. Cf. STNMCY.
5. Cf. Chi (1936), 129–33; P. T. Ho (1956).

6. Cf. L. S. Yang (1952).
7. Gernet (1962).
8. Cf. P. T. Ho (1962).
9. Cf. Kracke (1953); Menzel (1963); Eisenstadt (1963).
10. J. Liu (1957); J. Liu (1961); Eisenstadt (1963).
11. C. Y. Hsia (1937), 7–30; de Bary et al. (1960), 409–581; de Bary (1959).
12. Nivison (1959), 4–13; de Bary (1959).
13. De Bary et al. (1960), 491–509; Gardner (1961) Beasley and Pulleyblank (1961).
14. Hightower (1962), 72–75, 84–93.
15. WHTK, 30:285, CTYL, 130:2–5; Kracke (1953), 197–98; J. Liu (1957), 122–31; J. Liu (1959), chap. 5; J. Liu (1959a); S. P. Liu (1934).
16. K. C. Hsiao (1946), 2:143–89; J. Liu (1959), 22–30.
17. H. J. P'i (1923), 56; J. Liu (1959), 88–90.
18. H. J. P'i (1923), 56; M. Ch'ien (1953), 1:24–25; K. K. Sun (1953).

CHAPTER THREE

1. Aoyama (1951) (cf. WLCC, 90:68–69, 92:77–80, 84–85, 93:86–88).
2. C. M. Ch'en (1946); see also chap. 8 below.
3. OYYSC, 4:12–14, 8:98.
4. OYYSC, 3:99–102.
5. Ou-yang's father apparently had another son by a previous marriage, which was not generally known. See SJYS, 8:342–43; HCHL, 6:11–12; CWCW (Li), 2:9.
6. SCC, 21:35; LLHC, 16:5–6.
7. LLHC, 16:6–7; JCSP, 2d series, 16:153–54.
8. LLHC, 89:94.   9. SS, chap. 319.
10. LCIY, 2 (cf. SLYY, 10:10).   11. SS, chap. 294; OYYSC, 11:44–51.
12. S. Shimizu (1961); OYYSC, 7:102–3, 11:44–47; NKCML, 14:359–60.
13. SS, chap. 294; HCP, 118:2–3; OYYSC, 8:68–69; OYNP (Hua), 3.
14. SSWCL, 8:4–5 (cf. OYYSC, 11:52–53).
15. SS, chap. 319; see also chap. 10 below.
16. OYYSC, 2:17; 6:40–41.
17. OYYSC, 4:15–17, 26; WLHSC, "*Fu-lu,*" 4.
18. OYYSC, 6:46 (cf. HCP, 204:5).
19. SS, chap. 442; OYYSC, 1:10, 3:48, 14:106; MSYTL, 4:6; HWKC, 20:286.
20. Birch (1965), 366; OYYSC, 5:48–49.
21. CWCW, 3:21.
22. HCP, 114:21–22, 115:23; also Ou-yang's statement in OYYSC, 8:67.
23. OSSC, 3–4; SPLC, 4:64; SSWCL, 8:6; MSYTL, 4:5.
24. De Bary et al. (1960), 448 (cf. TSKY, 14; HCP, 275:11; KTL, 7).
25. SSCW, 10:2; JLKY, 1:24–25 (cf. FWCKC, 8:19–25; HCP, 108:13).

26. JLKY, 2:4–6; SS, chap. 314; HCP, 113:15–20; HCPPM, chap. 33.
27. HCP, 115:10.
28. SS, chap. 314; HCP, 118:9–10; HCPPM, chap. 37; CWCW (Li), 2:2; HTL, 4:10–11; SJYS, 8:309.
29. FWCKC, 5:24; SSCW, 3:6–9.
30. SS, chap. 311; SSWCL, 8:1–2; THPL, 3:8.
31. HWKC, 20:269; SS, chap. 311; SSHP, chap. 39; HCPPM, 29:13–14, 37:1–20; LCC, 36:1–11.
32. HCPPM, chap. 37; SS, chap. 288; M. Ch'ien (1947), 2:377–429; J. Liu (1957); J. Liu (1959), chap. 2; THPL, 14:10.
33. OYYSC, 8:41–43, 53 (cf. Locke (1951), 76–77; FWCKC, 18:3; SS, chap. 314).
34. SS, chap. 294; HCP, 118:2–3.
35. OYYSC, 8:59; MSYTL, 2:5; SSCW, "I-wen," 1.
36. SS, chap. 288.
37. OYYSC, 8:56–58 (cf. HCP, 118:12–13; Locke (1951), 82–88).
38. TCHKWC, 3:3–9.
39. OYYSC, 8:60–61, Nivison (1959), 19–20; see also chap. 8 below.
40. OYYSC, 8:64.
41. HWKC, "Chia-chuan," 10:163.
42. FWCKC, 5:20; CTYL, 129:2–3; SS, chap. 311; SSHP, chap. 39; HCPPM, 29:13–14, 37:1–20; LCC, 36:1–11.
43. FWCKC, 5:15; SSCW, 8:9–10; HTL, 1:6–7; HCP, 127–10; SWC, 113:6–7.
44. HNWC, 6:4–11, 28:10; FWCKC, 18:3; OYYSC, 6:1–2.
45. OYYSC, 17:38 (cf. OYNP (Hua), 11); 18:10, 25; SS, chap. 319; HCP, 127:16; 134:10.
46. PSLH, 2:4 (cf. OYYSC, 8:98, 16:80); OYNP (Yang), 33–34; FWCKC, "Pao-hsien-chi," 5:2.
47. OYYSC, 3:52.
48. OYYSC, 3:54, 8:79, 17:56; CSTP, 134:31–36, 40–41; FWCKC, "Pao-hsien-chi," 5:16; SSWCHL, 21:1–2.
49. LCPC, 1:12; OYYSC, 3:54 (cf. FWCKC, 9:13–16, 18:3–4; "Pao-hsien-chi," 5:23; PSLH, 3:34).
50. PSLH, 2:4.
51. Ibid. (cf. PLKT, 1:1; MCYHL, "Chien-lu," 6:56; Miyazaki (1953).
52. NCCT, 7; CTYL, 129:2–3 (cf. FWCKC, "Pao-hsien-chi," 5:16–23). On the importance of implications in Chinese historical writings, see J. Liu (1962).

CHAPTER FOUR

1. Cf. F. C. Wang (Ch'ing), 4:4; HCP, 138:4–6, 194:2–3; HHCY, 47:15–17; Fischer (1955).
2. HCP, 135:16.

3. HCP, 135:24–25, 142:3–4; OYYSC, 12:32–33; HCPPM, 48:1–4, 49:4–8 (cf. STNMCY).

4. OYYSC, 12:35.

5. Cf. G. W. Wang (1963).

6. OYYSC, 12:59, 61.

7. HCP, 142:3–4 (cf. OYYSC, 5:68–69, 9:69).

8. OYYSC, 18:34; for the nature of the draft biography, see L. S. Yang (1961), 45–46.

9. HCP, 126:12, 25; CCTY, 18:6–9.

10. OYYSC, 5:78–79; HCP, 137:13, 138:19, 139:8–10, 140:1, 8–10 (cf. SS, chap. 11); TCHKWC, 14:9–16.

11. OYYSC, 12:30–39; SS, chap. 11.

12. HCP, 140–1, 2, 152:3; FWCKC, 8:19–25 (cf. HWKC, "Chia-chuan," 10:161).

13. HWKC, "Chia-chuan," 20:269; SJYS, 7:260; SSWCHL, 20:3; HCP, 154:5–6; SSCW, 10:4; LCPC, 1:10.

14. SS, chap. 285; SJYS, 7:251–52.

15. HCP, 140:5; HWKC, "Chia-chuan," 12:183; OYYSC, 12:14.

16. HCP, 131:1, 140:7; THPL, 9:7–9; SJYS, 7:235–36. On Shih Chieh see TLC and chap. 7 below.

17. J. Liu (1957), 108; TLC, 1:7–10; HCP, 140:6, 11, 142:2; SS, chap. 432; FCHT, 1:8; PSLH, 2:19.

18. TCHKWC, 15:10–11; OYYSC, 12:14–15; LCC (Su), 36:1–2; HCP, 142:19, 21; SWC, 83:6–9.

19. OYYSC, 12:3–4; 18:40, 46; HCP, 141:9.

20. J. Liu (1963), 171; Buriks (1956); de Bary et al. (1960), 448–50; HCP, 143:1–4; FWCKC, "Tsou-yi," 1:1–16, "Pu-pien," 2:14–15. On the appointment of regional officials see Kracke (1953), 114, 141–42; J. Liu (1957), 120–22; HCP, 154:8–9, 163:9; on the controversy over the corvée see J. Liu (1959), chap. 5.

21. OYYSC, 12:45–46, 72 (cf. HCP, 144:4).

22. J. Liu (1957), 112–13; HCP, 145:8–11, 146:6.

23. JLKY, 1:14–16, 2:9–11; see also chaps. 7 and 10 below.

24. HCP, 141:12–13, 144:5, 146:21, 154:5–6, 8–9; FWCKC, "Tsou-yi," 1:18–24, 42–44, WHTK, 39:375.

25. OYYSC, 12:1, 7; HCP, 141:3–5; see also chap. 9 below.

26. FWCKC, "Tsou-yi," 1:47–50; HCP, 141:12–13, 146:12–13, 151:23–24; OYYSC, 12:48–49, 89, 99–100.

27. HCP, 155:4, 13–16, 157:7, 160:9 (cf. SSCW, 11:2–3; THPL, 13:1–2).

28. HCP, 148:8, 151:18, 156:3–4; OYYSC, 13:63–134, 14:1–18 (cf. HCP, 154:12–13).

29. OYYSC, 14:14–16 (cf. HCP, 156:3–6), 18:64, 200; chap. 9 below.

30. HCP, chaps. 142–46; SS, chap. 11; OYYSC, 4:63–64, 72–73 (cf. HCP, 139:1–5, 140:7–8, 141:2–3, 148:13, 188:9–10).

31. OYYSC, 13:8–10.

32. HCP, 142:8–28, 146:10–11; SS, chap. 11.
33. F. C. Wang (Ch'ing), 4:4, 26; HWKC, "Chia-chuan," 13:193 (cf. OYYSC, 4:53, 12:103; HCP, 155:6–8), "Pieh-lu," 20:267, 277.
34. HWKC, "Chia-chuan," 10:196; HCNP, 41–42.
35. HCP, 275:11, a comment by Wang An-shih.
36. OYYSC, 8:47, 12:54–55; TLC, 15:3–6; JLKY, 1:16; HCP, 143:24–26, 144:10–12, 146:1–4, 11, 14; 154:5–6; SSCW, 9:10; LCML, 8:1–2; SJYS, 4:145–47; HCPPM, 40:2–4; FWCKC, 7:4, "Tsou-yi," 2:30–35; SLYY, 10:10; KTL, 7.
37. HCP, 148–6; SSCW, 10:3 (cf. J. Liu (1957), 26; Kracke (1953), 130 n43).
38. OYYSC, 3:22; de Bary et al. (1960), 446–48; J. Liu (1957); HCP, 148:6–8.
39. The eunuch was Lan Yüan-chen, whose biography in SS, chap. 467, does not mention this episode. It may be found in OYYSC, 18:18–41 (which includes two draft biographies of Ou-yang originally from the Veritable Record), and in JLKY, 1:27–28.
40. HCP, 150:13–14; OYYSC, 8:48, 14:20, 24; HCPPM, 37:23–24; SSPM, 29:6. Hsia Sung later made another vicious accusation against Fu Pi and Shih Chieh, though Shih was dead at the time; for details, see J. Liu (1963), 179.
41. FCHKC, 17:14; JLKY, 1:27–28; HCP, 150:12, 151:9.
42. HCP, 150:30–32, 152:7–11.
43. LCML, 8:1–2; SJYS, 4:145–47.
44. HCP, 153:2–4; HCPPM, 38:9–11; OYYSC, 6:66, 8:61; YCYH, 4:9; J. Liu (1958).
45. HCP, 153:4.
46. HCP, 154:5–9; SSCW, 10:4.
47. HCPPM, 38:15–21; CTYL, 129:4–5; CTCS, 62:27-28.

CHAPTER FIVE

1. J. Liu (1957), 126; de Bary et al. (1960), 446.
2. FWCKC, 8:24.
3. SS, chap. 284; JKLY, 2:35.
4. SS, chap. 269.
5. HCP, 48:6; SSCW, 10:3; J. Liu (1957), 126.
6. SWC, 45:8–15; HNWC, 18:6–7; HCP, 135:4–5, 154:5–9, 157:10; CCTY, 76:1–4; KSC, 31:1–9.
7. De Bary et al. (1960), 446–47 (cf. OYYSC, 3:22–23; HCP, 148:6–9; J. Liu (1959a)).
8. OYYSC, 12:103; HCP, 155:6–8; SWC, 46:7–10; CCTY, 76:4–10; see also OYYSC, 4:53; FWCKC, "Pao-hsien-chi," 5:23–24, "Tsou-yi," 2:30–35; HCP, 143:24–26, 146:1–4, 150:5–10, 15, 155:8.
9. HWTS, chap. 35.

10. OYYSC, 13:37–38; see also 8:61; PSLH, 2:19.
11. FWCKC, *"Pao-hsien-chi,"* 5:25.
12. HHCY, 50:10.
13. J. Liu (1959), 7–10.
14. WKWCC, 71:8–9 (cf. CCTY, 76:10–14, 21–23).
15. HHC, 13:6–8.
16. CCTPWC, 4:58–59.
17. PKTY, 1:9, cf. HCP, 172:5; HWKC, *"Chia-chuan,"* 13:193–96; CCTY, 76:4–5.
18. CCTY, 76:16–18, see also 20; TTSL, 71:9; J. Liu (1960); Toyama (1950).
19. HHCY, 47:15; SPLC, 2:1; THPL, 14:7; KSYL, 3:5–6; F. C. Wang (Ch'ing), 4:17; cf. G. W. Wang (1963).
20. SWC, 83:6–9; Teng (1943), 500–505.
21. JCSP, 4th series, 14:5.
22. HCP, 118:9–10, 26:12; CCTY, 18:6–9; KSYL, 3:5–6; OYYSC, 18:46; LCC (Su), 36:1–2.
23. PKTY, 1:10, 2:5.
24. HLYL, 14:1; HWKC, 1:10–11.
25. F. C. Wang (Ch'ing), 4:17, 14:12–13.
26. OYYSC, 10:99.
27. LCC, 24:17.
28. HCP, 184:3.
29. HCP, 163:16 (cf. SS, chap. 302), 194:2–5; HHCY, 47:15–16; J. Liu (1962), 144.
30. LCC, 18:17–18; HCP, 163:13.
31. HCP, 166:1, 6–9 (cf. CCTY, 76:10–11).
32. HCP, 191:15, 192:3–4, 194:2–5; HHCY, 47:15–16.
33. OYYSC, 12:115 (cf. HCP, 172:3, 179:17; Wen (1965)).
34. HWKC, 9:151–52; HHCY, 47:15–17; J. Liu (1962), 144.
35. F. C. Wang (Ch'ing), 4:24–25; M. Ch'ien (1952), 1:59–62.

CHAPTER SIX

1. HWKC, *"Yi-shih,"* 20:281; OYYSC, 10:102–3, 12:14–15; MC, 2:1–2.
2. OYYSC, 11:6, 18:12, 20, 27, 59; SHY:CK, 64:3846; MC, 2:1–5; SJYS, 8:346–47; HYTL, 18; CSSC, 4.
3. OYYSC, 10:102–3, 18:12.
4. FCL, 32:38; SJYS, 8:357; Tanaka (1953); S. Hu (1921), 3:909–10; MC, 2:1–5; OYYSC, 10:102–3, 11:6, 18:12, 59; CSSC, 4.
5. MC, 2:1–5.
6. HCP, 157:3; WLCC, 9:81–82; PSLH, 3:24; MC, 2:1–5; HTL, 2:11; OYNP (Yang), 12–13; SS, chap. 379; SHY:CK, 64:3846.
7. SSCW, 3:8; HTL, 1:4; SWC, 148:13 (cf. CHTC, 8:6; MSYTL, 4:11); HCP, 163:12–13; J. Liu (1962), 140; LCC, *"Fu-lu,"* 9–10.

8. SHY:CK, 64:3846; HCP, 157:3; OYYSC, 1:17–20, 18:36, 42, 47.

9. OYYSC, 5:36–37, 10:107; YCFC, 6:16–17.

10. SS, chap. 319.

11. HCP, 176:18; OYYSC, 14:20, 24, 18:20–21, 36.

12. MC, 2:9–10.

13. HCP, 176:18, 19, 22, 204:12; OYYSC, 2:19.

14. HCP, 163:13, 177:17–18, 178:4–11, 180:2–5, 18–19, 184:3, 191:15, 192:3–4; SS, chap. 285; OYYSC, 12:110–12; SSCW, 4:10.

15. HCP, 181:2–4, 15–18, 184:7–8, 187:10; SS, chap. 285; OYYSC, 13:8–9; SJYS, 7:251–52.

16. HCP, 185:1.

17. HCP, 187:11, 16, 189:7; OYYSC, 13:21; LCC (Su), 25:7; see also chap. 9 below.

18. FWCKC, *"Pao-hsien-chi,"* 5:19; NKCML, 10:30, 39; SHC, 1:10; PSLH, 2:19; OYYSC, 8:28–29, 11:84, 13:46; also 3:59, 68–69, 4:88 (cf. HCP, 195:2, 201:8); for a negative evaluation, see C. I. Wen (1965).

19. OYYSC, 18:12, 37, 38, 70; HCP, 196:8, 205:5; see also chap. 8 below.

20. HCP, 177:4, 190:13; see also 144:6, 192:19–20; OYYSC, 12:68–69, 13:40–41.

21. OYYSC, 14:20–21.

22. HCP, 208:15–17 (cf. OYYSC, 18:38, 69; PSLH, 3:14); TYL, 16.

23. HCP, 237:8; PSLH, 2:14–15; OYYSC, 13:12–13, 45, 57.

24. WKWCC, 30:1–5.

25. OYYSC, 13:46 (cf. WHTK, 31:292).

26. Cf. WKWCC, 19:6–8, 35:2, 39:7–14, 52:1–6, 53:12–13.

27. CCTPW, 29:493–98; WHTK, 31:292; F. C. Wang (Ch'ing) 4:21–24.

28. Nivison (1960), 177–201.

29. SHC, 5:3.

30. OYYSC, 14:20–21.

31. HCP, 209:9.

32. OYYSC, 18:20.

33. HHCY, 48:9–10.

34. HCP, 190:24, 193:12.

35. HCP, 193:3, 12; SHY:CK, 77:1.

36. HCP, recovered passages from *Yung-lo ta-tien,* 12429:11; LCPC, 2:4.

37. HCP, 182:1–2, 11ff, 183:1–11, 189:16, 191:3, 193:12–15, 194:10, 195:2–7, 201:6; OYYSC, 14:24–26; HWKC, *"Chia-chuan,"* 14:210–13.

38. OYYSC, 14:24–26.

39. HCP, 506:4.

40. HWKC, *"Chia-chuan,"* 14:214; HCP, 199:15–16; OYYSC, 18:69; LCC (Su), 25:7 (cf. CCTY, 9:1–22, 10:1–5).

41. HCP, 201:6; HCPPM, 54:1–4; HWKC, *"Chia-chuan,"* 14:215; SSWCL, 3:1.

42. HCP, 201:6, 16–21, 205:14–15; CCTY, 14:12–16; SSWCL, 3:2–3; SJYS, 8:337; F. C. Wang (Ch'ing), 4:31; MSYTL, 4:12; CTYL, 129:8 (cf. Miyazaki (1953)).

43. HCP, 201:11, 204.21, 205:9–14, 206:18, 207:8–9, 11–22, 208:2, 8–9; HYC, 33:8–14; OYYSC, 14:29–55; HCNP, 30:1; WKWCC, 33:8–9, 34:8–10,

35:2-3; CCTPWC, 24:392-93. For a detailed account of the controversy see HCP, chaps. 205-7; HCPPM, 55:1-16; CCTY, chaps. 89-90; K. Y. Ch'eng (1964).

44. OYNP (Yang), 28; HCP, 207:3-4, 13; OYYSC, 14:29-55; SSWCL, 3:2, 16:4-5; HLYL, 14:2.

45. OYYSC, 10:123, 136-42; 11:1-7, 18:39, 48; HCP, 209:2, 5-6.

46. HCP, 209:6-7.

47. HCP, 166:1 (cf. JCSP, 4th series, 11:8).

48. CHFT, 2:11; SJYS, 8:349; HCP, 209:6, 7; OYYSC, 11:7, 18:54; OYNP (Yang), 30; SHY:CK, 65:27.

49. ECWC, 3:4-5; OYNP (Hua), 3 (cf. ECWC, 4:7-11; CTYL, 127:3).

50. OYYSC, 18:48; TCCS, 3:5; TCML, 1; SHY:CK, 67:6.

51. OYYSC, 5:74-76, 8:68, 11:8-12; YCFC, 9:13-15; MSYTL, 7:7; HCHL, 1:29-30.

52. OYYSC, 11:30-31, 13:58, 60.

53. HCPPM, 69:6.   54. OYYSC, 11:31-32.

55. OYYSC, 11:34-35.   56. OYYSC, 11:35-36.

57. HCP, 209:9; OYYSC, 11:36-40, 18:30, 39.

CHAPTER SEVEN

1. T. H. Ma (1936), 109-10.

2. WHTK, 30:286 (cf. CTYL, 129:7).

3. Pulleyblank (1960).

4. HCP, 192:11.

5. Nivison (1959).

6. H. J. P'i (1923), 47-48; J. Liu (1957), 109-10.

7. OYYSC, 3:98-99 (cf. 13:10); HCP, 184:14-15; SS, chap. 432; WHTK, 46:431-32; T. H. Chao (1953).

8. SYHA, 1:25-31; CTYL, 129:6-7; de Bary et al. (1960), 439-41.

9. OYYSC, 9:109, 4:17-18 (cf. HCP, 149:11, 186:12; SS, chap. 432; WHTK, 42:395; JLKY, 1:14-16).

10. SYHA, 4:67.

11. CTYL, 129:7.

12. OYYSC, 13:15-16 (cf. HCP, 191:13-14; CTYL, 129:6).

13. OYYSC, 8:46-48 (cf. OYNP (Hua), 8; SYHA, 2:96-104; SS, chap. 432).

14. OYYSC, 9:62 (cf. T. H. Ma (1936), 109-11; OYNP (Hua), 41; OYYSC, 8:64; SYHA, 4:67).

15. OYYSC, 8:70-71.

16. OYYSC, 3:29, 36, 5:73, 18:9.

17. OYYSC, 6:10.

18. OYYSC, 5:67-68 (cf. LCC (Su), 22:9; Y. T. Lin (1947), 291).

19. OYYSC, 5:50-52.

20. SS, chap. 319 (cf. OYYSC, 18:36); OYYSC, 8:72.
21. OYYSC, 1:11, 9:63, 14:134.
22. OYYSC, 8:45–46.
23. OYYSC, 3:33 (cf. preface by Su Shih (Su Tung-p'o), also 18:3, 9, 54).
24. OYYSC, 5:67 (cf. 5:73; M. Ch'ien (1953) 1:11–12), 6:17; see also 2:52.
25. OYYSC, 13:35–36 (cf. 5:67–68, 14:57–60; OYNP (Hua), 40–41; T. H. Ma (1936), 110–11).
26. OYYSC, 6:12–13 (cf. Uno (1942)), 7:69.
27. OYYSC, 3:28–30, 6:16, 7:75–78, 8:33–35, 9:62 (cf. H. J. P'i (1923), 47; T. H. Ma (1936), 124; Fung (1948), 138–42, 166).
28. OYYSC, 5:60–61.
29. OYYSC, 3:33, 5:73.
30. MTHH, 1:1–2; HHCY, 47:10, 50:11; SYHA, 4:66.
31. OYYSC, 14:124.   32. HCP, 135:9–10.
33. SYHA, 4:66.   34. OYYSC, 6:2–4.
35. CS, 2:8; YKSC, 2:32.
36. OYYSC, 5:69–70 (cf. J. J. Y. Liu (1963), 67), 7:77, 81.
37. SSWCL, 10:1; SYJS, 6:209–10, 8:309, 344–48, 354; HCL, 8:1; Lin (1947), 183; CSSC, 3–4; MSYTL, 4:5; MTHH, 8:3–4; TCML, 1; Tanaka (1953); see also chaps. 5 and 6 above.
38. CTCS, 59:4; CTWC, 12:447.
39. OYYSC, 2:4, 5:52, 8:64, 70–71.
40. HHCY, 39:14; T. H. Ch'ien (Ch'ing), 6:142; Takeuchi (1954).
41. LCC (Su), 37:9–10.
42. Cf. Sun (1953).

CHAPTER EIGHT

1. Demiéville (1961), 178–81 (cf. Nivison (1966)).
2. Y. F. Chin (1957), 233.   3. I. C. Y. Hsü (1959), 138n5.
4. OYYSC, 8:45.   5. OYYSC, 3:32–34, 36, 9:13–14.
6. OYYSC, 3:35–36; see also 2:4, 3:31–32.
7. OYYSC, 5:71–72; see also 8:45.
8. OYYSC, 15:49–50 (cf. SS, chap. 319; Needham (1956), 2:394).
9. OYYSC, 15:50.
10. OYYSC, 14:57–60 (cf. WHTK, 207:1710–11; HCP, 134:18; OYNP (Hua), 7); Teng and Biggerstaff (1950), 18–19.
11. WHTK, 174:1509.
12. HCP, 193:5; SHY:CJ, 2234.
13. L. S. Yang (1961), 46–68.
14. OYYSC, 12:108–9 (cf. HCP, 282:6–7; L. S. Yang (1961), 45–65; Gardner (1961), 88–94).
15. HCP, 190:16.
16. Franke (1961), 116.

17. OYYSC, 5:74.
18. SLYY, 4:3–4; MCML, 8:10 (cf. HCP, 192:2; Y. F. Chin (1957), 104).
19. OYYSC, 4:25–26, 8:60 (cf. HNWC, 28:40; OYNP (Hua), 9; MSTYL, 6:3).
20. OYSSC, 17:43.
21. OYSSC, 13:35.
22. SHY:CJ, 2259; HCP, 263:21; Y. F. Chin (1957), 136–37.
23. L. S. Yang (1961), 49; Y. F. Chin (1957), 104–5; M. S. Wang (Ch'ing), 93:4.
24. Y. F. Chin (1957), 104–5.
25. Pulleyblank (1961), 149–50.
26. Y. F. Chin (1957), 104–5, de Bary et al. (1960), 493.
27. L. S. Yang (1961), 43; Pulleyblank (1961), 157.
28. G. W. Wang (1958); Y. F. Chin (1957), 106.
29. Y. F. Chin (1957), 137 (cf. FTTC, 49:364, 474; SSCKL, 49:870; JCSP, 1st series, 4:38, 3d series, 7:65, 9:81).
30. Gardner (1961), 12–14; Y. F. Chin (1957), 136–38, 229–30; M. S. Wang (Ch'ing), 51:8, 93:4; I. C. Liu (1948), 177; J. Liu (1959a); L. S. Yang (1961), 52; I. C. Liu (1948), 177–80.
31. G. W. Wang (1962).
32. L. S. Yang (1961), 52.
33. *Ibid.*; I. C. Liu (1948), 177–80.
34. Y. F. Chin (1957), 136–38.
35. L. S. Yang (1961), 49; Pulleyblank (1961); de Bary et al. (1960), 448–50, 493–94.
36. OYYSC, 3:10–11, 7:53–61 (cf. LCC, 17:13–15).
37. OYYSC, 3:12–13; see also 3:16–17, 7:54–57, 61–62.
38. Cf. de Bary et al. (1960), 503–9.
39. OYYSC, 6:8, 8:76 (cf. HWKC, 1:11–14, 8:120, 10:153–55; PSLY, 2:13; Aoyama (1951), 19–37; Sudō (1950), 9–76).
40. Makino (1949); Shimizu (1942).
41. CYC, 13:1–8 (cf. CCTPWC, 17:257–59; CCLHSC, 15:11–14; WHTK, 207:1705; CS, 2:1; K. T. P'an (1933); T. H. Yang (1941)).
42. H. C. W. Liu (1959), (1959a).

CHAPTER NINE

1. Translated as "On Parties" in de Bary et al. (1960), 446–48; see also 441–45.
2. NKCML, 10:39; PLHH, 2:19.
3. De Bary et al. (1960), 441–45.
4. OYYSC, 5:60.
5. OYYSC, 6:12–13 (cf. H. J. P'i (1923), 47–48; T. H. Ma (1936), 111; Morohashi (1926), 464–65; Morohashi (1948), 145–60); see also 3:18–19, 7:49.

6. OYYSC, 6:15-16 (cf. Nishi (1951)).
7. OYYSC, 6:12-13 (cf. Uno (1942)); see also 11:30-31, 35, 13:58-60.
8. SS, chap. 319; JCSP, 1st series, 4:31.
9. OYYSC, 7:65.   10. OYYSC, 5:85.
11. OYYSC, 1:13.   12. OYYSC, 5:89.
13. OYYSC, 3:24-25; for a partial translation see Locke (1951), part 1, p. 94.
14. FWCKC, 5:4; HCP, 118:10; J. Liu (1957) (cf. de Bary et al. (1960), 448-50).
15. OYYSC, 3:24-25; see also 5:87-88. Wang An-shih later argued the same point: WLCC, 39:83 (cf. de Bary et al. (1960), 468-74).
16. See chap. 4 above.
17. OYYSC, 8:72, 5:34-35, 13:46 (cf. HCP, 195:2), see also 3:59, 68-69, 4:88, 8:17.
18. OYYSC, 7:49 (cf. HCP, 136:9-10).
19. OYYSC, 12:68-69 (cf. HCP, 144:6).
20. OYYSC, 13:40-41 (cf. HCP, 192:19-20).
21. OYYSC, 3:24, 26-27, 8:29; see also 8:46-48.
22. OYYSC, 8:28-29 (cf. HCP, 201:8).
23. OYYSC, 18:32 (cf. HCP, 187:11); see also 18:21-23.
24. OYYSC, 18:32.
25. SS, chap. 319 (cf. J. Liu (1959a), 176); CSPPL, 14:15-30, 15:11-16.
26. OYYSC, 6:13-14 (cf. HCP, 187:7).
27. OYYSC, 2:12.
28. OYYSC, 3:69, 4:40-41, 81, 14:85.
29. OYYSC, 3:58, 4:14-15, 52, 66 (cf. HCP, 143:27).
30. OYYSC, 4:96 (cf. HCP, 120:15; SSCW, 7:4-5).
31. OYYSC, 4:22.   32. OYYSC, 4:81.
33. OYYSC, 4:4, 59, 72.   34. OYYSC, 5:27.
35. OYYSC, 3:46-49.   36. OYYSC, 5:25.
37. OYYSC, 4:52, 63 (cf. HCP, 140:8, 148:13).
38. OYYSC, 2:12.
39. *Ch'ien Han shu* (*Standard History of the Former Han*), chap. 89 (cf. J. Liu (1959a)).

CHAPTER TEN

1. For translations of Ou-yang's works into Western languages, see Davidson (1957), 437-40; for an example of translations into vernacular Chinese, see K. C. Huang (1958).
2. Hightower (1962), 84.
3. T. P. K'o (1934), 97-99; K. Liang (1938), 39-51, 74-77.
4. OYYSC, preface by Su Shih; SS, chap. 319; MTHH, 8:3 (cf. HHCY, 4:7).
5. Rexroth (1955), 58; OYYSC, 7:31.

6. *Ibid.*, 57; OYYSC, 2:64. 7. *Ibid.*, 59; OYYSC, 2:77–78.

8. *Ibid.*, 61; OYYSC, 15:12. 9. *Ibid.*, 60; OYYSC, 2:77.

10. OYYSC, 15:27; my translation. 11. Lin (1947), 224.

12. OYYSC, 14:111–19. Cf. T. P. K'o (1934), 6–7; K. Liang (1938), 39–51, 74–77.

13. Unpublished paper by Adele A. Rickett of the University of Pennsylvania, and my own interpretation as well.

14. J. J. Y. Liu (1963), 63.

15. OYYSC, 1:16, 2:52, 14:114; SJYS, 4:148.

16. OYYSC, 4:77, 9:11, 14:114.

17. KHCW, 18:1387.

18. OYYSC, 14:114; see also 14:97 (cf. WHTK, 234:1868–69; SS, chap. 443; S. Y. Kuo (1934), 1:397–401; Y. I. Hu (1930), 43–48).

19. OYYSC, 4:76; see also 5:64.

20. J. J. Y. Liu (1963), 30.

21. Hightower (1962), 90 (cf. MTHH, 8:34; K. C. Huang (1958), preface, p. 3).

22. *Ibid.*, 91–92.

23. K. C. Huang (1958), 13–20; Tanaka (1953); SJYS, 8:348.

24. Tanaka (1953); Y. T. Lin (1947), 154.

25. TH, preface, p. 12 (cf. H. J. P'i (Ch'ing), "*Shih-ching*," 65).

26. Hightower (1962), 28–29.

27. Birch (1965), 368; OYYSC, 15:3.

28. Waley (1925), 99–102; OYYSC, 15:1–2.

29. Locke (1951).

30. Hightower (1962), 72–74 (cf. Pulleyblank (1959); M. Ch'ien (1957); C. S. Chin (1963)); SHY:CJ, 2247.

31. SS, chap. 293 (cf. HCC; SSWCL, 7:5, 15:5–6; SSCW, 2:9; T. P. K'o (1934), 17–20).

32. SS-R, chap. 440 (cf. HTHSC; NKCML, 10:245–46; MHPT, 9:18; JCSP, 2d series, 9:12; Chin (1963), 80–89).

33. SWC, 85:12–13, 112:14–16 (cf. MTCC; SS, chap. 442; FWCKC, 6:10–11; SSWCL, 15:5–6, 16:3; THPL, 3:6–7; CWCW, 4:32; Locke (1951), part 2, pp. 36–59; C. S. Chin (1963), 89–95).

34. OYYSC, 9:17–18 (cf. Nivison (1960), 177–78; JCSP, 2d series, 9:88–89).

35. OYYSC, 4:15–17, 6:40–41, 50–51 (cf. Locke (1951), part 2, p. 39ff).

36. SSWCL, 8:5; SPLC, 5:3.

37. HHCY, 49:10 (cf. MKHH, 2:2; SPLC-P, 5:2; HLYL, 5:10; S. M. Lü (1931), 8–15).

38. SS, chap. 295 (cf. HNWC); MTHH, 5:1 (cf. HNWC, 28:26–27); OYYSC, 4:25, 9:13–15 (cf. FWCKC (preface to HNWC), 6:10–11).

39. SSWCHL, 15:2.

40. OYYSC, 6:61.

41. Chin. Lit. (1961), 54–55.

42. HLYL, 5:10; S. M. Lü (1931), 8–15.
43. JCSP, 5th series, 8:4 (cf. OYYSC, 18:58; CWCW, 3:22).
44. OYYSC, 5:61; see also 3:36, 87, 6:61, 8:53, 79; NCCT, 2; CTCW, 7:1; MTHH, 5:3.
45. KTL, 8 (cf. OYYSC, 5:44).
46. Nivison (1959), 8–9; OYYSC, 6:5; T. C. Ch'en (1945), 7; Locke (1951), part 2, pp. 34–36.
47. HCP, 108:1.
48. HCP, 101:1, 9–11, 109:1, 11 (cf. SS, chap. 311; FWCKC, "Nien-pu," 10), 121:6.
49. HCP, 147:9–11 (cf. OYYSC, 9:72, 12:76–80; WHTK, 31:290; FWCKC, 9:1–2).
50. HCP, 147:10–11; OYYSC, 9:72.
51. HCP, 155:4; WHTK, 31:290.
52. HCP, 155:4, 158:4–6 (cf. LCC, 20:11–12, "Fu-lu," 12).
53. HCP, 164:3–5, 190:20–21 (cf. SS, chap. 155; JLKY, 1:14–16, 2:9–11).
54. HCP, 185:1; OYYSC, 6:17–19, 9:47.
55. CS (Yüeh), 9:2; SJYS, 6:232–33.
56. HCP, 185:1; SS, chap. 319; CCTPWC, 41:715–16; CSSC, 3–4; Tanaka (1953).
57. OYYSC, 18:67 (cf. LCC (Su), 22:1–2; Y. T. Lin (1947), 28, 38–40, 53).
58. OYYSC, 18:6, 36, 44–48, 53, 67 (cf. CCTPWC, 41:715–16; SS, chap. 319; WHTK, 31:290; HCP, 185:1).
59. OYYSC, 9:15 (cf. THPL, 4:1–2).
60. MCPT, 9:2–3 (cf. Tanaka (1953), KHCW, 20:1514).
61. OYYSC, 13:34; 18:58–59; YFLK, 18:3, 51:9; TKNP (Yang), 2–4, 13, 19, 22, 25; LCC (Su), 22:1–2; KSC, 12:741; PLKT, 2:2.
62. YFLK, 15:8; see also 15:10, 18.
63. YFLK, 16:5–6 (cf. SSWCHL, 14:2; MTHH, 6:1; JCSP, 3d series, 1:9, 1:18).
64. OYYSC, 13:12; see also 2:26, 47, 13:45, 16:102, 17:16 (cf. HCP, 190:3; WLCC, 2:28, 3:55; NKCML, 3:54).
65. WLCC, 9:24–25 (cf. OYYSC, 16:127–28, 18:2–3).
66. KHCW, 18:1381; OYYSC, 18:5–6; see also 13:40, 14:133, 16:89; SSWCHL, 15:24; CYC, 1:2, HCP, 192:5–6; LCC, 39:58; LCC (Su), 22:1–2; Y. T. Lin (1947), 35–36, 42, 183.
67. CTYL, 139:10–12 (cf. HLYL, 14:4–5, 15:5; HHCY, 47:8–10, 50:1–4).

CHAPTER ELEVEN

1. De Bary et al. (1960), 441–45.
2. OYYSC, 3:2, 5:10–20.
3. OYYSC, 10:1–95.
4. OYYSC, 6:20–24, 37, 7:13–14, 8:86–87.

5. OYYSC, 5:70; see also 12:65–66, 117–18 (cf. HCP, 145:20–21).
6. For this and the following quotations, see OYYSC, 6:20–24, 8:86–87.
7. OYYSC, 13:1–6, 14:24.
8. OYYSC, 14:124.
9. OYYSC, 2:55, 56; see also 1:2, 2:16.
10. OYYSC, 8:31–32.
11. OYYSC, 5:29.
12. K. Ch'en (1964), 213, 258–96.
13. OYYSC, 5:29.
14. OYYSC, 4:37.
15. OYYSC, 4:4, 67.
16. OYYSC, 1:13, 3:20–21, 4:93, 7:63, 8:2, 12–13 (cf. FWCKC, 8:8–9).
17. OYYSC, 4:12–14; SCC, 21:35.
18. MHPTCC, 1:418–19, item 205; L. S. Yang (1957).
19. OYYSC, 5:22, 14:22, 18:70; HCP, 106:14.
20. Nivison (1959), 5–9 (cf. de Bary et al. (1960), 438–45).
21. PSLH, 2:19 (cf. OYYSC, 1:14, 4:83).
22. De Bary et al. (1960), 441–42 (cf. MTHH, 11:3).
23. De Bary et al. (1960), 442.
24. De Bary et al. (1960), 445; OYYSC, 3:18–20; SS, chap. 319; CTYL, 126:25–34; MTHH, 11:3.
25. OYYSC, 3:20–21.
26. SYYS, 8:351; HLYL, 1:8; PSLH, 1:6; WWCKC, 26:24; OYNP (Yang), 43–44; SJYS, 8:358–59.
27. OYYSC, 5:56, 18:72–74.
28. OYYSC, 1:10, 3:84, 13:112, 14:131; OYNP (Hua), 12.
29. OYYSC, 5:48–49 (cf. Birch (1965), 366).
30. OYYSC, 5:45–50.
31. OYYSC, 1:13, 2:2, 3:6 (cf. CCTPWC, 56:912–13), 7:24.
32. OYYSC, 5:30, 8:64, 14:74–75.
33. OYYSC, 5:75; see also 5:60–61, 9:39–40.
34. OYYSC, 6:26.
35. OYYSC, 2:48.
36. OYYSC, 3:100, 101, 4:44, 14:81; TCPL, 3:8.
37. OYYSC, 3:101; see also 3:57, 8:16.
38. OYYSC, 4:15.   39. OYYSC, 4:23, 6:25.
40. OYYSC, 4:24.   41. OYYSC, 5:66.
42. S. Hu (1921), 4:105–18.
43. SSWCL, 18:7; CHTC, 10:4; SPLC, 6:3; PSLH, 1:7, 2:17; see also SJYS, 8:359–60; FTTC, 49:364, 474; SSCKL, 49:869–72.
44. LHAPC, 6:1, OYYSC, 18:72–74; SSWCL, 16:2; SSCW, 10:7.
45. LCC (Su), 24:8.
46. PSLH, 1:6; see also SJYS, 8:359–60.
47. MSYTL, 7:7, 10:2; SJYS, 8:257.
48. YKSC, 3:53–55.

49. K. Ch'en (1964), 395; de Bary et al. (1960), 525–81; Fung (1948), 294–318.

50. For favorable comment on Ou-yang, see CYC, 11:3; OYYSC, preface by Su Shih; Takeuchi (1934), 15; Chu Hsi's own comment in CTWC, 22:447. For Chu Hsi's criticism of Ou-yang, see CTYL, 126:31–32, 137:25.

51. CTYL, 126:34.

CHAPTER TWELVE

1. PSLH, 2:14–15.
2. CCTPWC, 56:912–13.
3. SYHA, 4:44–81.
4. SS, chap. 319 (cf. YFLK, 11:2–4, 51:2); CTYL, 126:25–34.
5. Cf. HHCY, 39:14.
6. OYYSC, 18:39.

GLOSSARY AND BIBLIOGRAPHY

GLOSSARY

The Glossary is divided into two sections, one giving Chinese characters for the Chinese names and terms used in the text, the other giving Chinese characters for the authors' names, for titles, and in some cases for editions of Chinese- and Japanese-language works listed in the Bibliography. These works are listed alphabetically by the abbreviations used in the Notes; primary and secondary sources are listed separately.

CHINESE NAMES AND TERMS

Chang Fang-p'ing　張方平

Chang Hsüeh-ch'eng　章學誠

Chang Hui-yen　張惠言

Chang Te-hsiang　章得象

Ch'ang-li　昌黎

Chao I　趙翼

Chao Kai　趙槩

Chen-tsung　眞宗

Ch'en Chih-chung　陳執中

cheng-t'ung　正統

Ch'eng Hao　程灝

Ch'eng I　程頤

Chia Ch'ang-ch'ao　賈昌朝

Chiang Chih-chi　蔣之奇

Chien-yü　鑒聿

Ch'ien Wei-yen　錢惟演

Ch'in Kuan　秦觀

Ch'ing-li　慶曆

ch'ing-tz'u　青詞

Chu Hsi　朱熹

Ch'uchow　滁州

Ch'ung-wen tsung mu　崇文總目

Fan Ch'un-jen　范純仁

Fan Chung-yen　范仲淹

Fu Pi　富弼

Fuyang　阜陽

Han Ch'i　韓琦

Hanyang　漢陽

Han Yü　韓愈

Hangchow　杭州

Ho-tung　河東

Hsi Hsia　西夏

Hsi-k'un　西崑

Hsia Sung　夏竦

199

Hsiang-kuo-ssu 相國寺

hsien *and* tan 閒淡

hsin-li 性理

Hsü Yen 胥偃

Hsüeh K'uei 薛奎

Hua-chien 花間

Huchow 湖州

Hu Yüan 胡瑗

Hui-ch'in 慧勤

I-ling 夷陵

Jen-tsung 仁宗

Kaifeng 開封

Kao Jo-no 高若訥

Li Shang-yin 李商隱

Li Ting 李定

Lin-an (Hangchow) 臨安

Liu-i-shih-hua 六一詩話

Liu K'ai 柳開

Liu K'ang 劉沆

Liu Tsung-yüan 柳宗元

Liu Yung 柳永

Loyang 洛陽

Luling 廬陵

Lü I-chien 呂夷簡

Lü Kung-chu 呂公著

Lü Hui-ch'ing 呂惠卿

Mei Yao-ch'en 梅堯臣

Mien-chou 綿州

Mu Hsiu 穆脩

Ou-yang Hsiu (*courtesy name* Yung-shu) 歐陽修 (永叔)

Ou-yang Hsiu ti chih-hsüeh yü ts'ung-cheng 歐陽修的治學與從政

Pao Cheng 包拯

P'eng Ssu-yung 彭思永

Pi Yen 秘演

Pochow 亳州

P'u-i 濮議

shen *and* yüan 深遠

Shih Chieh 石介

Shih Yen-nien (*courtesy name* Man-ch'ing) 石延年 (曼卿)

Soochow 蘇州

Ssu-ma Kuang 司馬光

Su An-shih 蘇安世

Su Ch'e 蘇轍

Su Hsün 蘇洵

Su Shih (*courtesy name* Tung-p'o) 蘇軾 (東坡)

Su Shun-ch'in 蘇舜卿

Suichow 隨州

Sun Fu 孫復

Sun Ho 孫何

tao-hsüeh chia 道學家

T'eng Tsung-liang 滕宗諒

Ting Wei 丁謂

Ts'ai Hsiang 蔡襄

Tseng Kung 曾鞏

Tseng Kung-lian 曾公亮

Tseng Pu 曾布

tsu 族

Tu Yen 杜衍

tz'u 詞

Wang An-shih 王安石

Wang Chao-ming 王昭明

Wang Ch'in-jo 王欽若

Wang I-jou 王益柔

Wang Kung-ch'en 王拱辰

Wang Lun 王倫

Wang Tan 王旦

Wang Yang-ming 王陽明

Wang Yu-ch'eng 王禹偁

wei 緯

Wei-yen 惟儼

wen-fu 文賦

Wu Ch'ung 吳充

Yangchow 揚州

Yang Shih	楊時	Yingchow	潁州
Yeh Meng-te	葉夢得	Ying-tsung	英宗
Yeh Shih	葉適	Yü Ching	余靖
Yen Shu	晏殊	Yung-cheng	雍正
Yin Shu	尹洙		

CHINESE- AND JAPANESE-LANGUAGE WORKS

Primary Sources (Chinese)

CCC	滁州志 (1879)
CCLHSC	李覯，直講李先生集 (四部叢刊)
CCTPWC	蘇軾，經進東坡文集事略 (1957)
CCTSC	晁公武，郡齋讀書志 (四部叢刊)
CCTY	趙汝愚，國朝諸臣奏議 (明刊)
CHFT	高晦叟，珍席放談 (叢書集成)
CHTC	吳處厚，青箱雜記 (涵芬樓)
(CIT)	(正誼堂本)
CPTC	周煇，清波雜志 (裨海)
CS (Wang)	王得臣，麈史 (涵芬樓)
CS (Yüeh)	岳柯，桯史 (裨海)
CSPPLC	陳仁錫，經世八編類集 (1626)
CSSC	錢世昭，錢氏私誌 (學海類編)
CSTP	王昶，金石粹編 (淸刊)
CTCS	朱熹，朱子全書 (1713)
CTCW	何薳，春渚紀聞 (涵芬樓)
(CTTS)	(昭代叢書)
CTCW	朱熹，朱子文集 (叢書集成)
CTYL	──，朱子語類 (1876)
CTYY	周密，齊東野語 (涵芬樓)
CWCW (Chu)	朱弁，曲洧舊聞 (叢書集成)
CWCW (Li)	李心傳，舊聞證誤 (榕園叢書)
CYC	蘇洵，嘉祐集 (四部叢刊)
ECWC	程顥，程頤，二程文集 (正誼堂)
FCHK	范純仁，范忠宣公集 (1910)
FCHT	袁褧，楓窗小牘 (裨海)
FCL	元懷 (輾然子)，附掌錄 (說郛)
FTTC	志磐，佛祖統紀 (大正大藏經卷49)
FWCKC	范仲淹，范文正公集 (1910)

HCC 王禹偁，小畜集（叢書集成）

HCHL 王明清，揮麈後錄（四部叢刊）

HCL 趙德麟，侯鯖錄（裨海）

HCNP 楊希閔，韓忠獻公年譜（1879）

HCP 李燾，續資治通鑑長編（1881又1962輯永樂大典本）

HCPPM 楊仲良，通鑑長編紀事本末

(HFL) （涵芬樓）

HHC 秦觀，淮海集（四部叢刊）

HHCY 葉適，習學紀言（1885）

(HHLP) （學海類編）

HLYL 羅大經，鶴林玉露（涵芬樓）

HNWC 尹洙、河南文集（四部叢刊）

HTHSC 柳開，河東先生集（四部叢刊）

HTL 李元綱，厚德錄（裨海）

HWKC 韓琦，韓魏公集（叢書集成）

HWTS 歐陽修，新五代史（四部備要）

HYC 王珪，華陽集（武英殿聚珍全書）

HYTL 趙葵，行營雜錄（歷代小史）

ICFC 宜昌府志（1866）

ICHC 宜昌縣志（1931）

JCSP 洪邁，容齋隨筆（四部叢刊）

JLKY 田況，儒林公議（裨海）

(KHCPTS) （國學基本叢書）

KHCW 王應麟，困學紀聞（國學基本叢書）

KSC (Chang) 張耒，柯山集（叢書集成）

KSC (Liu) 劉敞，公是集（武英殿聚珍全書）

KSYL 楊時，龜山先生語錄（四部叢刊）

KTL 范公稱，過庭錄（裨海）

(KYTS) （廣雅叢書）

LCC (Chang) 張方平，樂全集（四庫珍本）

LCC (Su) 蘇轍，欒城集（四部叢刊）

LCIY 蘇籀，欒城先生遺言（叢書集成）

LCML 費袞，梁谿漫錄（涵芬樓）

LCPC 蘇轍，龍川別志（涵芬樓）

LHAPC 陸游，老學庵筆記（涵芬樓）

LLHC 廬陵縣志（1920）

(LTHS) （歷代小史）

MC 王銍，默記（涵芬樓）

MCML 張邦基，墨莊漫錄（裨海）

MCYHL	朱熹，名臣言行錄 (1661)
(MHCH)	(墨海金壺)
MHPT	沈括，夢溪筆談 (裨海)
MHPTCC	——，夢溪筆談校證 (1955)
MKHH	彭乘，墨客揮犀 (裨海)
MSTYL	王闢之，澠水燕談錄 (涵芬樓)
MTCC	穆修，穆參軍集 (四部叢刊)
MTHH	陳善，捫蝨新話 (涵芬樓)
NCCT	南窗紀談 (墨海金壺)
NKCML	吳曾，能改齋漫錄 (叢書集成)
OYNP (Hu)	胡柯，廬陵歐陽文忠公年譜 (歐陽永叔集)
OYNP (Hua)	華孳亨，增訂歐陽文忠公年譜 (昭代叢書)
OYNP (Yang)	楊希閔，歐陽文忠公年譜 (1879)
OYYSC	歐陽修，歐陽永叔集 (國學基本叢書)
(PH)	(裨海)
PKTY	包拯，包公奏議 (奧雅堂叢書)
PLKT	陳長方，步里客談 (墨海金壺)
PSLH	葉夢得，避暑錄話 (涵芬樓)
SCC	隨州志 (1869)
(SF)	(說郛)
SHC	葉適，水心集 (四部備要)
SHSC	蘇舜欽，蘇學士集 (四部叢刊)
SHY	宋會要輯稿 (1936)
SHY : CJ :	——：崇儒
SHY : CK :	——：職官
SHY : HC :	——：選舉
SJYS	丁傳靖，宋人軼事彙編 (1935)
(SKCP)	(四庫珍本)
SLYY	葉夢得，石林燕語 (裨海)
SPLC	潘永因，宋裨類鈔 (1669)
(SPPY)	(四部備要)
(SPTK)	(四部叢刊)
SS	脫脫 (等)，宋史
SSCKL	覺岸，釋氏稽古略 (大正大藏經卷49)
SSCW	司馬光，涑水紀聞 (涵芬樓)
SSHP	柯維祺，宋史新編 (1557)
SSPM	馮琦，宋史紀事本末 (萬有文庫)
SSWCHL	邵博，邵氏聞見後錄 (涵芬樓)
SSWCL	邵伯溫，邵氏聞見錄 (涵芬樓)

STNMCY 蘇金源, 李春圃, 宋代三次農民起義史料彙編(1963)

SWC 呂祖謙, 宋文鑑（四部叢刊）

SYHA 黄宗羲（等）, 宋元學案（萬有文庫）

TCCS 范鎮, 東齋記事（墨海金壺）

TCHKWC 蔡襄, 蔡忠惠公文集（1734）

TCML 曾慥, 東齋漫錄（墨海金壺）

TH 張惠言, 詞選（四部備要）

THPL 魏泰, 東軒筆錄（裨海）

TKNP（Wang）王煥鑣, 曾南豐先生年譜（1943）

TKNP（Yang）楊希閔, 曾文定公年譜（1879）

TLC 石介, 徂徠集（1884）

TPCL 蘇軾, 東坡志林（涵芬樓）

（TSCC）（叢書集成）

TSKY 晁說之, 晁氏客語（叢書集成）

TTSL 王偁, 東都事略（1883）

TYL 龔鼎臣, 東原錄（涵芬樓）

WCKNP 蔡上翔, 王荆公年譜考略（1930 或 1958）

WHTK 馬端臨, 文獻通考（萬有文庫）

WKWCC 司馬光, 温国文正集（四部叢刊）

WLCC 王安石, 王臨川集（萬有文庫）

WLHSC 梅堯臣, 宛陵先生集（四部叢刊）

WWCKC 吳澄, 吳文正公集（1756）

（WYTCCCS）（武英殿聚珍全書）

（WYWK）（萬有文庫）

YCFC 潁州府志（1752）

YCHC 王明淸, 玉照新志（涵芬樓）

YFLK 曾鞏, 元豐類稿（四部叢刊）

YKSC 楊時, 楊龜山集（叢書集成）

（YYTTS）（奧雅堂叢書）

（YYTS）（榕園叢書）

Secondary Sources (Chinese and Japanese)

Aoyama (1951) 青山定雄, "五代宋に於ける江西の新興官僚", 和田博士還曆紀念東洋史論叢, 19-37

T. H. Chao (1953) 趙鐵寒, "宋代州學", 大陸, 1：305-9, 341-43

C. M. Ch'en (1946) 岑仲勉, "元和姓纂四校記", 中央研究院歷史語言研究所專刊29號

T. C. Ch'en (1945) 陳子展, 宋代文學史

Y. H. Ch'en (1957) 陳元暉, 范縝的无神論思想

K. Y. Ch'eng (1964) 程光裕, "北宋臺諫之爭與濮議," 宋史研究集, 2：213-34

M. Ch'ien (1947) 錢穆, 國史大綱

M. Ch'ien (1952) ——, 中國歷代政治得失

M. Ch'ien (1953) ——, 宋明理學概述

M. Ch'ien (1957) ——, "雜論唐代古文運動", 新亞學報, 3：1：123-68

M. Ch'ien (1959) ——, "讀詩經", 新亞學報, 5：1：1-48

T. H. Ch'ien (Ch'ing) 錢大昕, 十駕齋養新錄 (國學基本叢書)

C. S. Chin (1963) 金中樞, "宋代古文運動及發展研究", 新亞學報, 5：2：80-95

C. S. Chin (1964) ——, "北宋科舉制度研究", 新亞學報, 6：1：211-81 又 6：2：165-242

Y. F. Ch'in (1957) 金毓黻, 中國史學史

C. Y. Hsia (1937) 夏君虞, 宋學概要

K. C. Hsiao (1946) 蕭公權, 中國政治思想史

L. J. Hsüeh (1955) 薛礪若, 宋詞通論

S. Hu (1921) 胡適, 胡適文存

Y. I. Hu (1930) 胡雲翼, 宋詩研究

K. C. Huang (1958) 黃公渚, 歐陽修詞選評

Japanese Committee (1961) 日本宋史提要編纂協力委員會, 宋代研究文獻提要

C. I. K'o (1936) 柯昌頤, 王安石評傳

T. P. K'o (1934) 柯敦伯, 宋文學史

S. Y. Kuo (1934) 郭紹虞, 中國文學批評史

C. C. Liang (1920) 梁啓超, 王荊公傳

K. Liang (1938) 梁崑, 宋詩派別論

I. C. Liu (1948) 柳詒徵, 國史要義

J. Liu (1958) 劉子健, "梅堯臣碧雲騢與慶曆政爭中的士風", 大陸, 17：341-46

J. Liu (1960) ——, "王安石曾布與北宋晚期官僚的類型", 清華學報, 2：1：109-29

J. Liu (1961) ——, "儒教國家の雙重性格", 東方學, 20：119-25

J. Liu (1963) ——, 歐陽修的政治學與從政

S. P. Liu (1934) 劉師培, "漢宋學術異同論", 劉申叔遺書, 卷15

S. M. Lü (1931) 呂思勉, 宋代文學

T. H. Ma (1936) 馬宗霍, 中國經學史

Makino (1949) 牧野巽, 近世中國宗族研究

Miyazaki (1953) 宮崎市定, "宋代の士風", 史學雜誌, 62：139-69

Morohashi (1926) 諸橋轍次, "儒學史に於ける李泰伯の特殊地位", 斯文, 8：445-67

Morohashi (1948) ——, 儒教の諸問題

J. S. Mou (1952) 牟潤孫, "兩宋春秋學的主流", 大陸, 5：113-17, 170-72

C. C. Nieh (1939) 聶崇岐, "宋詞科考", 燕京學報, 225：107-52

Nishi (1951) 西順三, "三人の北宋士大夫思想", 一橋論叢, 26：30-52

K. T. P'an (1933) 潘光旦, "中國家譜學略史", 東方雜誌, 26：1：107-20

H. J. P'i (Ch'ing) 皮錫瑞, 經學通論 (四部叢刊)

H. J. P'i (1923) ——, 經學歷史

Saeki (1954) 佐伯富, 中國隨筆索引

Saeki (1960) ——, 中國隨筆雜著索引

M. Shimizu (1942) 清水盛光, 支那家族の構造

S. Shimizu (1961) 清水茂, "北宋名人の姻戚關係", 東洋史研究, 20：3：59-69

Sudo (1950) 周籘吉之, 宋代官僚制と大土地所有

K. K. Sun (1953) 孫克寬, 元初儒學

K. K. Sun (1965) ——, 宋元道教之發展

Takeuchi (1934) 武內義雄, "宋學の由来及び其特殊性", 東洋思潮, 11：1-50

Tanaka (1953) 田中謙二, "歐陽修の詞について", 東方學, 7：50-62

K. M. Teng (1943) 鄧廣銘, "宋史職官志考正", 中央研究院歷史語言研究所集刊, 10：433-593

Toyama (1950) 外山軍治, "靖康の變に於ける新舊兩黨の勢力關係", 羽田博士還曆紀念東洋史論叢, 663-88

Uno (1942) 宇野精一, "周禮の實施について", 東方學, 13：83-108

F. C. Wang (Ch'ing) 王夫之, 宋論 (四部備要)

M. S. Wang (Ch'ing) 王鳴盛, 十七史商榷 (廣雅叢書)

C. I. Wen (1965) 文崇一, "評歐陽修的治學和從政", 思與言, 3：511-13

T. H. Yang (1941) 楊殿珣, "中國家譜通論", 圖書季刊, 3：52：9-35；又 4：3-4：17-35

BIBLIOGRAPHY

Works of the Sung period, works written shortly after it, and selections from such works in later compilations (such as local gazetteers), are listed here as primary sources, with the editions or titles of the collectanea in which they appear listed in parentheses. Works of the Ch'ing period and of modern times are listed as secondary sources. All entries are listed alphabetically under the abbreviations used in the Notes: primary sources under initial letters of their romanized titles; secondary sources under authors' surnames and publication dates. Titles having the same initials are distinguished by authors' names: thus the three chronological biographies of Ou-yang Hsiu are given as OYNP (Hu), OYNP (Hua), and OYNP (Yang).

Primary Sources

CCC	*Ch'u-chou chih* (1879).
CCLHSC	Li Kou, *Chi-chiang Li hsien-sheng chi* (SPTK).
CCTPWC	Su Shih, *Chin-ching Tung-p'o wen-chi shih-lüeh* (Peking, 1957).
CCTSC	Ts'ao Kung-wu, *Chün-chai tu-shu chih* (SPTK).
CCTY	Chao Ju-yü, comp., *Kuo-ch'ao chu ch'en tsou-yi* (Ming ed.).
CHFT	Kao Hui-sou, *Chen hsi fang t'an* (TSCC).
CHTC	Wu Ch'u-hou, *Ch'ing hsiang tsa-chi* (HFL).
(CIT)	(Cheng-i-t'ang ed.).
CPTC	Chou Hui, *Ch'ing po tsa-chih* (PH).
CS (Wang)	Wang Te-ch'en, *Chu shih* (HFL).

CS (Yüeh)   Yüeh Ko, *Ch'eng shih* (PH).

CSPPLC   Ch'en Jen-hsi, comp., *Ching-shih pa pien lei-chi* (1626).

CSSC   Ch'ien Shih-chao, *Ch'ien-shih ssu-chih* (HHLP).

CSTP   Wang Ch'ang, *Chin shih ts'ui-pien* (Ch'ing ed.).

CTCS   Chu Hsi, *Chu-tzu ch'üan-shu* (1713).

CTCW   Ho Yüan, *Ch'un tu chi-wen* (HFL).

(CTTS)   (*Chao tai ts'ung-shu*).

CTWC   Chu Hsi, *Chu-tzu wen-chi* (TSCC).

CTYL   Chu Hsi, *Chu-tzu yü-lei* (1876).

CTYY   Chou Mi, *Ch'i-tung yeh-yü* (HFL).

CWCW (Chu)   Chu Pien, *Ch'u-wei chiu-wen* (TSCC).

CWCW (Li)   Li Hsin-ch'uan, *Chiu-wen cheng-wu* (YYTS).

CYC   Su Hsün, *Chia-yu chi* (SPTK).

ECWC   Ch'eng Hao and Ch'eng Yi, *Erh Ch'eng wen-chi* (CIT).

FCHK   Fan Ch'un-jen, *Fan Chung-hsüan-kung chi* (1910).

FCHT   Yüan Chiung, *Feng ch'uang hsiao-tu* (PH).

FCL   Yüan Huai (or Chan-jan-tzu), *Fu-chang lu* (SF).

FTTC   Chih-p'an, *Fo-tsu t'ung-chi* (*Taishō Daizōkyō* or *Tripitaka,* chap. 49).

FWCKC   Fan Chung-yen, *Fan Wen-cheng-kung chi* (1910 ed.).

HCC   Wang Yü-ch'eng, *Hsiao-ch'u chi* (TSCC).

HCHL   Wang Ming-ch'ing, *Hui chu hou-lu* (SPTK).

HCL   Chao Teh-lin, *Hou ch'ing lu* (PH).

HCNP   Yang Hsi-min, *Han Chung-hsien-kung nien-p'u* (1879 ed.).

HCP   Li T'ao, *Hsü Tzu-chih-t'ung-chien ch'ang-pien* (1881 ed. or 1962 reprint containing material recovered from the encyclopedia *Yung-lo ta-tien*).

HCPPM   Yang Chung-liang, *T'ung-chien ch'ang-pien chi-shih pen-mo* (1893), which is a topical summary of HCP.

(HFL)   (*Han-fen-lou* ed.).

HHC	Ch'in Kuan, *Huai-hai chi* (SPTK).
HHCY	Yeh Shih, *Hsi hsüeh chi-yen* (1885).
(HHLP)	(*Hsüeh hai lei-pien*).
HLYL	Lo Ta-ching, *Ho lin yü lu* (HFL).
HNWC	Yin Shu, *Ho-nan wen-chi* (SPTK).
HTHSC	Liu K'ai, *Ho-tung hsien-sheng chi* (SPTK).
HTL	Li Yüan-kang, *Hou teh lu* (PH).
HWKC	Han Ch'i, *Han Wei-kung chi* (TSCC).
HWTS	Ou-yang Hsiu, *Hsin Wu-tai shih* (SPPY).
HYC	Wang Kuei, *Hua-yang chi* (WYTCCCS).
HYTL	Chao K'uei, *Hsing ying tsa-lu* (LTHS).
ICFC	*I-ch'ang fu-chih* (1866).
ICHC	*I-ch'ang hsien chih* (1931).
JCSP	Hung Mai, *Jung-chai sui-pi*, 5 series (SPTK).
JLKY	T'ien K'uang, *Ju-lin kung-yi* (PH).
(KHCPTS)	(*Kuo-hsüeh chi-pen ts'ung-shu*).
KHCW	Wang Ying-lin, *Kun hsüeh chi-wen* (KHCPTS).
KSC (Chang)	Chang Lui, *K'o-shan chi* (TSCC).
KSC (Liu)	Liu Ch'ang, *Kung-shih chi* (WYTCCCS).
KSYL	Yang Shih, *Kuei-shan hsien-sheng yü-lu* (SPTK).
KTL	Fan Kung-ch'eng, *Kuo t'ing lu* (PH).
(KYTS)	(*Kuang-ya ts'ung-shu*).
LCC (Chang)	Chang Fang-p'ing, *Lo ch'üan chi* (SKCP).
LCC (Su)	Su Ch'e, *Luan-ch'eng chi* (SPTK).
LCIY	Su Chou, *Luan-ch'eng hsien-sheng i-yen* (TSCC).
LCML	Fei Kun, *Liang-chi man-lu* (HFL).
LCPC	Su Ch'e, *Lung-ch'uan pieh-chih* (HFL).
LHAPC	Lu Yu, *Lao-hsüeh-an pi-chi* (HFL).
LLHC	*Lu-ling hsien chih* (1920).
(LTHS)	(*Li-tai hsiao-shih*).
MC	Wang Chih, *Mo chi* (HFL).
MCML	Chang Pang-chi, *Mo-chuang man-lu* (PH).
MCYHL	Chu Hsi, comp., *Ming-ch'en yen-hsing lu* (1661).
(MHCH)	(*Mo hai chin hu*).
MHPT	Shen Kua, *Meng-hsi pi-t'an* (PH).

MHPTCC   Shen Kua, *Meng-hsi pi-t'an chiao-cheng* (annotated ed., Peking, 1955).

MKHH   P'eng Ch'eng, *Mo-k'e hui hsi* (PH).

MSYTL   Wang P'i-chih, *Mien-shui* (sometimes read as *Sheng-shui*) *yen-t'an lu* (HFL).

MTCC   Mu Hsiu, *Mu Ts'an-chün chi* (SPTK).

MTHH   Ch'en Shan, *Men tsao hsin hua* (HFL).

NCCT   Anonymous, *Nan-ch'uang chi-t'an* (MHCH).

NKCML   Wu Tseng, *Neng-kai-chai man-lu* (TSCC).

OYNP (Hu)   Hu K'o, *Lu-ling Ou-yang Wen-chung-kung nien-p'u* (included in OYYSC).

OYNP (Hua)   Hua Tzu-heng, *Tseng-ting Ou-yang Wen-chung-kung nien-p'u* (CTTS).

OYNP (Yang)   Yang Hsi-min, *Ou-yang Wen-chung-kung nien-p'u* (1879).

OYYSC   Ou-yang Hsiu, *Ou-yang Yung-shu chi* (KHCPTS).

(PH)   (*Pei hai*).

PKTY   Pao Cheng, *Pao-kung tsou-yi* (YYTTS).

PLKT   Ch'en Ch'ang-fang, *Pu li k'e t'an* (MHCH).

PSLH   Yeh Meng-te, *Pi shu lu hua* (HFL).

SCC   *Sui-chou chih* (1869).

(SF)   (*Shou fu*).

SHC   Yeh Shih, *Shui-hsin chi* (SPPY).

SHSC   Su Shun-chin, *Su Hsüeh-shih chi* (SPTK).

SHY   *Sung hui-yao chi-kao* (1936).

SHY:CJ   Section in SHY titled *ch'ung ju* (scholarship and education).

SHY:CK   Section in SHY titled *chih-kuan* (government organization and operation).

SHY:HC   Section in SHY titled *hsüan-chü* (selection of officials).

SJYS   T'ing Ch'uan-ching, comp., *Sung jen yi-shih hui-pien* (1935).

(SKCP)   (*Ssu-k'u chen-pen*).

SLYY   Yeh Meng-te, *Shih-lin yen yü* (PH).

SPLC P'an Yung-yin, comp., *Sung pei lei-ch'ao* (1669).

(SPPY) (*Ssu-pu pei-yao*).

(SPTK) (*Ssu-pu ts'ung-k'an*).

SS T'o-t'o, Ou-yang Hsüan, et al., *Sung shih*.

SSCKL Chüeh-an, *Shih-shih chi ku lüeh* (*Taishō Daizōkyō* or *Tripitaka*, chap. 49).

SSCW Ssu-ma Kuang, *Su-shui chi-wen* (HFL).

SSHP K'o Wei-ch'i, *Sung-shih hsin-pien* (1557).

SSPM Feng Ch'i, *Sung-shih chi-shih pen-mo* (WYWK).

SSWCHL Shao Po, *Shao-shih wen-chien hou-lu* (HFL).

SSWCL Shao Po-wen, *Shao-shih wen-chien lu* (HFL).

STNMCY Su Chin-yüan and Li Chun-p'u, comps., *Sung-tai san tz'u nung-min chi-yi* (1963).

SWC Lü Tsu-ch'ien, comp., *Sung wen chien* (SPTK).

SYHA Huang Tsung-hsi et al., comps., *Sung Yüan hsüeh-an* (WYWK).

TCCS Fan Chen, *Tung-chai chi-shih* (MHCH).

TCHKWC Ts'ai Hsiang, *Ts'ai Chung-hui-kung wen-chi* (1734).

TCML Tseng Ts'ao, *Tung-chai man lu* (MHCH).

TH Chang Hui-yen, comp., *Tz-u hsüan* (SPPY).

THPL Wei T'ai, *Tung-hsüan pi-lu* (PH).

TKNP (Wang) Wang Huan-piao: *Tseng Nan-feng hsien-sheng nien-p'u* (Shanghai, 1943).

TKNP (Yang) Yang Hsi-min, *Tseng Wen-ting-kung nien-p'u* (1879).

TLC Shih Chieh, *Tsu-lai chi* (1884).

TPCL Su Shih, *Tung-p'o chih-lin* (HFL).

(TSCC) (*Ts'ung-shu chi-ch'eng*).

TSKY Ts'ao Shui-chih, *Ts'ao-shih k'e yü* (TSCC).

TTSL Wang Ch'eng, *Tung-tu shih-lüeh* (1883).

TYL Kung Ting-ch'en, *Tung-yüan lu* (HFL).

WCKNP Ts'ai Shang-hsiang, *Wang Ch'ing-kung nien-p'u k'ao-lüeh* (Shanghai, 1930, or the Peking, 1958 reprint).

WHTK   Ma Tuan-lin, *Wen-hsien t'ung-k'ao* (WYWK).
WKWCC   Ssu-ma Kuang, *Wen-kuo Wen-cheng chi* (SPTK).
WLCC   Wang An-shih, *Wang Lin-ch'üan chi* (WYWK).
WLHSC   Mei Yao-ch'en, *Wan-ling hsien-sheng chi* (SPTK).
WWCKC   Wu Ch'eng, *Wu Wen-cheng-kung chi* (1756).
(WYTCCCS) (*Wu-ying-tien chü-chen ch'üan-shu*).
(WYWK) (*Wan-yu wen-k'u*).
YCFC   *Ying-chou fu chih* (1752).
YCHC   Wang Ming-ch'ing, *Yü chao hsin-chih* (HFL).
YFLK   Tseng Kung, *Yüan-feng lei-kao* (SPTK).
YKSC   Yang Shih, *Yang Kuei-shan chi* (TSCC).
(YYTTS) (*Yüeh-ya-t'ang ts'ung-shu*).
(YYTS)   (*Yung-yüan ts'ung-shu*).

Secondary Sources

Aoyama (1951). Aoyama Sadao, "Godai Sō ni okeru Kōsei no shinkō kanryō," in *Wada Hakushi kanreki kinen Tōyōshi ronsō*, 19–37.

Balazs (1964). Etienne Balazs, *Chinese Civilization and Bureacracy: Variations on a Theme* (New Haven, Conn.).

Beasley and Pulleyblank (1961). W. G. Beasley and E. G. Pulleyblank, eds., *Historians of China and Japan* (London).

Birch (1965). Cyril Birch, *Anthology of Chinese Literature from Early Times to the Fourteenth Century* (New York).

Buriks (1956). Peter Buriks, "Fan Chung-yen's Versuch einer Reform des chinesischen Beamtanstaates in den Jahren 1043–44," *Oriens Extremes*, 3:57–90, 153–84.

T. H. Chao (1953). Chao T'ieh-han, "Sung-tai chou-hsüeh," *Ta-lu*, 7:305–9, 341–43.

C. M. Ch'en (1946). Ch'en Chung-mien, "Yüan-ho hsing tsuan ssu chiao chi" (*Academia Sinica Special Bulletin*, No. 29).

K. Ch'en (1964). Kenneth Ch'en, *Buddhism in China: A Historical Survey* (Princeton, N.J.).

T. C. Ch'en (1945). Ch'en Tzu-chan, *Sung-tai wen-hsüeh shih*.

Y. H. Ch'en (1957). Ch'en Yüan-hui, *Fan Chen ti wu-shen-lun ssu-hsiang*.

K. Y. Ch'eng (1964). Ch'eng Kuang-yü, "Pei-Sung t'ai chieh chih cheng yü P'u-yi," in *Sung-shih yen-chiu chi*, 2:213–34.

C. T. Chi (1936). Chi Ch'ao-ting, *Key Economic Areas in Chinese History* (London).

M. Ch'ien (1947). Ch'ien Mu, *Kuo-shih ta-kang*, 2 vols.

M. Ch'ien (1952). ——, *Chung-kuo li-tai cheng-chih te-shih*.

M. Ch'ien (1953). ——, *Sung Ming li-hsüeh kai-shu*, 2 vols.

M. Ch'ien (1957). ——, "Tsa-lun T'ang-tai ku-wen yün-tung," *Hsin-ya hsüeh-pao*, 3:1:123–68.

M. Ch'ien (1959). ——, "*Tu Shih-ching*," *Hsin-ya hsüeh-pao*, 5:1:1–48.

T. H. Ch'ien (Ch'ing). Ch'ien Ta-hsin, *Shih-chia-chai yang hsin lu* (KHCPTS).

C. S. Chin (1963). Chin Chung-shu, "Sung-tai ku-wen yün-tung chih fa-chan yen-chiu," *Hsin-ya hsüeh pao*, 5:2:80–95.

C. S. Chin (1964). ——, "Pei-Sung ko-chü chih-tu yen chiu," *Hsin-ya hsüeh-pao*, 6:1:211–81, 6:2:165–242.

Y. F. Ch'in (1957). Chin Yü-fu, *Chung-kuo shih-hsüeh shih* (reprint).

Chin. Lit. (1961). *Chinese Literature Monthly*, 10 (Peking, Oct. 1961).

De Bary (1953). Wm. Theodore de Bary, "A Reappraisal of Neo-Confucianism," in Wright (1953), 81–111.

De Bary (1959). ——, "Some Common Tendencies in Neo-Confucianism," in Nivison and Wright (1959), 25–49.

De Bary et al. (1960). ——, Wing-tsit Chan, Burton Watson et al., comps., *Sources of Chinese Tradition* (New York).

Davidson (1952). Martha Davidson, *A List of Published Translations from Chinese into English, French, and German Literature* (Washington).

Davidson (1957). ——, *A List of Published Translations from Chinese into English, French, and German Poetry* (Washington).

Demiéville (1961). P. Demiéville, "Chang Hsüeh-ch'eng and His Historiography," in Beasley and Pulleyblank (1961), 167–85.

Eisenstadt (1963). S. N. Eisenstadt, *The Political Systems of Empires: The Rise and Fall of the Bureaucratic Societies* (New York).

Fairbank (1957). John K. Fairbank, ed., *Chinese Thought and Institutions* (Chicago).

Fischer (1955). "Fan Chung-yen (989–1052): Das Lebensbild eines chinesischen Staatsmannes," *Oriens Extremes,* 2:74–85.

Franke (1961). Herbert Franke, "Some Aspects of Chinese Private Historiography in the 13th and 14th Centuries," in Beasley and Pulleyblank (1961), 115–27.

Fung (1948). Fung Yu-lan, *A Short History of Chinese Philosophy,* trans. Derk Bodde (New York).

Gardner (1961). Charles S. Gardner, *Chinese Traditional Historiography* (Cambridge, Mass.), rev. ed.

Gernet (1962). Jacques Gernet, *Daily Life in China on the Eve of the Mongol Invasion, 1250–1276* (New York).

Hightower (1962). James Robert Hightower, *Topics in Chinese Literature* (Cambridge, Mass.), rev. ed.

P. T. Ho (1956). Ping-ti Ho, "Early Ripening Rice in Chinese History," *Economic History Review,* 9:200–218.

P. T. Ho (1962). ———, *The Ladder of Success in Imperial China: Aspects of Social Mobility* (New York).

C. Y. Hsia (1937). Hsia Chün-yü, *Sung-hsüeh kai-yao.*

K. C. Hsiao (1946). Hsiao Kung-ch'üan, *Chung-kuo cheng-chih ssu-hsiang shih,* 2 vols.

I. C. Y. Hsü (1959). Immanuel C. Y. Hsü, trans. *Intellectual Trends in the Ch'ing Period* (Cambridge, Mass.).

L. J. Hsüeh (1955). Hsüeh Li-jo. *Sung tz'u t'ung-lun.*

S. Hu (1921). Hu Shih, *Hu Shih wen-ts'un.*

Y. I. Hu (1930). Hu Yün-i, *Sung-shih yen-chiu.*

K. C. Huang (1958). Huang Kung-chu, comp., *Ou-yang Hsiu tz'u hsüan p'ing.*

Japanese Committee (1961). Japanese Committee for the Sung Project (Nihon Sōshi Teiyō Kyōryōku Iinkai), *Sōdai kenkyū bunken teiyō.*

C. I. K'o (1936). K'o Ch'ang-i, *Wang An-shih p'ing chuan.*

T. P. K'o (1934). K'o Tun-po, *Sung wen-hsüeh shih.*

Kracke (1953). E. A. Kracke, Jr., *Civil Service in Early Sung China, 960–1067* (Cambridge, Mass.).

Kracke (1955). ———, "Sung Society: Change Within Tradition," *Far Eastern Quarterly,* XIV, No. 4, 479–88.

S. Y. Kuo (1934). Kuo Shao-yü, *Chung-kuo wen-hsüeh pi-p'ing shih.*

C. C. Liang (1920). Liang Ch'i-ch'ao, *Wang Ching-kung chuan.*

K. Liang (1938). Liang K'un, *Sung-shih p'ai-pieh lun.*

Y. T. Lin (1947). Lin Yutang, *The Gay Genius: The Life and Times of Su Tungpo* (New York).

H. C. W. Liu (1959). Hui-chen Wang Liu, *The Traditional Chinese Clan Rules* (Association for Asian Studies monograph studies).

H. C. W. Liu (1959a). ———, "An Analysis of Chinese Clan Rules," in Nivison and Wright (1959), 63–96.

I. C. Liu (1948). Liu I-cheng, *Kuo-shih yao-i.*

J. Liu (1957). James T. C. Liu, "An Early Sung Reformer: Fan Chung-yen," in Fairbank (1957), 105–31.

J. Liu (1958). ——— (as Liu Tzu-chien), "Mei Yao-chen, *Pi-yün-hsia,* Ch'eng-li cheng-cheng chung ti shih-feng," *Ta-lu,* 17:341–46.

J. Liu (1959). ———, *Reforms in Sung China: Wang An-shih (1021–86) and his New Policies* (Cambridge, Mass.).

J. Liu (1959a). ———, "Some Classifications of Bureaucrats in Chinese Historiography," in Nivison and Wright (1959), 165–81.

J. Liu (1960). ———, "Wang An-shih, Tseng-pu, yü Pei-Sung wan-ch'i kuan-liao ti lei-hsing," *Tsinghua hsüeh-pao, new series,* 2:1: 109–29.

J. Liu (1961). ——— (as Ryū Shi-ken), "*Jūkyō kok'a no sōjū seisaku,*" *Tōhōgaku,* 20:119–25.

J. Liu (1962). ———, "An Administrative Cycle in Chinese History," *Journal of Asian Studies,* XXI, No. 2, 137–51.

J. Liu (1963). ———, *Ou-yang Hsiu ti chih-hsüeh yü ts'ung-cheng* (Hong Kong).

J. Liu (1963a). ———, a review of Wright and Twitchett (1962), in *American Historical Review,* 144–45.

J. Liu (1964). ———, "The Neo-Traditional Period (ca. A.D. 800–1900) in Chinese History," *Journal of Asian Studies,* XXIV, No. 1, 105–7.

J. J. Y. Liu (1963). James J. Y. Liu, *The Art of Chinese Poetry* (New York).

S. P. Liu (1934). Liu Shih-p'ei, "Han Sung hsüeh-shu i-t'ung lun," in *Liu Shen-shu i-shu* (1934–1938), vol. 15.

Locke (1951). Marjorie A. Locke, "The Early Life of Ou-yang Hsiu and His Relation to the Rise of the *Ku-Wen* Movement of the Sung Period" (University of London, unpublished Ph.D. dissertation).

S. M. Lü (1931). Lü Ssu-mien, *Sung-tai wen-hsüeh.*

T. H. Ma (1936). Ma Tsung-ho, *Chung-kuo ching-hsüeh shih.*

Makino (1949). Makino Tatsumi, *Kinsei Chūgoku sōzoku kenkyū.*

Menzel (1963). Johanna M. Menzel, ed., *The Chinese Civil Service: Career Open to Talents?* (Boston).

Miyazaki (1953). Miyazaki Sadao, "Sōdai no shifū," *Shigaku zasshi,* 62:139–69.

Morohashi (1926). Morohashi Tetsuji, "Jūgakushi jō ni okeru Li T'ai-p'o (or Li Kou) no tokushu chii," *Shibun,* 8:445–67.

Morohashi (1948). ———, *Jūkyo no sho-mondai.*

J. S. Mou (1952). Mou Jun-sun, "Liang Sung *Ch'un-ch'iu* hsüeh ti chu-liu," *Ta-lu,* 5:113–17, 170–72.

Needham (1956). Joseph Needham, *Science and Civilization in China,* vol. 2 (Cambridge).

C. C. Nieh (1939). Nieh Ch'ung-ch'i, "Sung tz'u-k'o k'ao," *Yenching hsüeh-pao,* 25:107–52.

Nishi (1951). Nishi Junzō, "Sanin no Hoku-Sō shidafu shisō," *Hito-tsubashi ronsō,* 26:30–52.

Nivison (1959). David S. Nivison, Introduction to Nivison and Wright (1959), 3–24.

Nivison (1959a). ———, "Ho-shen and His Accusers: Ideology and Political Behavior in the Eighteenth Century," in *ibid.*, 209–43.

Nivison (1960). ———, "Protest Against Conventions and Conventions of Protest," in Wright (1960), 177–201.

Nivison (1966). ———, *The Life and Thought of Chang Hsüeh-ch'eng (1738–1801)* (Stanford, Calif.).

Nivison and Wright (1959). ——— and Arthur F. Wright, *Confucianism in Action* (Stanford, Calif.).

K. T. P'an (1933). P'an Kuang-tan, "Chung-kuo chia-p'u hsüeh-lüeh-shih," *Tung-fang tsa-chih*, 26:1:107–20.

H. J. P'i (Ch'ing). P'i Hsi-jui, *Ching-hsüeh t'ung-lun* (SPTK).

H. J. P'i (1923). ———, *Ching-hsüeh li-shih*.

Pulleyblank (1959). Edwin G. Pulleyblank, "Liu K'o, a Forgotten Rival of Han Yü," *Asia major*, 7:145–60.

Pulleyblank (1960). ———, "Neo-Confucianism and Neo-Legalism," in Wright (1960), 77–114.

Pulleyblank (1961). ———, "Chinese Historical Criticism: Liu Chih-chi and Ssu-ma Kuang," in Beasley and Pulleyblank (1961), 135–66.

Reischauer and Fairbank (1960). Edwin O. Reischauer and John K. Fairbank, *East Asia: The Great Tradition* (Boston).

Rexroth (1955). Kenneth Rexroth, *One Hundred Poems from the Chinese* (New York).

Rudolph (1963). Richard C. Rudolph, "Preliminary Notes on Sung Archaeology," *Journal of Asian Studies*, XXII, No. 2, 169–77.

Saeki (1954). Saeki Tomi, *Chūgoku zuihitsu sakuin*.

Saeki (1960). ———, *Chūgoku zuihitsu zassho sakuin*.

M. Shimizu (1942). Shimizu Morimitsu, *Shina kazoku no kōzō*.

S. Shimizu (1961). Shimizu Shige, "Inter-Marriages Between Eminent Families in the Northern Sung Period," *Tōyōshi kenkyū*, 20:3:59–69.

Sudō (1950). Sudō Yoshiyuki, *Sōdai kenryosei to dai tochi shoyū*.

K. K. Sun (1953). Sun Ke-k'uan, *Yüan ch'u ju-hsüeh*.

K. K. Sun (1965). ———, *Sung Yüan tao-chiao chih fa-chan*.

Takeuchi (1934). Takeuchi Yoshio, "Sōgaku no yurai oyobi sono toku-shusei," *Tōyō shichō*, 11:1–50.

Tanaka (1953). Tanaka Kenji, "Ou-yang Hsiu no shi ni tsuite," *Tō-hōgaku*, 7:50–62.

K. M. Teng (1943). Teng Kuang-ming, "*Sung-shih* chih-kuan-chih-k'ao-cheng," *Bulletin, Institute of History and Philology, Academia Sinica*, 10:433–593.

Teng and Biggerstaff (1950). Ssu-yü Teng and Knight Biggerstaff, *An Annotated Bibliography of Selected Chinese Reference Works* (Cambridge, Mass.), rev. ed.

Toyama (1950). Toyama Gunji, "Seiko no hen ni okeru shin kyū ryō tō no seiryoku kankei," *Haneda Hakushi kanreki kinen Tōyōshi ronsō*, 663–88.

Twitchett (1961). Denis Twitchett, "Chinese Biographical Writing," in Beasley and Pulleyblank (1961), 95–114.

Twitchett (1962). ———, "Problems of Chinese Biography," in Wright and Twitchett (1962), 24–42.

Uno (1942). Uno Seichi, "Shūrei no jisshi ni tsuite," *Tōhō gakuhō*, 13:83–108.

Waley (1925). Arthur Waley, *The Temple and Other Poems* (London).

F. C. Wang (Ch'ing). Wang Fu-chih, *Sung lun* (SPPY).

G. W. Wang (1958). Wang Gung-wu, "The *Chiu Wu-tai Shih* and History-Writing During the Five Dynasties," *Asia Major* 6:1:1–22.

G. W. Wang (1962). ———, "Feng Tao: An Essay on Confucian Loyalty," in Wright and Twitchett (1962), 123–45.

G. W. Wang (1963). ———, *The Structure of Power in North China During the Five Dynasties* (Kuala Lumpur).

M. S. Wang (Ch'ing). Wang Ming-sheng, *Shih-ch'i-shih shang-chüeh* (KYTS).

C. I. Wen (1965). Wen Chung-i, "Review: Ou-yang Hsiu's Academic Achievements and Political Life," *Ssu yü yen* (*Though and Word*), 3:511–13.

Wright (1953). Arthur F. Wright, ed., *Studies in Chinese Thought* (Chicago).

Wright (1960). ———, ed., *The Confucian Persuasion* (Stanford, Calif.).

Wright and Twitchett (1962). Arthur F. Wright and Denis Twitchett, eds., *Confucian Personalities* (Stanford, Calif.).

L. S. Yang (1952). Lien-sheng Yang, *Money and Credit in China: A Short History* (Cambridge, Mass.).

L. S. Yang (1957). ———, "Economic Justification for Spending—An Uncommon Idea in Traditional China," *Harvard Journal of Asiatic Studies*, XX, Nos. 1–2, 36–49.

L. S. Yang (1961). ———, "The Organization of Chinese Official Historiography," in Beasley and Pulleyblank (1961), 44–59.

T. H. Yang (1941). Yang Tien-hsün, "Chung-kuo chia-p'u t'ung-lun," *T'u-shu chi-k'an,* new series, 3:1–2:9–35, 4:3–4:17–35.

INDEX